Brand
esSense

Brand esSense

Using sense, symbol and story to design brand identity

Neil Gains

LONDON PHILADELPHIA NEW DELHI

Publisher's note

Every possible effort has been made to ensure that the information contained in this book is accurate at the time of going to press, and the publishers and author cannot accept responsibility for any errors or omissions, however caused. No responsibility for loss or damage occasioned to any person acting, or refraining from action, as a result of the material in this publication can be accepted by the editor, the publisher or the author.

First published in Great Britain and the United States in 2014 by Kogan Page Limited

2nd Floor, 45 Gee Street
London EC1V 3RS
United Kingdom
www.koganpage.com

1518 Walnut Street, Suite 1100
Philadelphia PA 19102
USA

4737/23 Ansari Road
Daryaganj
New Delhi 110002
India

© Neil Gains, 2014

The right of Neil Gains to be identified as the author of this work has been asserted by him in accordance with the Copyright, Designs and Patents Act 1988.

ISBN   978 0 7494 7001 2
E-ISBN   978 0 7494 7002 9

British Library Cataloguing-in-Publication Data

A CIP record for this book is available from the British Library.

Library of Congress Cataloging-in-Publication Data

Gains, Neil.
 Brand esSense : using sense, symbol and story to design brand identity / Neil Gains.
    pages cm
 ISBN 978-0-7494-7001-2 – ISBN 978-0-7494-7002-9 (ebook)   1. Branding (Marketing)
2. Brand name products.   3. Logos (Symbols)   4. Corporate image.   I. Title.
 HF5415.1255.G35 2013
 658.8'27–dc23

                                                                          2013026092

Typeset by Graphicraft Limited, Hong Kong
Print production managed by Jellyfish
Printed and bound by CPI Group (UK) Ltd, Croydon, CR0 4YY

Dedicated to the memory of my brother Peter, 1971–2012

CONTENTS

List of figures   x
List of tables   xi

Introduction   1

01   The reality of perception   8

Signal and noise   8
Patterns in the world   10
Perception is an active construction   13
Nature and nurture   18
Matching the right patterns   20
Experience and memory   22
Associating with the right memories   24

02   The senses close up   27

Five and counting   27
The primal sense   30
Basic taste   36
The touch of reality   41
Touching sight   42

03   Sensing from a distance   47

Touching space   47
The rhythm of life   52
The dominant sense   60
The colour of experience   65
Integrating the senses   69

04   Symbols and signs   72

Symbols of life   72
The colour of meaning   74
Identity matters   75
Signifying something   78
Understanding your category   80
The structure of signs   82
The story of meaning   84
Changing times   85
Metaphor and meaning   87
Opposites matter   89
Squaring the circle   92
Blending identity   94

05   Story and archetypes   97

Causality and the mind   97
The meaning of stories   99
Story and myth   100
Brand archetypes   105
Archetypal frameworks   107

06   Using archetypes in branding   115

Archetypes of belonging   115
Archetypes of freedom   124
Archetypes of ego   132
Archetypes of order   141

07   Finding the esSense of your brand   150

Building a brand back story   151
Cracking the category codes   153
Uncovering consumer stories and underlying conflicts   156
Building transformational stories   161
Moving to the senses   165
Building the story of an Asian food brand   167
Making rice 'nice' for a snack brand   168

08   Applying the esSense framework   171

The esSense of branding   171
Brand colours   172
Brand senses   175
Symbolic names   180
Brand symbols   185
How archetypes answer why   192
Telling the brand story   195
Using sense, symbol and story to build brand esSense   202

References   205
Index   213

LIST OF FIGURES

FIGURE 0.1 Golden circle of brand esSense 5

FIGURE 1.1 Müller-Lyer illusion and perception of interior space 17

FIGURE 1.2 Context and memory 21

FIGURE 1.3 Emotion and memory 22

FIGURE 2.1 Henning's smell prism 35

FIGURE 2.2 Ney's flavourgram 38

FIGURE 2.3 Sensory homunculus on the somatosensory cortex 45

FIGURE 3.1 Human spatial zones 51

FIGURE 3.2 *Bouba* and *kiki* 70

FIGURE 4.1 Semiotic square of sexuality 93

FIGURE 5.1 The hero's journey from Campbell, 1993 101

FIGURE 5.2 Chinese zodiac 105

FIGURE 5.3 Ten human values from Schwartz, 1993 112

FIGURE 5.4 Twelve archetypes 114

FIGURE 8.1 esSense framework 172

FIGURE 8.2 Distinctive typefaces 188

LIST OF TABLES

TABLE 1.1   Information flow in sensory systems and conscious perception   9

TABLE 2.1   Relative importance of the five main senses   29

TABLE 4.1   Colour meanings in Asian cultures   76

TABLE 4.2   Moments of truth for functional and beauty shampoo   83

TABLE 4.3   The structure of stories   84

TABLE 4.4   Mythic oppositions   90

TABLE 4.5   Global themes of beer advertising   96

TABLE 5.1   The hero's journey and *Star Wars*   103

TABLE 5.2   Seven archetypal plots   104

TABLE 5.3   Rokeach's terminal and instrumental values   110

TABLE 7.1   Key binary oppositions of StoryWorks model   154

TABLE 7.2   Summary of 12 archetypes   162

TABLE 7.3   Playing the journalist questions   165

TABLE 7.4   Summary of the meanings of rice   169

TABLE 8.1   Stella Artois pouring ritual   198

Introduction

> *If I eat pink cake, the taste of it is pink.* JEAN PAUL SARTRE

In 2012, Cadbury finally won a lengthy court battle to trademark their distinctive purple colour for packaging milk chocolate. They first applied for the trademark in October 2004, registering their own right to use Pantone 2685c, but their rival Nestlé had argued that colours could not be practically trademarked for commercial advantage. Why such a fuss about a particular shade of the colour purple?

Cadbury's purple is a distinctive asset for the brand, with huge importance in making Cadbury memorable and recognizable to customers, hence building mental availability and commercial value. The *Guardian* (2 October 2012) reported the appeal judge's verdict as, 'the evidence clearly supports a finding that purple is distinctive of Cadbury for milk chocolate'. The judge added that Cadbury had used purple for its Dairy Milk chocolate bars since 1914.

The ruling means that the particular shade of purple has become specific to milk chocolate bars and tablets, milk chocolate for eating and drinking chocolate, delighting Cadbury. The *Guardian* also quoted a Cadbury spokesman as saying, 'Our colour purple has been linked to Cadbury for more than a century and the British public has grown up understanding its link with our chocolate'.

Unsurprisingly, Nestlé retaliated in 2006 by filing a trademark application for the distinctive four-finger shape of Kit Kat, which they won earlier this year (reported in the *Daily Telegraph* on 2 January 2013). In similar applications, Christian Louboutin has secured the trademark for the distinctive red that marks the soles of the shoes he designs, Harrods has secured its own distinctive shade of green, and Tiffany owns the rights to the distinctive egg shell blue which wraps every package coming out of their stores.

Building successful brands is about building availability: physical availability in the marketplace and mental availability in the mind (Franzen and Bouwman, 2001; Sharp, 2010). Byron Sharp defines physical availability as 'making a brand as easy to notice and buy as possible, for as many consumers as possible, across as wide a range of potential buying situations as possible' (2010: 196). He adds that this includes retail penetration, store presence, hours of availability and facilitation of purchase. This definition is close to the famous quote from Robert Woodruff (1923), former Chairman of Coca-Cola, that his brand should be 'always within an arm's reach of desire'. The company's channel and distribution strategy reflects their continuing focus on physical availability.

Byron Sharp defines mental availability, also called brand salience, as 'the propensity for a brand to be noticed and thought of in buying situations' (2010: 191). He points out that salience is much more than simple top-of-mind awareness, and is a more general reflection of the network of associations with the brand in a buyer's memory. The larger and 'fresher' this network of memories is, the greater the chance that the brand will be noticed across different buying situations. This depends on the quantity and quality of those associations, and quality comes from distinctive and consistent icons, imagery and experiences that are relevant to the brand and the buying contexts.

This book focuses on building availability in the mind through quantity and quality of associations. These associations are built using experiential clues that send a consistent and strong message to the minds of customers and prospects, maximizing the signal and minimizing the noise that reaches consumers.

The messages are built around the brand's core values (esSense), combining the brand story with symbols and sensory cues that unify, simplify and amplify those values, creating an impression that is far more than the sum of the individual parts.

Sense, symbol and story

The American Marketing Association has defined sensory marketing as 'marketing techniques that aim to seduce the consumer by using his or her senses to influence feelings and behaviour'. Although this captures the importance of non-functional aspects of experience, I prefer the Wikipedia definition (from the article 'Sensory branding', 4 April 2013), which says,

> Sensory branding is a type of marketing that appeals to all the senses in relation to the brand. It uses the senses to relate to customers on an emotional level. Brands can forge emotional associations in the customers' minds by appealing to their senses. A multi-sensory brand experience generates certain beliefs, feelings, thoughts and opinions to create a brand image in the consumer's mind.

Much has been written about the importance of sensory marketing, and brands are starting to wake up to the vital role that the senses play in building brand identity. The majority of brand communication continues to focus on the visual appearance of brand experience; although sound and smell are often much more effective in engaging the human senses and emotions, and even images are more distinctive when they are matched with a second sense.

Although there is general agreement that multi-sensory experiences create stronger engagement and more powerful memories (Hill, 2008; 2010), relatively few books or articles have addressed how and why this can be achieved. Certainly the most famous, and a pioneer in the field, is *Brand Sense* by Martin Lindstrom (2005, second edn 2010). In the book, Lindstrom introduces his test of the 'smashability' of a brand's sensory signatures, based on the iconic story of the creation of the Coca-Cola bottle.

Lindstrom's book is full of examples of sensory branding, using the results of a Millward Brown research study to focus on some of the most successful examples of sensory marketing, including Coca-Cola, Singapore Airlines, Apple and Disney. Singapore Airlines is certainly a case study close to my heart, as I live in Singapore and I love travelling with them. Much has been written about their success, both in terms of their business model and their experience design (Rolls, 2006; Lindstrom, 2010).

Lindstrom takes a traditional view of the senses, focusing on the classical five senses of smell, taste, touch, hearing and vision, as many other authors do. Before his breakthrough book, a few authors had addressed the importance of sensory engagement, primarily through the lens of customer experience management (Schmitt and Simonson, 1997; Schmitt, 1999; Pine and Gilmore, 2011; Gobé, 2009; Jackson, 2003). All of these works describe sensory marketing as a part of the total customer experience.

Following Martin Lindstrom's work, other books and articles have looked at different aspects of sensory branding, although often through an academic lens or a specific focus on one of the senses (Brynie, 2009; Hultén, Broweus and van Dijk, 2009; Krishna, 2010; Lusensky, 2011; Treasure, 2011). Dan Hill (2008, 2010) has also written about the importance of the senses in the context of building emotional salience. Most recently, Aradhna Krishna has summarized much of the academic literature on sensory marketing in a more business friendly form (Krishna, 2013).

Most of the published work on sensory branding and marketing focuses on the importance of the senses in creating customer engagement, with less emphasis on the symbolic value of sensory experience in creating brand meaning. The topic of brand meaning has often been left to the more academic world of semiotics, although some authors have tried to make these ideas accessible to broader audiences. Marcel Danesi, in particular, has written many articles and books explaining semiotic thinking and its application to the meaning of brands in layman's language (Danesi, 2006, 2007, 2008).

Virginia Valentine was a tireless champion of the application of semiotic thinking in market research, and Laura Oswald (2012) has written about the application of semiotics in marketing. Mark Batey manages to cover aspects of perception, semiotics and storytelling in his book *Brand Meaning* (2008) which is both scholarly and very wide ranging in the range of topics, ideas and theories that are covered.

Storytelling has now become a very popular topic for business and branding literature, with an avalanche of books on storytelling in branding over the last 12 months (for example: Cooke, 2013; Gottschall, 2012; Sachs, 2012; Signorelli, 2012; Smith, 2012; Sykes, Malik and West, 2013). Is there a pattern here, with so many surnames that start with an 'S'? The ability of brands and businesses to tell relevant and engaging stories is fundamental to success.

Building brand esSense

Although brand experience, brand meaning and brand stories are often discussed as separate elements of marketing strategy, is there a common ground between them? Experience, meaning and story are different manifestations of a brand's core esSense. Simon Sinek has written convincingly about the importance of 'why?' in defining business strategy, and his TED talk has been watched by almost 10 million viewers as I write this (in late March 2013). In his book *Start With Why* (2011), Sinek writes about the golden circle of why, how and what and I have taken the liberty of adapting the circle to express brand esSense in terms of the underlying brand story, the meaning of the brand and the brand's physical presence.

FIGURE 0.1   Golden circle of brand esSense

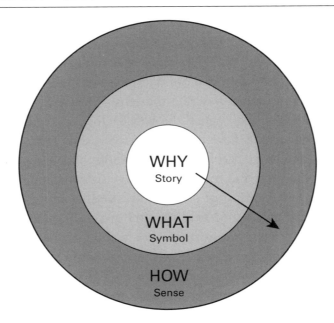

Sensory branding speaks to the most direct and physical manifestations of a brand. However, the physical experience of the brand must reflect the meaning of the brand to customers, which in turn is ultimately defined by an underlying brand story.

To rephrase this, story helps define why a brand exists, symbols help communicate a brand's meanings, and the senses help a brand to make these meanings real and tangible through direct engagement with customers. Sense, symbol and story define the physical, cognitive and emotional value of a brand to consumers, and are intimately linked in shaping the way that brands are perceived.

Language itself has limited impact on brand perceptions and it is well understood that the brain 'thinks' primarily in images and not words (Zaltman, 2003). However the two are intimately linked and Benjamin Bergen argues strongly that experience comes before language. He writes, 'Maybe we understand language by simulating in our minds what it would be like to experience the things that the language describes' (2012: 13).

The story of Brand esSense

Chapter 1 of *Brand esSense* describes the reality of perception, revealing the importance of expectations in shaping how we experience the world around us with profound implications for brand management. Chapters 2 and 3 describe the senses in detail; starting with those senses which experience the world close up, and moving to those senses that can help us perceive the world from a distance. Chapter 4 describes the world of symbols and signs, and how brands can interpret and leverage these to create meaning. Chapter 5 describes the importance of story in creating meaning for humans and references models of evolutionary psychology, emotion and behaviour that relate to customer goals. Chapter 6 builds on the importance of story, outlining 12 archetypal brand personalities that tell the stories of the most common customer goals. Chapter 7 details the process by which a brand can identify and realize the most relevant archetype for their category and customers. Finally, Chapter 8 integrates sense, symbol and story into the esSense framework, providing examples of 30 brand touch points and how they can be leveraged to build brand identity.

When combined, sense, symbol and story create a complete picture of a brand and its role in a consumer's life. Story links directly to consumer goals that are the most important motivation for using any brand. Successful brands align their brand story with customer goals, and then ensure that the brand's symbols and sense (experiential) cues are consistent with them. Customer goals should be at the heart of the meanings and experiences that any brand seeks to build.

Successful branding comes from understanding customer goals and linking these concretely to the stories, symbolism and experience of using the brand. I hope you enjoy reading how sense, symbol and story can work together to bring your brand the success it deserves.

01 The reality of perception

> *Life is not all that we think it is, it's only what we imagine it to be and for us what we imagine becomes mostly so.*
>
> **CHARLES BUKOWSKI**

Signal and noise

The world rushes past us every second of every day. How much do we take in? It has been understood for many years that we are consciously aware of very little of what happens around us. In the words of Professor Manfred Zimmerman, 'What we perceive at any moment, therefore, is limited to an extremely small compartment in the stream of information about our surroundings flowing in from the sense organs' (Nørretranders, 1999: 124–26; Zimmerman, 1989: 166–73).

Professor Zimmerman has written elsewhere that the maximal conscious information flow from sensory perception is around 40 bits per second (Zimmerman, 1986; Nørretranders, 1999: 124) and other estimates vary from 16 to 50.

This is in contrast to the millions of pieces of information that flood into the brain from our senses. Our eyes send at least 10 million bits of information to the brain every second, the skin around 1 million, the ears 100,000, smell 100,000 and the taste buds a much more limited 1,000. And Professor Zimmerman estimates that we are conscious of no more than 40, containing very little information compared with the richness of the world.

Professor Zimmerman has gone further to estimate the 'conscious' bandwidth of each of the five classic senses as in Table 1.1. Although visual perception dominates the total amount of sensory information, the table highlights the importance of hearing and touch in our conscious perception of the world around us.

Every second, many millions of pieces of information are being 'compressed' into a tiny handful that we might be aware of. All of this compression happens outside our consciousness. Language can never possibly capture the richness of our individual experience of the world through our senses, but it can capture those things that we are consciously aware of, raising a number of questions about the difference between the real world and our perception of the world. Are we conscious of the most important things that are happening around us? How much information about experience is stored in

TABLE 1.1   Information flow in sensory systems and conscious perception

Sensory system	Total bandwidth (bits/second)	Conscious bandwidth
Eyes	10,000,000	40
Ears	100,000	30
Skin	1,000,000	5
Smell	100,000	1
Taste	1,000	1

SOURCE: Zimmerman, 1989: 172

our unconscious brain outside awareness? Is there any way to access this unconscious information?

Much of what we perceive, learn and understand remains unspoken, and is written into the mind in the language of the senses. That said, it remains true that even the briefest piece of spoken or written language can often capture a rich network of ideas and associations. This is something that great storytellers and great brands have always known. When Carl Jung (1968) published a study of Hans Christian Andersen's fairy tales he wrote, 'Any viable work of poetry (and work of art in general) rests on archetypal foundations'. The power of archetypes in great stories is their ability to tap into a rich vein of unspoken associations, in the same way that our limited conscious memory taps into the rich vein of our experienced world.

The capacity or bandwidth of our conscious mind is limited to around one millionth of the capacity of our body to sense the world around us. Yet the world appears rich, detailed and coherent to us. How does this happen?

Patterns in the world

Although the unconscious brain processes a huge amount of information, it can only do this by simplifying. In essence, the brain is a very sophisticated pattern recognition machine and scientists from a wide range of disciplines have written about this in the context of the role of expectations, the relationship between mind and brain, artificial intelligence and empirical studies of visual perception (Berdik, 2012; Frith, 2007; Gregory, 2009; Hawkins, 2005; Purves and Lotto, 2011).

Our brain does not trawl through every piece of information coming from the senses. Rather, it uses very fast, highly intelligent and constantly adapting algorithms to search for meaningful patterns in the world. Meaningful in this sense is the ability to help the brain predict future events and adapt to a changing environment with successful strategies that are likely to lead to positive outcomes.

There are more than five senses, but in some respects the brain sees only one sense. All sensory data arrive as patterns of information for the brain to check, filter and build into hypotheses about the world outside. Most sensory information has undergone a great deal of processing before we are conscious of it and this processing happens at different levels in the brain, some much quicker than others.

For example, if my unconscious brain notices a suspicious object in the grass that is long and thin, I may immediately stop or even start to take flight before I am fully conscious of anything at all. Later, my brain will fill in the details, perhaps finally working out that it's a branch of a tree rather than a dangerous snake. But all that happens after I have already taken evasive action.

Our brains are constantly trying to spot patterns in the world. In the Second World War, the bombing of London was random, but somehow experts were able to pick out clusters and patterns in the randomness, just as we can all see faces on the Moon's surface (this effect is called the Law of Prägnanz and is one of the principles of Gestalt psychology). That's why expectations play such a large role in sensory perception.

The best-known example of the role of expectations is the placebo effect, documented across hundreds of studies. The placebo effect is largely attributed to a combination of expectancy and classical conditioning, and some of the most recent and interesting studies of placebo and expectations have been those documented by Dan Ariely and co-workers across a series of experiments (Shiv, Carmon and Ariely, 2005; Lee, Frederick and Ariely, 2006; Ariely, 2008).

In one experiment, Ariely and colleagues demonstrated that members of a fitness centre worked out less and were more fatigued when they had purchased a reduced-price energy drink compared with when they had purchased a full-price energy drink. That is, price discounts led to a behavioural effect (marketers take notice).

In further experiments, Ariely and co-workers investigated intrinsic expectation effects (eg an active drug 'should' work) and extrinsic expectation effects (eg injections and capsules have different levels of effect) as well as the role of existing beliefs (eg brand name, ingredients) and new knowledge (eg price). They demonstrated in three follow up studies that:

- Participants solved fewer puzzles when given a discounted energy drink compared with a full-price drink (and they were unaware of the effect).

- This effect was eliminated if participants' attention was drawn to the link between price and efficacy.

- The same effects could be seen when participants were given new information about the efficacy of the drink (ie additional marketing information) and this was independent of the price effect.

In a separate experiment, Ariely and co-workers were able to repeat the price effects on the efficacy of a drug, with reduced price drugs providing a lower level of pain relief. The significance of these studies and others is that it proves that price not only affects perceptions of quality, but also influences *actual* quality. That is, changes in price can actually change the experience of a product.

This was proved in a more entertaining experiment with beer, where the addition of small amount of balsamic vinegar to a beer increased preferences for it when tasted blind. However, when participants were informed before tasting the beer, their preferences switched. In a follow up experiment, Ariely and co-workers tested whether the information was just another input variable to participants' judgments or whether it had actually changed perceptions. They found that the timing of the information was very important, and if the information was given after the beer had been tasted, then preferences were much closer to the blind experimental condition. Thus, it was not the information which had changed the preferences, but the experience of drinking. The information had the effect of profoundly changing experience.

In the next chapter you will read of many instances when our brains can be fooled by our senses, most frequently in the visual illusions that are common in psychological literature. The point is not to prove how easily the brain can be fooled, but rather to demonstrate the fundamental role of prior information in shaping our experience of the world. We experience what we expect to experience, not what is really out there.

Behavioural economists refer to effects like the beer experiments as 'priming' (Kahneman, 2012). They are the reason that you rate someone as more friendly after being given a warm drink compared with when you are given a cold drink; why you are more flexible in negotiations when sitting in a soft chair rather than a hard chair;

and why even wine experts can be fooled into describing white wine as 'rounded' and 'red fruit' when a small amount of red colouring is added.

Perception is an active construction

Our vision seems vivid and real, and directly related to the things we see around us, but perhaps this is one of the greatest visual illusions of all. Is vision passive or does it actively construct a version of reality from small pieces of evidence?

Richard Gregory (1998) believes that our vision and other senses have evolved from passive responses (ie reception) to active constructions (ie perception). Our perceptions are hypotheses about the world around us, probabilistic computations designed to help our embodied brains maximize the effectiveness of our behaviour as we navigate our environment, our cultures and relationships with the other people around us. As Gregory puts it, 'perception is a bunch of guesses'.

In the 17th century, John Locke (1632–1704) and Sir Isaac Newton (1642–1727) argued that colour is created in our brains and that light and objects do not have colour in themselves. Colour only exists through the interaction of light with objects, in terms of which parts of the light spectrum are absorbed or reflected by an object. George Berkeley (1685–1753) believed that we do not really see shape and space at all, but we feel them in the sense that we see coloured 'patches' and associate these with shapes and spaces through our experience of the world, much like the experience of a Cézanne painting with its rough shaped splashes of paint forming a vision of a mountain (Locke, 1979; Berkeley, 1922; Hume, 1993; Gregory, 2009; Hoffman, 1998; Frith, 2007; Purves and Lotto, 2011). Berkeley was far ahead of his time, and in the 21st century we know where the sensation of colour is produced in the brain, but we still do not understand how this happens. Similarly, loudness is just the sensation created by moving air. So are the perceptions of colour and sound an illusion? Why does the sky look blue and thunder sound loud?

The world we see is really a construct of our brain, which does not produce a picture or video image in the way a camera does, but

checking predictions against reality

actively creates a model of the world from the information provided by the different modules of the senses. In the case of vision this includes light and shade, edges, curvature and many other sensations. Integrated together, all these pieces of information allow the brain to 'fill in' the blind spot in the middle of our eyes (the part of the retina where the optic nerve joins the brain), compensate for the rapid eye movements ('saccades') that our eyes makes around five times each second, and still produce a steady and coherent picture of the world around us. Consider how we can 'see' in a dark room, where the colour receptors in our eyes do not function at all. We are still able to recreate a coloured world based on our memory of experiences in daylight.

In *Visual Intelligence* (1998), Donald Hoffman discusses how our eye and brain interact to put together 'patches of colour' to see a coherent picture of the world. The fundamental problem of perception is that any image on our retinas is not unique and can be interpreted in countless different ways. Hoffman argues that we all build a set of visual rules of thumb through which construct our visual world.

The perception of depth and distance demonstrates how the brain uses such rules to predict the reality of the world outside. Although depth perception is often considered a result of binocular vision, this plays a lesser role than monocular vision in how we perceive distance. Here is a non-exhaustive list of the clues that are used in determining depth, with only the last three dependent on having two eyes (Gibson, 1950; 'Depth perception' article from Wikipedia, accessed on 4 April 2013):

1 **Relative size** of objects known to be similar provides clear evidence of relative depth or distance.

2 **Familiar size** of objects helps the brain determine distance based on the object's size on the retina. That is, our brain knows the size of cars and people and can extrapolate distance based on perceived size.

3 **Perspective** gives clues based on the brain's experience that parallel lines converge in the distance at infinity.

4 **Motion parallax** depends on the relative motion of stationary objects against a background when we move as observers to give clues about distance.

5 Depth from motion gives clues based on the changing size of objects when observer or object are moving.

6 Aerial perspective uses the lower luminance contrast and saturation of distant objects (due to light scattering in the atmosphere) to determine the 'distance fog' and, therefore, likely depth. For example, Cézanne and other painters used 'warm' pigments (red, orange, yellow) to bring features nearer the viewer and 'cool' pigments (blue, green, violet) to make features recede into the distance.

7 Accommodation is based on feedback from the eye's muscles, which contract and relax when looking at short distances in order to make the eye lens thinner.

8 Occlusion is based on the knowledge that objects closer to you block (or occlude) objects that are farther away, allowing the brain to create a ranking of objects in the distance.

9 Curvilinear perspective is based on the curving of parallel lines at the extremes of visual perception, giving the brain clues about our position in three dimensions.

10 Texture gradient uses the fact that we can perceive the details of near objects much more clearly than those of more distance objects. For example, we can see the details of nature (size, shape, colour) with much more clarity in the near distance than farther away.

11 Lighting and shading are used to determine distance from the way that light falls on an object and reflects off its surfaces.

12 Defocus blur is used to determine depth as there is less focus and more blur the farther an object is from us.

13 Elevation gives clues as to the position of an object relative to the horizon, with those closer to the horizon farther away from us.

14 Stereopsis is the use of the information from both eyes to infer distance based on the relative size and angle of the image in each retina.

15 Convergence happens as both eyeballs focus on an object, allowing the brain to infer distance based on the feedback from the muscles in the eyes.

16 Shadow stereopsis uses disparities in the perception of shadows across retinas to infer depth.

James Gibson's comments from 1950 on the importance of binocular vision are still relevant today, and should be compulsory reading for the advocates of 3D cinema and television:

> It has been commonly believed for many years that the only important basis for depth perception in the visual world is the stereoscopic effects of binocular vision... It is the belief of photographers, artists, motion picture researchers, and visual educators that a scene can be presented in true depth only with the aid of stereoscopic techniques... This belief is based on the assumption that there exists a class of experiences called innate sensations. With the increasing tendency to question this assumption in modern psychology, the belief is left without much foundation. Depth, we have argued is not built up out of sensations, but is simply one of the dimensions of visual experience.

The brain has many clues that it uses to make predictions based on limited (and often corrupted or conflicting) sensory inputs. The process of perception is efficient and based on years and years of experience. The downside of these (highly efficient) rules of thumb is that it is very easy to fool our eyes. TV, films and optical illusions work by misleading the brain about what is out there. This is why the Moon appears larger than it really is, and varies in size when its real size is about the same as a hole made by a hole punch held at arm's length. It is also why we see films as continuous and moving, although they are only composed of 24 images each second, and why we hear actors speaking from their mouths, although the sound is coming from the speakers behind us.

These processes are also the basis of many visual illusions and magic tricks. Richard Gregory spent his life studying visual illusions in order to understand how perception works, and the hollow face illusion described by him is a perfect example of the paradoxes of perception. You can see the illusion by searching for 'hollow face illusion' on YouTube. It shows the power of prior probabilities, in the best sense of Bayesian statistics. Humans are experts at interpreting faces, as we see thousands of different faces from different angles throughout our life, and all of those faces are convex. Therefore, when the brain sees a stimulus that is concave, it overrides the information from the senses, which clearly do not make sense, and interprets the information as a normal convex face (Gregory, 2009: 127–29).

The majority of other illusions work in this way. One of the most famous is the Müller-Lyer illusion, which consists of a stylized arrow. When viewers are asked to place a mark on the figure at the midpoint, they invariably place it more towards the tail end. Franz-Carl Müller-Lyer devised the illusion in 1889. A more common variation of the illusion consists of a set of arrow-like figures, with straight-line segments comprising the shafts of the arrows, while fins protrude from the ends of the shafts (see below). The fins can point towards or away from the shaft, forming a head or a tail to the arrow. The line segment with two 'tails' is perceived to be longer than that with two heads ('Müller-Lyer illusion' article from Wikipedia, accessed on 4 April 2013). You can see the illusion in Figure 1.1.

FIGURE 1.1 Müller-Lyer illusion and perception of interior space

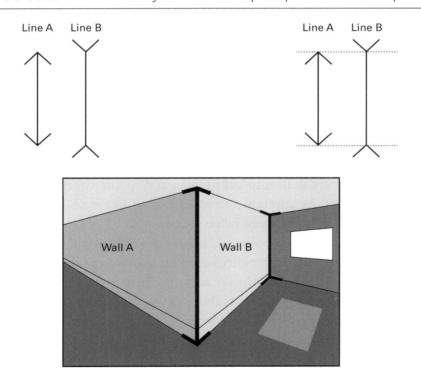

Richard Gregory hypothesized that the basis of this illusion was the brain's interpretation of depth and distance (perspective), and that the lines in or out are interpreted as signalling a three dimensional object. You can see this in the visual of an interior space in Figure 1.1.

Gregory's theory may or may not be true, but it has been demonstrated that the illusion varies across culture and age groups and, specifically, that the illusion is more powerful for older people brought up in more urban areas, where there are a lot more 'straight line' three-dimensional objects in the environment, and less powerful for younger children and those from rural areas. Whatever the reasons, it is clear that differences in the environment lead to differences in perception. Perception is learnt from experience.

The reality is that although the senses work from the bottom up, providing a rich source of information about the world, our perception is driven by top-down knowledge. This is the progression of evolution, from a simple bottom-up view of the world, to a sophisticated bottom-down view that uses a vast databank of information to make highly informed predictions. Our experience of the world has developed from 'reception' to 'perception' over millions of years. That's why we need such a large and interconnected brain, which uses far too much of our body's energy to make sense unless it can help us to survive, reproduce and lead successful lives.

Nature and nurture

How much innate knowledge of the world do we have? Neonate babies already know to respond to faces and to like sweet tastes and avoid sour ones. As adults we have learned to like both, using both prior knowledge and learned behaviours.

In 1955, George Kelly published his *Theory of Personal Constructs*, an original theory of personality based on the concept that there are many alternative solutions to the way in which any of us construct our world. His basic premise is that our perception of the world is guided by the way we anticipate what will happen, rather than how we react to it. This is again a more active, rather than passive, view of perception and behaviour.

Kelly coined the term 'constructs' to label the dimensions through which we structure the world. The way Kelly sets out his theory in postulates reflects his background in physics and mathematics before he moved into aviation psychology in the Second World War and ultimately into psychotherapy.

He saw humans as naïve scientists who see the world through their own lens and based on their own unique system of constructs. These constructs are only useful as far as they help us to anticipate future events, and in mental illness they have often been distorted by experiences that are atypical of normal social situations.

This view has been incorporated into many subsequent theories including cognitive-behavioural theory, and was a reaction against earlier theories that focused on drives or behaviour only, most especially those of BF Skinner. Importantly, Kelly took a less deterministic view of human behaviour, and was also driven by the need for reflexivity in psychology. It was important to him to be comfortable with describing his own behaviour in the same way as that of his patients. As Kelly put it,

> Theories are the thinking of men who seek freedom amid swirling events. The theories comprise prior assumptions about certain realms of these events. To the extent that the events may, from these prior assumptions, be construed, predicted, and their relative courses charted, men may exercise control, and gain freedom for themselves in the process (1955: 22).

Kelly's constructs are bipolar categories, or as he put it, 'the way two things are alike and different from a third'. For example, 'attractive', 'intelligent' and 'kind' always imply a contrast with an opposite meaning, such as 'ugly', 'stupid' or 'cruel'. Bipolar constructs describe a mental world very similar to that of semiotic theory that will be discussed in Chapter 5. Just like semiotic theory, constructs are always context specific or in Kelly's words, each construct has a 'range of convenience'.

Humans who are well adapted are continually revising and updating their own constructs to match new information that they encounter through new sensory data. Kelly's theory and related repertory grid technique assume that you can understand an individual's world view if you can understand the constructs that they use to evaluate the world.

Although the theory is abstract, the practical application is straightforward and has been used widely in clinical and commercial research. More importantly, Kelly's view of the process of evaluating experiences through a set of hypotheses in order to predict likely futures is consistent with the view of sensory perception discussed here.

Matching the right patterns

Perception is really a pattern matching system and memory is intimately linked to how we see the world. The brain uses past memories to predict future outcomes, and our perception of our any situation and our behaviour in response to that situation depend on which memories are used to match the current pattern.

It is well known that contextual cues are important in memory, which is why witnesses are taken back to the scene of the crime. In market research, it has been shown that placing people in a relevant environment improves the quality of their responses – you remember the names of more alcoholic drink brands when you are in a bar than when you are in a more artificial environment.

In one classic experiment, divers learnt lists of words in two environments, on dry land and underwater. They were later asked to recall the words in one of the two environments: either the original environment in which the words were learnt or in the alternative environment. Lists learnt underwater had higher recall underwater, and lists learnt on dry land had higher recall on dry land. The experimenters later proved that this effect was one of context-dependent memory and not related to the disruption of moving environments, as you can see in Figure 1.2.

Some companies have used these effects to their advantage. In *The Experience Economy*, Pine and Gilmore (2011) quote the example of Standard Parking of Chicago, who had a parking garage at O'Hare Airport. To help customers remember on which floor they parked their car, they play a different signature tune at each level of the garage, and decorated the walls with the icons of different local

FIGURE 1.2 Context and memory

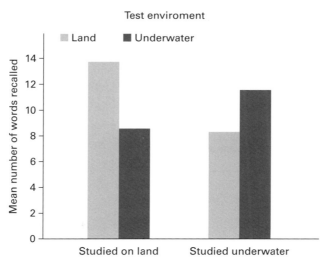

Test enviroment

■ Land   ■ Underwater

Mean number of words recalled

SOURCE: Godden and Baddeley, 1975

sports franchises, so the Bulls were on one floor and the Blackhawks on another. They quote one local resident saying, 'You never forget where you parked!' (Pine and Gilmore, 2011: 5).

Other studies have shown that memory recall can also depend on physiological state and mood state. Pamela Kenealy (1997) demonstrated that recall was dependent on mood state, although only for free recall and not cued (prompted) recall. In the study, participants looked at a map and learned a set of instructions about a particular route, until their performance on recall tasks exceeded 80 per cent accuracy. They were brought back one day later and given tests of free recall and cued recall on the visual outline of the map. It was shown that mood state effected memory, but only for free recall and not cued recall. Those induced into a sad mood had higher recall when in a sad mood on the following day, and lower recall when in a happy mood (and vice-versa) as you can see in Figure 1.3.

The brain is a prediction machine, and prediction of the future is and should be sensitive to mood state and environment. Our emotions and context are important determinants of what is appropriate behaviour. If you want your brand to be recalled, then create associations with the relevant emotions and contexts. As Dan Hill says,

FIGURE 1.3   Emotion and memory

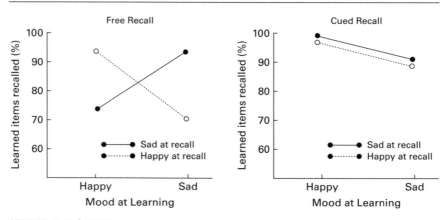

SOURCE: Kenealy, 1997

'be on-emotion (and not just on message)' (2010: 171). There are also some important lessons for market research here too: if you want to predict behaviour more accurately, ensure that your respondent is in the right place and the right mood.

Experience and memory

In *Thinking, Fast and Slow* (2012), Daniel Kahneman discusses the difference between our experience of events and what we remember later. They are not the same. We tend to remember only key parts of our experiences, and most especially the very first time we come into contact with someone or something ('priming'), the most extreme moments and the end of the experience ('peak-end rule'). In addition, our memory for individual events is much better than our memory of time ('duration neglect').

Kahneman discusses examples and experiments that involve the evaluation of pain. In one quoted experiment, participants were asked to hold their hands in painfully cold water (14 °C). In one condition, participants were asked to do this for 60 seconds. In a second condition, participants were asked to do this for 60 seconds and then for a further 30 seconds as the temperature was increased by one degree – enough to perceive a slight decrease in pain. Participants experienced both these conditions, with a break in between, and were then asked to choose which condition they would prefer to repeat. Eighty per cent of participants chose to repeat the second condition rather than the first.

Objectively, this does not make sense, but remember that our memory is different from our experience, and what we remember most are the extremes and end points, and not the duration of the experience. So participants' memory told them that the second condition ended better, and that there was no difference in the duration of the experience. Therefore it made sense to go for the second. Kahneman puts it, 'The experiencing self is the one that answers the question: "Does it hurt now?" The remembering self is the one that answers the question: "How was it, on the whole?"' (2012: 38). As he says later, 'the remembering self is sometimes wrong, but it is the one that keeps the score and governs what we learn from living, and it is the one that makes decisions. What we learn from the past is to maximize the qualities of our future memories, not necessarily of our future experience. This is the tyranny of the remembering self.'

How does this apply to brand experience design? First impressions last, as do final impressions, so it pays to focus on beginning and end points. It also pays to surprise customers occasionally or provide occasional 'big moments'. These are the parts of the experience that will be remembered and therefore will guide future decision-making.

Kahneman's overall metaphor for the mind is as a dual system, with System 1 fast, intuitive, automatic, implicit and uncontrollable and System 2 slow, deliberate, explicit and directed by our conscious minds. The subtleness of Kahneman's description of independent parts of a whole system is best captured in the comment by Rory Sutherland of Ogilvy Group UK, 'System 1 is the Oval Office and System 2 is the press office. Of course, System 1 is always ultimately in charge of what happens, whatever System 2 decides to say.'

Associating with the right memories

How does System 1 work? We all store different ideas associatively. If I hear the word 'banana' a number of things come immediately to mind:

1 A picture of a banana (it is after all a fruit);

2 A jingle from a late 1960s children's programme which I used to watch avidly every Saturday morning (Fleegle, Bongo, Drooper and Snorky sang the theme tune 'One banana, two banana, three banana, four' every week);

3 The shopfront of Banana Republic (which I happened to pass yesterday).

In turn these trigger a further set of ideas:

4 A banana split (the dessert made from banana);

5 The smell of banoffee pie (another dessert made from banana – you can tell I have a sweet tooth);

6 The tune of 'Banana Republic' by the Boomtown Rats.

Our memory works by associating ideas or concepts with each other, when they have any kind of association or there is an analogy between the ideas. Although some of these ideas are made concrete by words, many of them are sensory experiences triggered by a certain stimulus, such as a picture, a tune or a smell.

The process of association mirrors the more fundamental neuronal processes that are the building blocks of our memories and behaviours. Neuroscientists use the expression, 'fire together, wire together' to describe how neurons work, meaning that if one set of neurons, linked to a specific experience, fire at the same time as another set of neurons, linked to a separate experience, the brain learns that there may be some connection between the two events. The more often this happens (fire together), the stronger the association between the two events becomes, until eventually the connection is so strong that only one event is needed to trigger those neurons linked to the second experience (the events are wired together). This is the basis of conditioning, where the body's behavioural response to one event comes to anticipate its response to a separate later event.

The associative basis of memory is why metaphors and archetypes are so powerful. Metaphors allow us to associate a rich vein of ideas and memories in our minds through one central 'idea', making that idea a powerful trigger of behaviour.

Gerald Zaltman (2003) has pioneered the use of metaphors in marketing and research, building on pioneering work in philosophy, psychology and linguistics (see also Lakoff and Turner, 1980). Zaltman argues that there are a number of 'deep metaphors' that are unconscious 'structures of human thought' and that these metaphors manifest themselves in surface metaphors used in everyday language. Furthermore, he argues that these metaphors can be used in marketing to communicate more effectively to consumers about a brand, product or topic using language that everyone can understand and appreciate.

Zaltman uses metaphors as the basis of his research to understand deeper beliefs and thinking patterns. He has written about seven fundamental metaphors that are common across cultures and categories: balance, transformation, journey, container, connection, resource and control (Zaltman and Zaltman, 2008). All are related to universal human traits, and our love of stories is really a love of extended metaphors. There are many common themes between these metaphors and the archetypes that will be the subject of Chapter 7.

Metaphors frequently use sensory terms, such as 'I see what you're saying' and 'I was touched by your words'. Many scientists have argued that the experience of synaesthesia is linked to the brain's use of analogy and metaphor, and that these processes are also deeply linked to creativity (Cytowic and Eagleman, 2011; Ramachandran, 2011).

Synaesthesia is much more prevalent among artists and poets than in the general population. For example, Wassily Kandinsky was synaesthetic, as was Richard Feynman, who was a highly creative scientist and bongo player and once described the experience of synaesthesia in this way: 'When I see equations, I see the letters in colours – I don't know why. As I'm talking, I see vague pictures of Bessel functions, with light-tan j's, slightly violet-bluish n's, and dark brown x's flying around. And I wonder what the hell it must look like to the students' (Ward, 2008: 11).

"the sound of feeling"

One theory of synaesthesia is that cross-wiring in the brain leads it to learn to associate one sensory impression with another from a different sensory modality. This means that the colour can help the brain predict the letter or word (or vice-versa). As we have learnt, the brain is above all a sophisticated pattern recognition machine, designed to make predictions about the world in order to optimize our behaviour to achieve the best possible outcomes. As Richard Gregory said more succinctly, '[Sensation] is a bunch of hypotheses'.

Perception, memory and action are all part of the same integrated system. We remember experiences that have meaning, in order to make future predictions by matching current perceptions to those past experiences. Meaning comes from predictive ability, emotional salience and context. Our senses help us create meaning, but they are far from perfect.

I will leave the final words of this chapter to Richard Gregory (2009) who wrote:

> We expect small things to be lighter than big things, to get smaller as they move away from us, and to grow larger as they get nearer... Though seeing and hearing and touch seem simple and direct, they are not. They are fallible inferences based on knowledge and assumptions which may or may not be appropriate to the situation. Listen to a tape recording of an audience clapping. In the kitchen, it sounds like bacon frying. In the garden, it sounds like rain.

The senses close up

02

> *Harry breathed in her aroma. Scientists still know very little about how the olfactory cortex in the brain converts impulses from the receptors into conscious senses of smell. But Harry wasn't thinking so much about the hows, he just knew that when he smelt her, all sorts of things started happening in his head and body. Like his eyelids closing halfway, like his mouth spreading into a broad grin and his mood soaring.*
>
> JO NESBO, THE BAT

Five and counting

Despite what we've all learnt, there are more than five senses. For example, if you place your hand a few centimeters away from a hot iron, none of your senses (sight, sound, touch, smell, taste) can warn you that the iron will burn you, yet you won't touch it as you can feel it is hot from a distance. That's due to the heat sensors in your skin. Other sensors can tell you if you are experiencing pain, or if you are upside down. All these senses and more will be explored in this chapter.

The word 'sense' is defined in the Oxford English Dictionary as 'any of the faculties, such as sight, hearing, smell, taste or touch, by which humans and animals perceive stimuli originating from outside or inside the body'. The Wikipedia entry for senses states that, 'Senses are physiological capacities of organisms that provide data for perception'. Above all, the senses are our connection with the outside world, through which we can build a store of memories to help us predict and control our future. For scientific introductions to each of the senses you can read Roberts (2002) and for a more poetic introduction Ackerman (1995).

The unique value of the human mind is to make our behaviour context sensitive. Context depends on what we sense around us, as described in one of the earliest references to the five senses from the *Katha Upanishad*. In the *Ratha Kalpana*, the teacher Yama compares the 'five material faculties' to five horses drawing the 'chariot of the body' ('Katha Upanishad' article on Wikipedia, accessed on 4 April 2013). The parable, describes the 'self' as the chariot's passenger, the body as the chariot itself, consciousness as the chariot driver, the mind as the reins, the five senses as the horses and the objects perceived by the senses as the chariot's path. The parable is roughly contemporary with Parmenides' and Plato's use of similar metaphors (eg in *Phaedra*), and the reference to the 'five organs of perception' predates Aristotle who is often credited with the idea.

In William Shakespeare's time there were believed to be five 'wits' (sense and wit were synonyms), and allegories based on the five senses were common in 17th-century painting. For example, in Gérard de Lairesse's *Allegory of the Five Senses* (1668), each of the main figures allude to one of the senses, with a reclining boy with a mirror representing sight, a cupid-like boy with a triangle representing hearing, a girl with flowers representing smell, a woman with a fruit representing taste and a woman holding a bird representing touch. You can see the painting and read more about it in the Wikipedia article on 'Gérard de Lairesse'.

In *Audio Branding*, Karsten Kilian estimates the importance of each of the five main senses to the overall impact of a brand as shown in Table 2.1.

The table shows the importance of the eyes and ears relative to other senses, and reinforcing the view of the conscious 'bandwidth' of the senses, although touch is given less prominence than in Zimmerman's data or my personal experience.

Whatever the relative importance of the senses, it is critical to remember that they are not separate and independent systems. The

TABLE 2.1   Relative importance of the five main senses

Eyes (visual)	83.0%
Ears (acoustic)	11.0%
Nose (olfactory)	3.5%
Skin/movement (tactile/kinesthetic)	1.5%
Tongue (gustatory)	1.0%

SOURCE: Bronner and Hirt, 2009

senses work together to provide a more holistic picture of the world, adding up to much more than 100 per cent, (see 'Gestalt psychology' article on Wikipedia for more on this topic). Although product design is typically a separate function from branding, the most successful brands are based on identities or personalities that span across design, communication and all aspects of experience.

Most of the senses comprise multiple feedback systems and are ultimately integrated in the brain, which checks for patterns that have been experienced before. Vision includes perception of motion, colour and luminance, while touch includes pressure, temperature, pain, vibration and movement (proprioception works from the nerve endings in our muscles and joints). Our ears help us keep a sense of balance as well as a sense of the rhythms of life.

In the 21st century, sight is the most used sense in marketing and the sense most stimulated by the environment. Arguably other senses could and should be better utilized by brands. The choice of colours and forms in the design of a product are perhaps the most critical choices in branding, along with the use of sound, smell and the naming of brands and products, which are important elements in the esSense template for experience design that will be discussed in the final chapter.

Let's begin our exploration of the senses with those senses that work close up and personal.

The primal sense

What is your favourite smell? I have many, although the smoky, velvet, roasted smell of freshly brewed coffee is high up the list (I have a pot in front of me as I write). The sharp earthy smell of freshly cut grass is also one that brings back memories of mowing the lawn with my father, when I struggled to push the manual lawnmower up and down the grass. Another very strong memory is the fragrant hops at Brakspear's brewery in Henley-on-Thames that I was lucky enough to visit before the original brewery was closed down in 2002.

Although many friends swear by it, one smell I can never learn to love is the durian, common in South East Asia. As Helen Keller once said, 'Smell is a potent wizard that transports you across thousands of miles and all the years you have lived'. Martin Lindstrom cites studies that have shown that 75 per cent of our emotions are generated by smell (2005: 84).

Smell is the oldest of the human senses, originating in the chemical detection systems found in our earliest ancestors. It is the only sense with a straight line to our emotions, as the olfactory bulb is directly connected to the limbic system (the centre of our brain's emotions). Although we are very poor smell detectors compared with many other animals, the system is still sophisticated enough to detect between 10–20,000 different odours (using an estimated 12 million olfactory receptor cells). To put this in context, cats have around five times as many receptor cells, and dogs have more than a billion. For cats and dogs, smell is much more important as they are closer to the ground where all the interesting smells are lurking.

Even our limited abilities mean that we can detect smells far better than we can describe them. For other animals, smell is a primary survival sense, while for humans vision has that role. However, smell still signals to us whether we should approach or avoid something in the environment, and is able to do this at a distance, unlike taste. Some of our primary emotions, such as disgust, are linked to our sense of smell, and our acceptance or rejection of different smells is usually cultural rather than innate (unlike taste). I love the smell of strong cheese, while many people, especially in Asia, are reminded of vomit and reject it. Chemically the smells are almost identical.

Some years ago, an interesting comparison of smells across cultures found huge differences in preferences for smells even in seemingly similar cultures. Wintergreen was rated as the best liked smell by Americans and almost the least liked by those from the UK. Why was this? Americans first encounter wintergreen as candy, whereas the British first encounter wintergreen as medicine. Our first experience with any smell has a powerful effect on whether we have positive or negative associations with it.

As Paul Rozin once said, the one piece of information that can help you understand someone's food likes and dislikes is their culture (Rozin and Vollmecke, 1986).

Vanilla is one of the smells that is popular across many cultures and countries, which is perhaps why Johnson & Johnson use this as the basis of their signature fragrance used across a wide range of their product line, and most noticeably baby products. Although not always popular, there is also no mistaking the signature smell of Dettol products too, designed to communicate the antiseptic and hygiene values of the brand.

In evolutionary terms, our brain evolved from our sense of smell, from the olfactory bulb in the limbic (basic emotional reaction) system of fish. Smell was (and is) a chemical detection system, and the nerve endings of smell receptors go straight from the top of the nose into the olfactory cortex, and in one more step directly on to the brain's emotion and memory systems. While other senses are mediated through the thalamus (which is responsible for language) and are integrated before reaching memory, smell has its own very direct route.

Richard Feynman was once asked if there was a single sentence that summarized all that humans understand about the world from science. His answer was, 'The world is made of atoms' (Feynman, 1995: 4). Smell and taste are very much about atoms, and smell can be described as a 'contact sport', where the receptors in our nose come into direct contact with molecules of whatever we smell. As long as a molecule is volatile, water soluble and capable of attaching to the surface of receptor cells then it can be detected.

Diane Ackerman uses another beautiful poetic phrase to describe this sense: 'Smells detonate softly in our memory like poignant land mines, hidden under the weedy moss of many years and experiences'

(1995: 5). Smells are not translated into language before they are stored in memory or activate our emotions, which may be one reason why, despite our detection abilities, we find it hard to describe smells in detail (in addition to the inadequacy of language itself). However, they are directly linked into our emotions and memories, and can therefore trigger very strong emotional responses.

Although memories that are triggered by smell are very powerful, research has shown that they are not more accurate – they just seem much more vivid and therefore make us more confident that we are right. If you have ever visited a Thomas Pink store, you will have smelt the distinctive whiff of fresh laundry, which triggers exactly the right vivid memories of freshly starched clean shirts.

A Swedish experiment compared the memories evoked by odours, words and pictures and found that odour cues triggered older memories than words or pictures, often from when participants had been younger than 10. They also found that odours alone were more evocative than odours paired with names, as the words got in the way (Brynie, 2009: 68).

Rachel Herz has studied the sense of smell extensively, and has found that odours trigger more emotional and evocative memories than other sensory cues, although they are no more or less specific or vivid than the memories triggered by other senses. She writes:

> What I found in these experiments is that, in terms of their accuracy, detail, and vividness, our recollections triggered by scents are just as good as our memories elicited by seeing, hearing, or touching an item – but no more so. Yet our memories triggered by odours are distinctive in one important way: their emotionality. We list more emotions, rate our emotions as having greater intensity, report our memories as being more emotionally laden, and state that we feel more strongly a sense of being back in the original time and place when a scent elicits the past than when the same event is triggered in any other way. (Herz, 2007: 67)

Proust famously wrote about his 'madeleine moment', and others have written similarly about the evocative nature of smell, perhaps because of the important role of context in both smell and memory. Memory is based on an emotional experience linked to a very specific context. Smell operates in the same way. The perception of a smell is highly dependent on the context in which we smell something, and evocative smells are usually linked to very positive emotional experiences (such as visiting Brakspear's brewery or helping my father mow the lawn). They can also be linked to very negative emotional experiences. For example, I remember vividly suffering from food poisoning on a picnic when I was seven or eight years old, and didn't eat another Cornish pasty for 20 years.

The importance of context may also be why aromatherapy works for some people, through association of particular smells with specific moods and positive experiences. Apart from its role in tasting food and drink (see below), smell also plays a role in sexual selection. Our body odours reflect our immune system, and we typically prefer the odour of partners who smell 'different' to us – meaning that they have different immune systems making them more compatible. If you want to choose the right partner, make sure that they are not wearing perfume or cologne on your first date.

Hotels and spas have long realized the power of using scents to create the right ambience. The Westin hotel chain has rolled out a Sensory Welcome programme across all its hotels, creating a relaxed mood in public spaces, blending carefully chosen soundtracks, and using infused scents and carefully designed visual cues in interior design. The company's White Tea fragrance has been such a hit that it can be bought as a stand-alone product line. This follows on the chain's successful tactile branding campaign with its Heavenly Bed and Heavenly Bath products (which are also sold in Nordstrom stores).

Closer to home, Marina Bay Sands, the iconic 'ship' hotel looking across Singapore's waterfront, offer guests a choice of three signature fragrances in their suites: masculine, feminine and neutral. Housekeeping staff in the hotel use portable scent machines to neutralize unpleasant odours. Meanwhile, the Equarius Hotel on Sentosa has developed a signature fragrance which is described as 'reminiscent of rainforest infused with floral and green top and mid notes, perfectly balanced with woody lower notes to compliment the design and bring out the elements of the resort's lush tropical greenery' (as reported in 'This is what sensory branding can do for your business' by Simon Faure-Field in Singapore Business Review, 25 September 2012).

Other businesses are catching on. BMW partnered with Austrian natural cosmetics brand Susanne Kaufmann and launched a hand sanitizer and moisturizer made entirely from herbal extracts. They describe how the collaboration is an example of how 'nature and technology can work together and effectively enhance each other'. More recently, Nissan have recently announced an 'official fragrance partner' in Air Aroma, developing a 'fresh, luxurious and oriental fragrance with hints of green tea' selected to reflect Nissan's target audience and brand identity (as reported in the articles 'Sensory Branding: Luxury Auto-Makers Woo with Smell and Sound', 5 December 2010, and 'Detroit Auto Show Preview: Nissan to debut Brand Scent', 9 January 2013, at **www.brandchannel.com**).

Similarly, Gillette and Schick have recently cottoned on to the power of scents in female razors (following Bic, which first launched a disposable woman's razor with a scented handle). Schick's Xtreme3 Refresh is claimed to be the world's first scented razor for men (as reported in the article 'Brands Smell Opportunity in Scent Marketing', 14 June 2011, at **www.brandchannel.com**).

Singapore Airlines are often cited as pioneers of fragrance marketing, with their signature Floridian Waters fragrance which is infused in the cabins, the stewardesses' perfume and the towels that are a ritual before take off and landing. My earliest memory of sensory marketing is my first experience of opening a jar of coffee for myself, and taking in the rich aroma of coffee that hit me as I peeled back the freshness seal. The true pioneer of fragrance marketing was Coco Chanel. Back in 1921 she reportedly sprayed Chanel No. 5 in the dressing rooms of her Paris boutique.

Like the colour system, some scientists have conjectured that there are 'basic' smells. In the 18th century, Linnaeus proposed seven categories: camphor, musk, floral, minty, pungent, putrid and ether. Almost 100 years ago, Hans Henning (a German philosopher) constructed a 'smell prism' with six basic odours: fragrant, putrid, fruity, spicy, resinous and burnt (see Figure 2.1). Henning claimed in his book *Der Geruch* that every odour could be placed within the three dimensional grid between these six reference points.

The most widely accepted explanation of how smell works is that the shape of molecules (or part of them) provides a 'key' used

FIGURE 2.1 Henning's smell prism

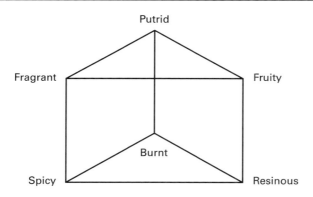

by smell receptors to measure 'fit' with specific smells. This means that different chemicals with similar shapes can have the same smell, while chemicals that differ very slightly (for example, different isomers) can have very different smells because of their shape. Most systems use a combination of size and or shape to predict the quality of smell, but no system has been developed that explains all smells. For example, perception of smell can also vary with amount. The chemical indole smells like flowers in small amounts, and putrid in high concentrations. The reality is perhaps that again, smell is as much a function of the mind as it is of molecular chemistry. Luca Turin writes more about the controversies around odour in *The Secret of Scent* (Turin, 2006).

Mood has been shown to have a big impact on our sense of smell. Research in Germany showed pleasant and unpleasant pictures to subjects before rating their performance on smell tests. Subjects rated test odours as less pleasant and more intense after viewing unpleasant pictures (and vice-versa). These effects were a function of changes in the mood of subjects.

There has long been a link between sense of smell and depression. Rachel Herz opens *The Scent of Desire* (2007) with the story of Michael Hutchence, the lead singer of INXS who took his life on 22 November 1997. After a freak traffic accident in 1992, his behaviour changed markedly, and this has been linked to the loss of his sense of smell. Michael Hutchence had lived his life as a hedonist and sensualist (he was definitely a 'Seducer' archetype as you will read later). His gourmand taste and lust for life were taken away from him, sending him into a spiral of depression. He reportedly broke down in tears and confessed to a friend, 'I can't even smell my girl-friend any more'.

Rachel Herz (2007) believes that anosmia (the loss of the sense of smell) was a crucial factor in Michael Hutchence's suicide, reflecting the unique interconnection between smell and emotion (via the brain's limbic system). Clinical research shows that patients who lose smell often also lose interest in normal pleasurable activities and are prone to depression, and these effects have also been observed in other animals who often stop eating and lie still oblivious to the world around them. Similarly, people suffering from depression often report a loss of sensitivity in smell. It seems that smell and emotion are intimately bound together in human behaviour.

Although it is common to talk about taste and flavour interchange-ably, taste is technically a different (and more basic) sense linked to actual ingestion of food. Flavour description comes from both taste (on the tongue) and smell (through the front of the nose and also via the back of the nose when we chew food). Most of us are very poor at describing flavour, just as we are poor at describing smells, how-ever good we are at detecting them.

There is considerable individual difference in ability to detect flavours, both qualitatively and quantitatively. This is because not everyone has exactly the same type and number of olfactory receptors; you may be able to smell things that I cannot and vice-versa. Those with more receptors typically may perceive things as more intense than those with fewer receptors.

Arguably, smell and taste are parts of the same integrated system, so it's time to discuss taste.

Basic taste

Close your eyes and hold your nose, and you will notice no effect on the sense of taste. However, you will be unable to detect the dif-ference between an apple and an onion, red and white wine, beef and lamb. You will also be unable to tell the difference between orange, mango, peach or a blend of juices. That is why you lose your 'taste' when you have a head cold.

Importantly, taste relies on foods being heated (to body temperature) and chewed in the mouth as well as aromas reaching the olfactory receptors via the back of the mouth to give food all its complex taste. Other senses play a role too, as pain (for example, the sting of capsaicin) works by reducing taste sensations and then enhancing them as the pain moderates (along with the endorphins which give eaters the chili buzz). Similarly, salt is a flavour enhancer, amplifying the taste of other ingredients.

Sound impacts our perception through the loudness and timbre (pitch) of the sound through the air and the vibration of our bones (when we eat crisps and other foods). Sound is related to texture, and one bizarre experiment measured the impact of texture on taste by asking participants to identify fruits and vegetables with the texture differences removed. Only 41 per cent of students could identify banana, 30 per cent could identify broccoli, 63 per cent could identify carrot and 7 per cent could identify cabbage. For elderly participants the accuracy was much lower at 24 per cent, 0 per cent, 7 per cent and 4 per cent.

Even music can affect the way food tastes. High-pitched music has been shown to make toffees taste sweeter. Sweetness is often linked to high notes, whereas savoury tastes are often linked to low brassy notes. For another example, try bacon and egg ice cream (yes, there is such a thing), and then play a sizzling sound alternated with farmyard music and you will notice the dominant flavour changing.

Ney's flavourgram captures the complexity of flavour combining the impact of smell, taste and consistency (texture) on its overall perception. You can see a version of the flavourgram in Figure 2.2. The top layer of boxes relate to the different classes of smells associated with foods. The middle layer incorporates the key taste sensations on the tongue including umami and the contribution of the sensations perceived through the trigeminal nerve such as astringency. The bottom layer references other important factors in experiencing the flavour of food including those related to mouth feel (Roberts, 2002: 332).

Our 'taste' relies on much more than taste. In contrast to smell, our sense of taste is limited to five (or perhaps six or seven) varieties. As

FIGURE 2.2 Ney's flavourgram

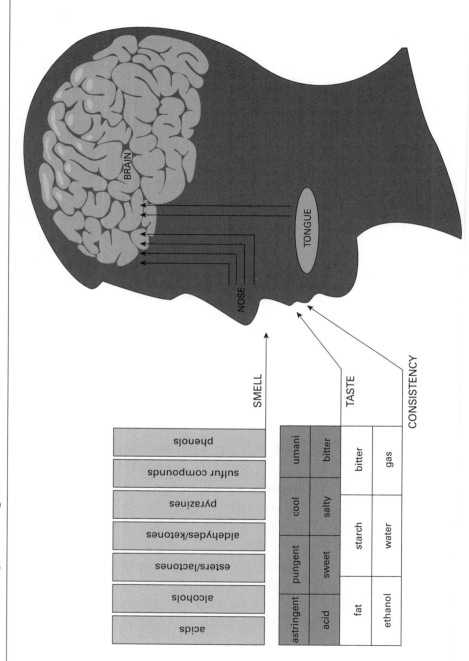

well as sweet, sour, salt and bitter, umami is the fifth taste. Each of the basic tastes reflects a basic detection (or signalling) system for the things we bring into our bodies.

On the positive side, sweetness indicates a source of energy, saltiness indicates mineral salts (important for body regulation), and umami indicates protein-rich food. Umami is a Japanese discovery and word, literally meaning 'savoury deliciousness' or, more simply, 'tasty' in reference to the rich and meaty quality of savoury foods.

On the warning side, sourness is associated with food that is unripe or 'off' and bitterness is associated with many of nature's poisonous creations. Newborn babies already know which of these to approach and which to avoid (except saltiness, which lags a few months behind the other tastes). Sweetness produces suckling, lip smacking and smiling in neonate infants, while bitterness (quinine) produces nose wrinkling, gaping and tongue protrusion (animals have similar reactions). This is why we all have to learn to love the bitterness of beer and coffee (Prescott, 2012: 32–36).

Have you ever asked yourself, why tomatoes are not in the fruit salad? This is something to do with glutamate (an amino acid), which produces the 'umami' taste, giving tomatoes the meaty, rich quality that means you can use them in sauces and stews. Glutamate increases savouriness, richness and a tactile mouth-filling quality in foods, which is why many Asians love to use monosodium glutamate (MSG) in cooking.

Although metallic and the drying, puckering quality of astringency have been suggested as tastes (for example, by Aristotle), they are now accepted as coming from odours and tactile sensations. However, recent research shows that fatty acids and calcium can be detected by certain receptors in the tongue and may therefore count as basic tastes (Brynie, 2009: 77).

Most brands, even foods, rely on more than taste to give them a sensory signature, although Tabasco is perhaps one example of a product that is all about taste. I have friends who cannot eat anything, especially pizza, without a liberal dosing of Tabasco sauce. The packaging and branding of Tabasco is also a masterpiece of simplicity and focus. Another brand that is all about taste is Coke Zero with its tagline, 'real Coca-Cola taste and zero calories'.

Taste's important role in our daily lives is evident in many of the metaphors we commonly use. We refer to the 'sweetness' of moments we treasure, the 'bitterness' of defeat, the 'souring' of a relationship and call a truly good friend 'the salt of the earth'.

The Greek philosopher Alcmaeon believed that the tongue had tiny holes that allowed tastes to reach the brain, and later Democritus explained taste qualities saying that sourness was related to angular shapes, sweetness to round shapes, and bitterness to round shapes with small hooks. Democritus clearly understood how to think synaesthetically. Aristotle identified the four basic tastes plus astringent, pungent and harsh.

As with smell, we all have much greater ability to experience the rich tastes of food than we do to describe those experiences (even for experts or 'supertasters' who are less than 20 per cent of the population). In work I have conducted in the UK, only 90 per cent of people accurately describe a sugar solution as 'sweet', with 67 per cent describing sourness, 53 per cent saltiness and 18 per cent bitterness. 'Supertasters' are usually identified by their sensitivity to 6-n-propylthiouracil (known as PROP for short), which is linked to the number of fungiform papillae on the tongue (genetically inherited). The detection thresholds between normal people and supertasters vary about 300 fold, which is the difference between not tasting it at all and wanting to threaten an experimenter's life (Prescott, 2012: 125–35).

The wine industry, along with coffee, perfumes and others, employs 'experts'. We all accept that some people have more taste ability than others, but a large part of the ability of expert tasters comes from their rich conceptual understanding of the language and meaning of the elements of anything they taste. This conceptual understanding comes from their experience. Brain imaging of wine tasters shows much greater brain activity in three areas and stages: the initial sensory impression (which creates a much stronger 'representation' in experts), analytic (left-brain) processing of the representation and in the final stage much greater activity in the memory and language areas of the brain (conceptualization).

This ability is because experts can describe what they taste without interfering with their ability to perceive the sensation. Several experiments have shown that non-expert tasters often have the same ability to *perceive* differences between wines, but lack the ability to *conceptualize* the differences. The inability to conceptualize can compromise their experience of tasting, changing their memory of the experience. This has also been seen in market research, where asking questions can change how participants remember and evaluate an experience.

In *The Physiology of Taste*, Jean Anthelme Brillat-Savarin says that taste can be reduced to 'in the last analysis, in the two expressions, agreeable or disagreeable' (Brillat-Savarin, 2009). Taste shows more clearly than any other sense the importance of environmental 'signals', mediated by the senses, to helping us understand the world and predict the future. We will turn to signs and signals in the next chapter.

The touch of reality

One of my most vivid memories of childhood is of a huge electric storm, when a sudden power cut meant that we all had to find our way around our home. I was very scared, especially as the power cut had interrupted our viewing of the film *Alien*. Of course, it was also exhilarating, using my hands to 'see' my way around the house and test my memory of the space I lived in. The exhilaration disappeared the moment I stepped into the kitchen, which was set a little lower than the other rooms in the house, and stepped into something cold and wet (the storm had also caused some minor flooding).

What makes Pringles and Toblerone unique? Why do Bang & Olufsen remote controls have such a feeling of quality about them? Shape and weight are all about how products feel in our hands. Research has shown that touch seems to improve integration of sensory inputs with personal thoughts and feelings, making a brand more tangible and increasing the customer's feeling of ownership (Peck and Shu, 2009).

Touch is in many ways different from other senses as it is really 'us'. Eyes, ears, tongue and nose are all specific organs with specific functions, but touch encompasses our whole body. Touch is how we 'know' what is really out there, and although we can see our environment, it doesn't become real until we touch it or hold it.

Without touch there would be no nurturing or relationships and touch develops early in the womb (along with hearing). Infants who experience more touching are healthier both physically and mentally, and babies who are massaged and nurtured have been shown to gain weight 50 per cent faster than those who are left alone. Brynie discusses an experiment in which pediatricians used a heel-stick procedure to take blood samples from very young babies. Those babies in contact with their mothers grimaced 65 per cent less and cried 82 per cent less than those in bassinets. Touch always brings comfort (Brynie, 2009: 7). Ashley Montagu provides a detailed and intimate portrait of this sense in *Touching: The Human Significance of the Skin* (1986).

The skin is our body's largest organ (by some stretch), encompassing the whole of our body and weighing between 2.7 and 4.5 kilograms. Moreover, touch is the only sense that gives us direct contact with the outside world, and not just small floating particles of it. Skin keeps us inside and safe from the outside world, acting as a wall between our bodies and our environment, just like a spacesuit. It is constantly growing and renewing with cells starting in lower layers of the skin and working their way to the outer layers as they age and eventually drop off to be replaced.

Our mental sense of our body's map is vitally important to navigating the world, and many modern neuroscientists speak of the brain more as an embodied organ than a stand-alone instrument. Touch is the one sense that we cannot do without. It is very hard to eliminate touch, in the same way that we can with the eyes, ears and other organs. Physical contact is always more powerful than verbal or even emotional communication, and it is possible to rely on touch if we lose other senses, but not the other way around.

Touching sight

Our powers of adaptation are astonishing. When we are artificially blinded, we quickly adapt to our changed circumstances and our sense of touch can improve dramatically within five days as our brain already starts to use its plasticity to make better use of our visual cortex. However, we can also start to hallucinate (see things in our minds) and our sense of taste can be dulled without the visual stimulus it is used to. At the same time, we develop heightened sensitivity to temperature and sound.

On the other hand, without touch we are completely lost. We have no sense of where we are in the world. Also, if we are not able to feel pain, we put ourselves in many very dangerous situations. This reflects the importance of touch in building our knowledge of how the other senses work. Richard Gregory argued that touch is uniquely important in providing the real physical evidence of what is 'out there', which we later rely on in order to make predictions based on what we see (2009: 98–99).

In this conclusion, Gregory followed George Berkeley, the 18th century Irish philosopher and clergyman who argued that our visual perception of materiality, distance and spatial depth would not be possible without haptic (touch) memory. He wrote that vision needs the help of touch to provide sensations of 'solidity, resistance and protrusion', and that sight detached from touch would not 'have any idea of distance, outness or profundity, not consequently of space or body' (Berkeley, 1922; Pallasmaa, 2005).

Gregory studied and wrote about a fascinating case study of a man blind from birth regaining his sight. He could immediately 'see' certain things that he had only previously 'felt', such as the time on his open-faced watch, based on his existing knowledge. There is an interesting parallel in more recent studies which have shown that when a right angle is drawn on the open palm of a normal sighted person it activates the visual cortex in exactly the same way as 'seeing' a right angle even when their palm is out of their sight (Gregory, 2009: 94–96; Stein and Meredith, 1993).

Young babies rely on this sense to learn (not the sense of sight) and R. Buckminster Fuller put this perfectly when he wrote in 1978, 'Children are born true scientists. They spontaneously experiment and experience and re-experience again. They touch-test for hardness, softness, springiness, roughness, smoothness, coldness, warmness: they heft, shake, punch, squeeze, push, crush, rub, and try to pull things apart'.

Touch is very much the exploratory sense. When you pick up a big green watermelon (or any other choice of fruit or vegetable) at the supermarket, you might give it a gentle squeeze, weigh it in your hands and use the pressure of your thumb to see if it is too soft, too hard or just the right ripeness. All of these behaviours depend on active touch and cannot be done passively by pushing a fruit against your hand. Our hands are adapted to perform active touch, working together to grasp, palpate, prod, press, rub and heft objects we want to test. The pulp of our fingers is equipped with a dense array of highly sensitive tactile receptors.

Touch comprises a number of different senses, mostly based in the layers of our skin below the surface:

- **Light touch** is the feeling of contact with the skin's surface (for example a kiss) where the skin is not deformed;

- **Touch pressure** is where skin deformation stimulates the nerves in the deeper layers of the skin;

- **Vibration** is felt by nerves in the skin and other body organs (including bones);

- **Heat and cold** are felt by specific receptors in the skin that are sensitive to heat and cold (but not to temperature in general);

- **Pain** is felt by tissue that has been damaged and is designed to warn you of possible injury;

- **Proprioception** is felt from nerve endings in muscles and joints and indicates position and movement of the body.

Figure 2.3 depicts how a sensory homunculus (human body) is represented in the somatosensory cortex of our brain. Most of our sense of touch is processed in the somatosensory cortex, where all the areas of our body are mapped on to the brain, although some parts are more equal than others. This map was developed by Wilder Penfield, and is commonly known as the Penfield Map (Roberts, 2002: 245–54).

You can see from the map that the most touch-sensitive parts of your body are hands, lips, face, neck, tongue, fingertips and feet. Brands need to pay attention to touch points that come into contact with these parts of the body as they create much greater impact on customers' perceptions of experience. That is why Apple's touch screens are so much more 'sticky' than a keyboard. There are interesting differences between men and women with regards to touch. Men

FIGURE 2.3 Sensory homunculus on the somatosensory cortex

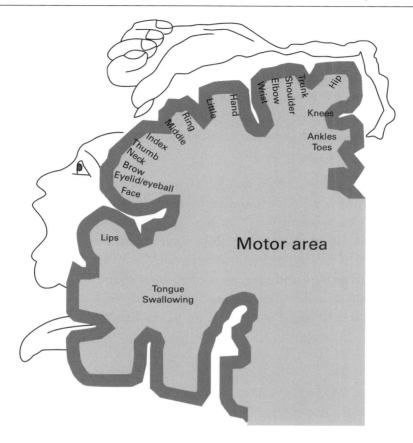

typically think of premium fabrics as fine and heavy (wool), while women think of them as fine and light (silk).

Proprioception is part of the touch sense and very important, but there is little general awareness about it. If you try and touch your nose with your eyes closed, this is the sense that tells you where the different parts of your body are relative to each other. It works by using your brain's knowledge of what muscles are doing with an awareness of the size and shape of your body. This makes sure that you can touch your nose in the dark even without the five classic senses.

Arguably all our other sense organs are really just specializations of skin. For example, our eyes developed from patches of light-sensitive skin (and some areas of our skin are still sensitive to light). As Ashley Montagu wrote:

> [The skin] is the oldest and the most sensitive of our organs, our first medium of communication, and our most efficient protector... Even the transparent cornea of the eye is overlain by a layer of modified skin... Touch is the parent of our eyes, ears, nose, and mouth. It is the sense which became differentiated into the others, a fact that seems to be recognized in the age-old evaluation of touch as 'the mother of the senses'. (Montagu, 1986: 3)

Our language reflects this, and is rich in metaphors involving touch. Most obviously we refer to our emotions as 'feelings', and talk about something or someone who 'touches' us. We all avoid touchy people, yet we talk about touchy feely in positive terms. Problems are often referred to as thorny, sticky or to be handled with kid gloves. We talk about touchstones, and marketers often refer to the 'touch points' of their brands. Finally, when we lose contact with old friends we say we have 'lost touch' and if we behave strangely, 'lose touch with reality'.

Sensing from a distance

03

As mathematics is the universal language of the mind, music is the language of the heart. ROBERT SCHUMANN

Touching space

Very few branding manuals consider the importance of space in relation to our sense of orientation and body extension as well as tactile experience. Arguably these are very separate senses, with one a distance sense and the other an immediate sense (Hall, 1982: 41). For those who want to stick to five senses, an alternative categorization that makes sense is to think of taste-smell, tactile, orientation, auditory and visual senses as the five main sensory systems, a system proposed by James J Gibson (1950). So what is known about the system of orientation and space?

Although our skin acts as an outer surface, and is the location of our touch sense, our body maps can be extended outside. In the simplest case, have you ever felt the wetness of water when wearing gloves to wash up? Our ability to sense beyond our body is powerful, relying particularly on proprioception to help us evaluate the size, shape, weight and movement of objects that we hold. If you hold a book between your fingers, somehow you can sense the whole of the book, its weight and centre of gravity, and just the amount of contact needed to hold it from falling.

I still prefer physical books, although e-books are much more convenient. One of the difficulties I find using digital devices to read is that I have lost the sense of where I am in the book, which I could physically feel with a real book by turning the pages.

When we use racquets, fishing rods, golf clubs or any equipment we have an almost uncanny knack of quickly understanding how they impact our body shape, reach and interaction with the outside world. We can grip and manipulate with incredible ease, and even novices can quickly 'feel' where the sweet spot of a tennis racquet is just as well as a professional player.

Our sense of touch can also cause distress through phantom limbs or create powerful illusions like the 'rubber hand' illusion. You can try the illusion for yourself, by simply sitting at a table and placing one of your hands under the table. You then place a rubber hand (perhaps a rubber glove) on top of the table where your missing hand should be. If you now stroke both your hand (under the table) and the rubber hand, within one or two minutes you will have the perception that the rubber hand is your own and is attached via a missing arm (Metzinger, 2009; Ramachandran, 2011).

The rubber hand illusion is caused by the change in your mind's self model, which has adapted to include the rubber hand. This is similar to the sensation that you get when using a tool, which eventually becomes an extension of your body. As David Katz (1925) put it, 'When one feels the world through a stick, one feels the world, not the stick' (Krishna, 2010: 45). For anyone designing a 'body extension', including mobile devices, it's important to think about how it will feel as an extension of the user, and not just how it will feel itself.

This mental adaptation is a phenomenally useful evolutionary development, giving humans the ability to easily use tools to perform a wide range of functions. Considerations of body extension are also important in designing architecture and spaces including retail outlets, as Juhani Pallasmaa has written.

Pallasmaa draws on the earlier work of Edward Hall, who developed the science of *Proxemics*, the study of measurable distances between people as they interact. In *The Hidden Dimension*, Hall discusses the psychology and cross-cultural significance of personal space and environment. Each of us keeps an invisible bubble of space around us to mark our personal 'territory', which impacts our business and personal relations, cross-cultural interactions, architecture and city planning.

All animals use space as a key part of their perceptual world, mediated by cultural 'rules of engagement'. Why is this important for sensory branding? Compare my personal experience of two airlines, asking a flight attendant for help or for an item of food or drink. On one airline, they stand over me in my seat and ask me to repeat the request. On a second airline, they bend down to ask me to repeat at my own eye level. The two create a completely different brand impression. The first example is the typical behaviour of most airlines, while the second happens on Singapore Airlines, although not always.

The Japanese have long been skilled at creating the feeling of openness, even in very confined spaces. The design of Japanese gardens in Kyoto and other Japanese cities, combine the experience of vision with movement and tactile involvement to create this illusion, using running water, irregularly spaced steps, the need to look down and placing objects in the middle of spaces rather than at the edges. The most successful retail outlets of the past few years, Apple stores, have learnt the importance of the design of space.

Apple follow the advice of Hall, who urged designers and engineers to use touch far more in order to help users relate to their designs and actively explore them, something that is also an important feature of their retail environments. Hall also argued that design and architecture do not take into account the 'design' of our sensory organs.

For example, only the central focus of eyes has a clear picture, whereas in the periphery movement can be greatly exaggerated. This means that straight edges and black and white bands are more noticeable in the periphery and movement becomes more apparent when the walls of a tunnel or hallway are closer to us. This is an effect that has been used to design more impactful road safety markings. The effect is similar to the impact of trees and regularly shaped pillars on the side of roads, which also creates a sense of movement (and causes drivers to slow down), whereas in closed public spaces, the removal of such visual distractions can increase perceptions of openness and reduce the feeling of crowding (Hall, 1982).

Perception of space is so important, that Edward Hall looked through the Oxford English Pocket English Dictionary to find the number of words related to space, and estimated that it accounted for around 20 per cent of the words listed. He also created a rule of thumb that 'the influence of two bodies on each other is inversely proportional to the square (or even cube) of the distance between them'. Proxemics is the language of the science of distance, built from work on animals into a science of human interaction. Work with animals has shown that there are four 'distances' which impact animal behaviour:

1 Flight distance is the boundary for running;

2 Critical distance is the boundary for attacking;

3 Personal distance is the boundary for separation of non-contact species;

4 Social distance is the boundary for intra-species communication.

Hall developed four levels of human inter-personal distance affecting body spacing, posture, pitch and loudness of voice and other aspects of interaction. The specific distances vary by culture and context and are seen across all human behaviour:

Intimate distance is for embracing, touching or whispering, and makes the presence of another person unmistakable and often overwhelming with greatly enhanced sensory inputs. Our vision is often distorted; we can smell and feel the heat of the other person's body and hear, smell and feel their breath. This is the distance of physical contact (love-making, wrestling, comforting, protecting), where touch is more important than sound. Some cultures (eg US) are very uncomfortable with such contact with anyone not in their very close circle, whereas other cultures are more tolerant.

Personal distance is the distance at which close friends and family members can interact and is the distance which reflects the 'personal bubbles' that we maintain around ourselves. At personal distance we are able to hold or grasp each other. The three-dimensional quality of objects is particularly pronounced at this distance as are surface textures. The far phase of this distance reflects the 'arm's length' expression that we use to describe something just outside touching distance and this is the limit of physical domination of our personal space.

Social distance is for interactions among acquaintances where we can no longer dominate (nor can they) and we lose intimate visual feedback on faces. At this distance we cannot touch or expect to be touched unless someone makes a conscious (physical) effort. This is a normal distance for conversation, social interaction, and impersonal business.

Public distance is the distance used for public speaking, well outside our circle of involvement. At this distance we can take evasive or defensive action (a reminder of the flight reaction of animals), and some linguists have observed a change in language to more careful use of words and phrases (a more formal style).

You can see Hall's diagram of the human spatial zones (with distances based on US culture) as Figure 3.1.

A study by JW Black, a phonetician, demonstrated that the size and reverberation time of a room affected reading rates, with reading slower in larger rooms with longer reverberation times (Hall, 1982: 44). Distance and space can have a profound effect on our behaviour and each culture has its own hidden rules about how space can be used. Branding needs to think more about orientation, movement and the use of space in designing engaging experiences.

FIGURE 3.1   Human spatial zones

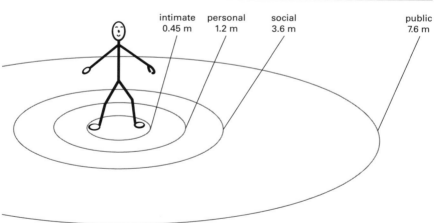

intimate 0.45 m   personal 1.2 m   social 3.6 m   public 7.6 m

SOURCE: Hall, 1982: 113–29

The rhythm of life

The Schweppes sound icon used to be a part of every advert, heard on television and seen on labels and posters. I say it used to be part as I haven't heard it for a long time, but 'Schhhh … you know who' was distinctive and successful. In a similar vein, I remember the 'Plink plink fizz' line of Alka Seltzer from the 1970s, which was written at the bidding of a psychologist who suggested that sales would double if you could create a social norm around using two tablets at a time (according to an interview with Rory Sutherland on the Indecision blog, 18 March 2013). Both are successful uses of sonic icons that made their brands memorable, just as music and song can also do.

Like many others, I love listening to music and can't imagine living without it. My tastes are very diverse, and my preferences are highly dependent on context. However, when working I can only listen to certain types of music which help me concentrate rather than distracting my mind. Vocal music is particularly distracting as my brain insists on interpreting the words that are sung. The lesson is that music can help or it can be a hindrance.

Research shows that despite much publicity, the Mozart effect does not exist, although it would be great if it were that easy to become intelligent (Levitin, 2006: 155). It is true that music has a profound influence on our physiology and, in the case of Mozart and others, music which makes us happy helps us to be more creative and productive (for example, we are faster and more accurate at mental tests). If you love heavy metal, it might even do the trick for you if it puts you in a good frame of mind!

If you go to the gym, you might have noticed that music with a faster beat influences the pace of your exercise, and you instinctively run faster. In fact, the body is sensitive to the rhythms around us. When that rhythm becomes higher than our heart rate our body gradually increases our own rhythm too, and similarly it decreases when the world around us slows down. Retail environments use these effects commonly, to make us get in and get out more quickly in fast food restaurants, or to linger longer, ideally spending more money, when buying gifts or wine for our dinner guests.

Several studies have shown that high volume music increases food consumption, and different genres of music can influence purchase behaviour. For example, fast tempo ambient music (high arousal) excites and energizes customers, which might be appropriate for an electrical store. In contrast, soothing and relaxed low tempo music is used when you want to slow a customer down and get them to spend more time in a certain environment, which might help if they are shopping for furniture or you want them to make more impulse purchases (North and Hargreaves, 1998; North, Hargreaves and McKendrick, 1999; North, Hargreaves and Shilock, 2003). We all know that music has a very strong influence on mood. It can calm a troubled child, rouse a crowd, or connect a group of people through a shared rhythm or vibe.

Although our ears also help us to keep balance and monitor the movement of our body (particularly acceleration) through the vestibular system, their most important function is to keep us in tempo with the world. We can sense frequencies as low as 20 Hz (one beat or event per second) and as high as 20,000 Hz (1 beat per millisecond). Hearing also helps us to determine direction, distance and speed through the difference in volume and timing between left and right ears, in conjunction with our vision. We can detect differences as little as 20 microseconds in the timing between ears, providing important information about where to check for obstacles and threats in the environment.

So, while vision helps us to see *where* things are happening, hearing helps us to understand when they happen, giving us a sense of time and causality. Several experiments have shown that the way we interpret music is directly related to the way we evaluate time. Hearing really helps us to place events in the outside world into order, and to understand the causes and effects of events around us. This helps us to make sense of the stories that our brain loves to learn.

If you long to return to the age of gramophone, you may be disappointed to learn that sound is the most digital of all the senses. In the cinema, film is typically shown at 24 frames per second, appearing to our eyes as a continuously moving image. However, if we listen to sounds at 24 clicks per second, we hear 24 clicks. Even at four times this speed, with 96 clicks per second, the clicks appear discrete and do not blur into a continuous sound.

This is in part because of the highly mechanical (physical) nature of hearing, which stems from the vibrations of bones and then hairs in our ears, along with the movement of liquid, which is ultimately converted into signals to the brain. The vibrations are of course linked to discrete events in the outside world, causing vibrations in the air around us as objects collide, move, explode, break, bang and change the world around us.

Through our hearing we even have the ability (although much less well developed) to use the echolocation that bats use to navigate their world. Of course, bats can hear a much wider range of frequencies (up to 110,000 Hz), using the timing, energy and frequency differences between the sounds they emit and the sounds that return to learn about the shape, composition, location, size and distance of objects in their environment.

However, if you make a 'ssshhh' sound (or even a 'Schhhh ...' sound) with your own mouth and then move your hand slowly closer to your mouth and then further away, you will also be able to hear changes in the sounds based on interference between sound waves that are leaving your mouth and bouncing off your hand. It has been demonstrated that blind people often develop a greater acuity for interpreting their surroundings in this way, and with the ever increasing focus of our eyes on small screens rather than the world around us, this could be an increasingly important skill to develop.

Car manufacturers have realized that we see with our ears too. Many have had to add engine noises to silent electric cars, so that pedestrians don't get run over by cars that they 'didn't see'.

There is a close connection between music and words, and although many other animals communicate through sound, human speech has been enabled by some very specific changes to human biology. In most animals, the larynx is much higher in the throat, to make it safer to eat without choking. In humans, the larynx is much lower, to enable us to make a greater variety of sounds, but at the risk of choking to death on food. Clearly there is an evolutionary advantage to producing language that outweighs this risk.

Hearing develops very early in the womb, and the myelination (insulation) of neurons associated with hearing is completed before that of any other sense. Ears start to form from as early as two months in the womb, and babies start to react to sounds from as early as four to five months before birth. Immediately after birth, we respond to loud and sudden sounds, turning our heads towards them, and from three to six months we start to recognize sounds and make them for ourselves, forming recognizable words at about one year old.

We all have innate musical ability, responding to frequency, harmony and rhythm, and as early as four years old we can label music with 'emotional' content. We can all recognize standard musical intervals, even without musical training. If you try singing (or humming) the first two notes of 'Somewhere Over the Rainbow', you will likely sing something very close to an octave. Opinions differ as to when musical instruments first developed, but there is evidence that it was at least 5,000–6,000 years ago and probably much earlier than that (Levitin, 2006).

As well as being the first sense to develop before birth, hearing is also the first sense to awaken when we become conscious in the morning and the last sense we lose when we fall asleep at night.

Music is a powerful branding tool, as we all know when struck by an 'earworm' (a jingle that you just cannot get out of your head). Earworm comes from the German expression 'ohrwurm'. Earworms typically have high, upbeat melodies and repetitive lyrics, verging between the catching and the annoying (Levitin, 2006: 55). Think of 'YMCA' by Village People, 'We Will Rock You' by Queen, 'The Lion Sleeps Tonight' by The Tokens, or 'Who Let The Dogs Out' by Baha Men, all of which are impossible to forget, even if you would like to.

One reason that earworms occur is that melodic music tends to have a rhythm that repeats. This cyclical nature can cause endless repetition, unless there is a way to break the cycle with a musical climax. I recently visited a Jakarta supermarket where a jingle was blasted out over the loudspeakers again and again. Although I would have described the repetition as 'ad nauseam', I couldn't get the tune out of my head for days afterwards! Jingles are essentially just ex-tended musical slogans or musical messages.

There are conflicting versions of the origins of jingles. The first ever jingle is usually attributed to General Mills, who advertised the Wheaties brand in 1926 with the following refrain, 'Have you tried

Wheaties? They're whole wheat with all of the bran. Won't you try Wheaties? For wheat is the best food of man'. The jingle was first aired on the WCCO radio station, incidentally owned by General Mills. The four male singers later became known as the Wheaties Quartet, and this is arguably the first piece of music written *specifically* for advertising.

'In My Merry Oldsmobile' is a popular song originally written in 1905, written by Gus Edwards and Vincent Bryan. The song (or rather the its chorus) was later co-opted by the marketing division of Oldsmobile (part of General Motors) as a marketing jingle. Oldsmobile dropped the more suggestive lyrics (the references to lovemaking were somewhat risqué for the time) and focused on the song's praise of cars. Although 'In My Merry Oldsmobile' was not written as a jingle, it eventually became one (Jackson, 2003).

More recently, many will remember, 'A Mars a day helps you work, rest and play', 'I'm lovin' it', and Léo Delibes and George Gershwin used to advertise airlines. First used in 2003, 'I'm Lovin' It' used a snippet from a Justin Timberlake song, which was later linked to sponsorship of a European tour and other promotional activities. More recently the jingle has been used in its own right, often omitting the slogan part of the jingle to leave customers to finish the 'ba da ba ba baa' intro.

For many years, United Airlines have been linked to George Gershwin's 'Rhapsody in Blue' (also used in Woody Allen's *Manhattan*). British Airways used the song 'Sous le dôme épais' from the opera Lakmé by Léo Delibes for many years, and became so strongly associated with it that they had to bring it back when passengers missed it (Bronner and Hirt, 2009: 80). The song was used in advertising, in the on-hold sound, and as background music while boarding and after landing, bringing a sense of peace, calm, beauty, class, distinction and refinement to the airline.

Wall's Cornetto's use of 'O sole mio' (or 'Just one Cornetto' in their version) has been cited as the best remembered advertising jingle of all time. In one study, 70 per cent of people remembered the song 24 years after the campaign finished (Treasure, 2011: 179). Hamlet cigar's use of Bach's 'Air on a g-string' remains unforgettable for me, and something I still remember from my childhood.

Leo Tolstoy said that 'music is the shorthand of emotion' and he was right. Music is often associated with rituals in our lives, and arguably developed from more primitive rituals thousands of years ago. Think of being in a large crowd at a Six Nations rugby match (or even watching on television) as English fans sing 'Swing low, sweet chariot', Welsh fans sing 'Land Of Our Fathers', Irish fans sing 'Ireland's call' or Scottish fans sing, 'Flower of Scotland'. As an Englishman, I have to admit that the Welsh always have the best voices!

Similarly, singing and music are associated with all the important rituals and rites of passage of life, such as birth, marriage and death. The importance of the music is its impact on our personal emotions and social bonding as well as the sheer enjoyment of letting go.

The National Academy of Sciences defines music as, 'a pattern of sounds that varies in time and which are driven by cultural, emotional, social and intellectual reasons', but music can be much more too. The components of music are rhythm, melody, harmony, dynamics and occasionally text, but the emotional content of music is almost always more than the sum of these parts.

Importantly, music is critical to the way we define our personal identity and the 'tribes' we belong to (Lusensky, 2011: 13–16). The majority of youth movements that have driven cultural change over the last 50 years have been primarily motivated by musical subcultures. Think of mods, punk rockers, hippies, metal heads and grunge. Our sense of personal identity is dominated by our musical taste, and this is always one of the first questions anyone asks of a new acquaintance, at least it's certainly one of the first that I always ask. In several studies, music has been cited as the one medium that people would least like to live without.

A Millward Brown study showed that the average person listens to six different music devices and that 80 per cent of young people (18–24 years) actively listen to music every day. Another study has shown that people think music reveals who they really are more than any other medium like books, film, etc (Rentfrow and Gosling, 2005).

Many social interactions revolve around musical tastes and sharing, which is why Myspace was initially so successful, and why Apple and

Facebook continue to place a premium on the sharing of musical tastes. Music tells other people who you are and just as importantly who you are not. It can do the same for brands too.

Many successful brands have built their business on a musical logo or 'musical signature'. Personal computer brands have used start up sounds to build their brands, and Nokia pioneered the use of the ringtone as part of the phone's identity. If you have never heard of Walter Werzowa, you have probably heard his most famous tune, which supports the 'Intel inside' campaign. The four-note theme is instantly recognizable and is one of the best examples of sonic branding from the last 20 years.

Mercedes is another brand that has developed its own acoustic trademark of a young choirboy singing three notes, linking to its three-pointed logo. The sonic icon is memorable and very human, but does the feeling of a guardian angel above fit comfortably with the brand's overall identity?

BMW has recently announced that it will be introducing a new auditory signal around the world, which will initially be heard in new television and radio adverts. According to its press releases, 'the line ends with two identical sounds that have a hammer-and-tongs tinge, a deep and highly resonant tone with a metallic edge'. The signal will replace the previously used 'double gong' that has existed since the late 1990s. BMW described the sonic logo in this way: 'The melody is introduced by a rising resonant sound and underscored by two distinctive bass tones that form the sound logo's melodic and rhythmic basis... the new sound represents "sheer driving pleasure" and has been composed to appeal to a wide variety of geographic markets'. The initiative is part of an overall sensory branding drive that introduced a co-branded line of hand sanitizers as discussed in Chapter 2 (reported in 'Audio Branding: BMW Uses New Sound Signature to Help Redefine the Brand' on 20 March 2013 at **www.brandchannel.com**).

Some of the earliest acoustic logos date back to the early days of cinema – who could forget the 20th Century Fox fanfare theme, or the roar of Leo the Lion's signal at the start of an MGM movie? The James Bond series of movies, perhaps the most successful franchise of all time, has a strong visual and acoustic branding and core motifs of the 'James Bond Theme' (written by Monty Norman in 1962) and

'007' (written by John Barry in 1963). Both of these motifs are typically written into the opening sequences of each film, which usually include a pre-title sequence before the main titles. Adele's hit single 'Skyfall', the Oscar winner in 2013, notably starts with the two note Bond motif, and has a sound and feel which is instantly recognizable.

One of the most successful brands of the last century, Coca-Cola, has built its value on strong associations with music, from the 1970s 'I'd like to buy the world a Coke' up to today with the different versions of 'Open happiness' and the use of 'Give a little bit' in their most recent campaign in 2013.

Starbucks is also strongly associated with music, both in the ambience of its cafes and in having its own music label, which has launched Grammy award winning CDs from Ray Charles, Joni Mitchell and Paul McCartney.

Songs live forever in our hearts and minds, connect with our deepest emotions, remind us of happy experiences and provoke an instant emotional reaction. Music is a great shortcut to the heart of a brand's customers.

However, song, jingle and sound logo are not the only ways that brands can leverage our sense of hearing to build brand equity. Brands can have a 'voice', a soundscape, an ambience, a product sound as well as being associated with specific melodies and rhythms.

Levi's (or specifically Levi's 501s) has been linked to music for a long time. It started its 'back to basics' campaign in 1986, using popular and lesser-known soul and rock classics corresponding to the brand identity of 501s. This fit very well with the 501s slogan, 'Originals stand the test of time', and led to the revival of the jeans model as well as many of the songs. It continues to use music and sponsor many musical events such as South by Southwest. Abercrombie & Fitch uses music from club and DJ culture in its stores to create a high-tempo wall of electronic sound that is a brand signature and an important part of the brand experience.

Venues such as Buddha Bar and Hotel Costes have used their association with a certain style of music to build their brands. Heineken along with many other drinks brands often associates itself with live music and even recorded music, as in Heineken's *The Sounds of Summer* CD. Red Bull set up a yearly music academy a few years ago too.

Other brands have used sound engineering as an essential part of the brand. Porsche spends 5 per cent of its research and development budget on sound (Bronner and Hirt, 2009: 166). The Porsche Carrera has a distinctive engine sound, very different from a BMW or a Ford. Likewise, BMW gives each of its model ranges a distinct sound profile, as well as its overall brand sonic logo. German biscuit brand Bahlsen has a development team of 16 researchers working on the sound design of pastry. Product tests make special efforts to measure biting and chewing noises, transmitted through loudspeakers into its research laboratory for analysis (Bronner and Hirt, 2009: 167).

Kellogg's was an early pioneer of sound engineering, analyzing the sound of its products to optimize crunchiness. Kellogg's worked with a Danish commercial music laboratory to engineer the crunch of Corn Flakes and the 'snap, crackle and pop' of Rice Krispies are trademarked. Martin Lindstrom quotes that 74 per cent of those interviewed in his Brandsense survey associated the word 'crunch' with Kellogg's (Lindstrom, 2010: 16–17). Kellogg's also uses sonic logos – Frosties have been 'gr-r-r-reat' for Tony the Tiger since 1951. Nestlé is trying to catch up, developing a 'Krustimeter' that allows them to analyze munching sounds while eating crackers and cookies, giving every tested product an acoustic fingerprint.

However, branding is not all about noise. Some brands make a point of advertising their lack of sound. Lexus advertises the silence of the car interior as a major point of difference, and the Airbus A330 is the 'quietest cabin in the sky'.

Importantly, our sense of hearing has a relatively high conscious bandwidth compared with the total amount of sensory information it represents. This is because of its important role in helping us unpick events in time. The sense of hearing helps us keep time with the world and to break events into cause and effect. Hearing is intimately linked to stories.

The dominant sense

When you see a white cross on a red tool what do you think of? Or when you see the classic wavy curves of a bottle or a ribbon based logo? Or a book or website with a strong yellow colour? A pink ribbon? A triangular-shaped chocolate bar? I am confident that many of the following brands came to mind: Swiss army knife (Victorinix), Coca-Cola, Yellow Pages, Breast Cancer Awareness and Toblerone.

Vision dominates the other senses, accounting for more than two thirds of all sensory processing in the brain, and therefore a large part of all brain activity. What we see dominates our memory of events. For example, body language is the most important aspect of presentation skills, accounting for more than half of communication, while language accounts for less than 10 per cent of overall impact (Mehrabian, 1972).

In *The Vision Revolution*, Mark Changizi argues that human colour vision is not just about picking out the right fruits in the forest, but gave more social evolutionary advantages. He claims that it developed to better interpret the feelings and intentions of others, as our eye's receptors are particularly well tuned to the range of colours that affect skin and complexion. This means that we can 'see' how other people feel through their skin colour, giving us great insight into how to react in any social situation (Changizi, 2010).

Changizi also shows that the position of our eyes is typical of a predator, a hunter rather than a gatherer, allowing us to have X-ray vision in certain environments and see behind obstacles, such as foliage, to what lies beyond. The advantage of this adaptation outweighs the loss of rear vision, something that animals with more lateral eyes have.

So vision has evolved to recognize other people, and their feelings, and we are all experts in facial recognition and emotional coding. Humans are instinctively drawn to faces immediately, recognizing them more quickly than any other objects. Take a look around you next time you are sat in your local coffee shop, and you will be able to read the feelings of others just from the expressions on their faces, whatever their age, sex or ethnicity, especially if they are interacting with others.

Even very young babies prefer looking at anatomically correct facial drawings, can spot their mother's face on video within four days, and start to imitate their parent's facial expressions after two weeks. This is an impressive feat given that their visual perception is not fully developed until much later, and is probably providing very 'fuzzy' images at best. The full range of our facial coding skills is only in place when we reach our teens, when we are tuned into the arrangement or configuration of faces as well as their individual features. That's why we find it very difficult to 'read' a face that is upside down, however sharp the image. However, we can still recognize a very blurry image of a face as long as we can make out its configuration.

A normal facial picture not only gives information about the configuration, but enhances our sensitivity to small facial details, so our memory of a nose or moustache (especially in November), is much better when we see it in the context of the full face rather than on its own. We also recognize faces by the way that they move. Young babies first recognize their mothers in video before static pictures. We can all recognize most of our friends and families just from dots placed randomly across their face, as long as we can see the face moving. We all have distinct and subtle ways of moving our facial muscles when we laugh, smile and yawn.

We detect faces twice as quickly as other images, and even faster if they show emotion, and it is almost impossible to ignore a face when it is in your field of view. From a face, we can determine who a person is, their gender and genetic health, their emotional state and intentions, and their reproductive potential. We can also understand their linguistic messaging if we lip read, as you will see later.

For this reason, faces are very important in advertising and branding, although they need to be the right face to create the right emotional impact. Dan Hill argues that using the right talent is critical along with ensuring that they show the right emotion. Fake emotion does not work and cold impassive faces are a real turn off, as we can all detect a fake smile from a mile away, creating a negative impression. Research shows that although celebrity spokespeople can work well, they have to be authentic. If a celebrity is not authentic, then it is usually better to have a more authentic and more anonymous personality (Hill, 2010: 55–70).

We use our own face to perceive the expressions of others and the most important information we see in a face are feelings. Do they intend harm or affection? Do they need consolation or privacy? Our reactions are automatically communicated in our own expressions, and so a loosely choreographed dance begins between two faces, out of which emerge empathy or antipathy. And perhaps even seduction or a battle for dominance?

Much of this is unconscious, in Kahneman's System 1, taking place even when we see subliminal expressions. It has been shown that if you see a face that expresses anger, disgust or sorrow, even when not aware of the face, you rate your mood more negatively than if you see more neutral expressions. We have all experienced the tendency to subtly mimic the expressions, accents and mannerisms of others (known as the 'chameleon effect'), which is partly about improving our own perceptual abilities, as memory and skills are all about repetition.

All perception, including vision, is a system for detecting threats and opportunities in the environment, including other people. Vision is one of the 'distance receptors' (Hall, 1982: 41–50), allowing us to see further into the future than perhaps any other sense by seeing further into the distance. Vision often dominates other senses because it is more salient (or more reliable) across many contexts.

It is easy to fool someone that an orange drink is lime flavoured by adding a green colour. In the real world a green coloured drink is lime flavoured in 99.99 per cent of cases, so the brain is making a very educated guess and rightly ignores our taste buds and nose! Indeed, vision often distracts the other senses, which is why we often close our eyes, to listen to music or to kiss or touch loved ones.

How does vision integrate with other senses? In reality, we all read the lips of others every day, without realizing it. Lawrence Rosenblum describes the McGurk effect, first discovered by McGurk and MacDonald in 1976. McGurk and MacDonald studied the relative contributions of audition and vision to speech perception. In the most famous experiment, participants were simultaneously presented with a voice uttering a particular syllable (eg 'ba') while they saw synchronized lip movements associated with another syllable (eg 'ga'). In the experiment, the majority of participants reported hearing a different syllable (eg 'da'), demonstrating that the sound that people hear can be modulated by seen lip movements (Rosenblum, 2010: Chapter 10).

The effect occurs even when people know that what they are seeing and hearing are incongruent, suggesting that integration happens automatically, and another example of the brain 'jumping to conclusions'. Other examples of such effects include the interpretation of the emotional tone of a sentence being modulated by the simultaneous presentation of a face showing happiness or fear.

We most often resolve situations of spatial conflict through visual perception, such as at the cinema when the soundtrack is perceived to be coming from the lips of the actors on screen, despite really coming from loudspeakers located elsewhere. This is akin to the 'ventriloquism' effect that mislocates sounds towards their apparent visual source. The 'rubber arm' illusion also described by Rosenblum shows that vision is very often the most 'salient' information and therefore overrides other sensory inputs.

The same drink can taste lime, cherry or orange depending on colouring (Roberts, 2002: 351). Colour can also be used to change perceptions of intensity and quality. In my own experience of sensory testing, I have run studies where the cocoa taste of chocolate and the alcoholic strength of beer were manipulated purely through the colour of the products. It is common when eating and drinking to associate darker colours with stronger and richer tastes. Darker colours are common 'signs' and mental shortcuts, with symbolic value in the language of the next chapter.

Research shows that the visual appearance of a product or experience is important in the short term, and of course is critical in shaping first perceptions (as in 'priming' discussed in Chapter 2). First impressions count, but the tactile feel of a product or service becomes increasingly important the longer you continue to experience it. Think of buying a pair of fancy shoes. You will love the way they look the first time you wear them, but you will not wear them very often if they are not comfortable on your feet.

There are some other key principles of visual appearance. Humans often prefer big objects to small ones, and round forms to sharp ones (sharp objects and straight lines are often more threatening). It is generally true that humans prefer complex designs to simple renditions, but this is not as important as shape and size. Symmetry is more important than complexity, and the combination is ideal. For example, we like symmetrical faces. They are a signal for good health and reproductive potential, although it is also true that symmetrical objects are quicker and easier to mentally process and the brain loves efficiency.

Ease of recognition is very important to likeability, and the exposure effect shows that familiarity is related to liking. This means that brands that have greater visibility have an advantage over brands with lower visibility, showing the double jeopardy effect in practice (Sharp, 2010). Robert Zajonc pioneered the study of exposure effects in the 1960s, and is famous for the statement that, 'preferences need no inferences'.

Exposure effects only work for things for which we have neutral or positive feelings and familiarity only 'breeds contempt' for things that we do not like anyway. Exposure effects have been confirmed for music, visual arts, images, people and advertisements. Robert Zajonc argued that his experiments also showed that many decisions have no cognitive component, but rather we know what we like and then rationalize our decisions later. Psychology is finally starting to come round to this point of view.

In designing experience there is always a trade off between familiarity and the urge for novelty, and research shows that humans best like classical (familiar) forms with small elements of novelty or surprise. This gives a sense of the known with an innovative appearance, or 'the most advanced yet acceptable'. This is common in car design, with updated models from the latest Aston Martin to the new Volkswagen Beetle, combining classic forms and innovative changes as in all best design.

The colour of experience

What colour are carrots? 'Orange, what other colour would they be?' I hear you say. In reality, they could be many other colours. Wild carrots were first found in Afghanistan and Iran more than 1,000 years ago, and the original cultivars were a range of colours including purple and yellow. So why are carrots orange today?

The colour of carrots is perhaps one of the greatest pieces of sensory branding of all time. And William of Orange is responsible. In the 17th century, Dutch farmers started cultivating carrots in the colour of orange to support the House of Orange and their struggle for independence. The Prince of Orange, Willem III, later became William II of Scotland and William III of England and Ireland, and is popularly known in Northern Ireland as King Billy (he is responsible for the colour of the Orange Order).

Somehow the cultivar they developed, with an abundance of carotene, has remained popular and is the colour by which much of the world identifies carrots today. In another strange twist, the flag of the Netherlands is red rather than orange, only because of the quality of orange dyes in the 17th century. However, the Dutch football team strip has the colour of the House of Orange, as does the whole country on the Queen's birthday.

Colour is such an important part of visual perception it is worth discussing in detail. Colour vision comes from three classes of photoreceptor in the retina with different sensitivities to wavelengths of light and is comprised of three dimensions: brightness, colourfulness (sometimes called intensity or saturation) and hue.

There are at least 8,000 colour names in the UK, although many have only a tenuous connection to the colour they describe. Humans can describe all the colours that we are able to discriminate by using only six terms and their combinations: red, yellow, green, blue, black and white. Arranging these six colours based on similarity leads to the classic colour wheel. In the circle, opposite colours are complementary, and if you look at a colour circle you will see that there are no yellowish blues or reddish greens. Grey is in the centre of the circle as an achromatic colour.

The best-known colour system is the Munsell colour-order system. Born in Boston, Massachusetts, in 1858, Albert Munsell was an artist and art teacher with an interest in colour. He developed his ideas on colour into the Munsell Colour System first published in 1905 (called *A Color Notation* at that time), and gave people the ability to see samples ordered on the basis of equal hue, value and chroma. It remains an important industrial standard (Roberts, 2002: 91–102).

Although we can discriminate many colours, studies of language indicate that there are 11 colour words that appear in most modern languages, and they seem to appear in language in a particular order as languages develop. White and black (or light and dark) appear first, followed by red, then yellow and green (or green and yellow), then blue. Thus, blue is the last of the primary colours to have its cultural importance rewarded with a generic colour word. After blue, brown appears next, then orange, followed by purple and finally pink and grey are the final colour words (Berlin and Kay, 1999; Deutscher, 2011).

Importantly, the oldest colour words in languages tend to have the richest meanings, and blue is therefore the least meaning-laden of the primary colours. This is perhaps why blue is often considered the most neutral colour globally, and is also the most popular colour in surveys of preferences. Colours are powerful weapons in any branding toolkit. Colours are rich with meanings, but those meanings do change from country to country and culture to culture. Marketers should always check colour meanings for their local market. As a starting point, here is a quick tour of the 11 named colours, and you can see a more detailed list of meanings in the next chapter.

White is often a sign of purity, cleanness and coolness. White is a basic colour, bringing out everything else. For service brands, white is used everywhere the customer expects cleanliness (kitchens, surgeries, etc). The Innocent brand of fruit smoothies uses the purity of white to great effect.

Black has become a regular symbol of top of the range, quality and sobriety, and can be used to create a very specific and exclusive environment. There is a reason that the 'little black number' is the iconic statement of Coco Chanel.

Red has the hue with the strongest stimulation, giving it the power to excite with increased pulse and heart rate and raised blood pressure. Women in red are rated more sexy than when wearing any other colour, while men in red are rated as more powerful, and it's not just a coincidence that drivers of red cars are more likely to be involved in car accidents. Red can stimulate appetite, making it popular in restaurants and bars.

Yellow is a comforting colour, which also means tangy, creamy or delicious in foods and drinks. It is very popular in food and drink outlets, but is also used by brands like Scholl (foot powder) for its connotations of warmth and comfort.

Green symbolizes ideas of refreshment and nature, and is also connected to ideas of healthiness. However, green is a delicate colour and can have strong negative connotations if misused, as it is also the colour of decay and putrefaction. Although BP has tried to hijack green to symbolize its environmental credentials, its behaviour hasn't always lived up to its ideals.

Blue is associated with the sea and sky and calmness, and often suggests trust and serenity. Some shades of blue (eg ice blue) reflect purity and coolness and are ideal for products like bottled water. Brands like Wall's in the UK use dark blue to signify the quality of sausages and other products, and brands like Bombay Sapphire have used the colour to forge a distinctive brand identity as well as to reflect their unique blend of ingredients.

Orange is a friendlier colour than red (which has a dangerous side), but is still stimulating and gets attention especially from kids and teens. Brands like Orange Mobile use these associations to signify the vitality and fun of their brand.

Brown is a wholesome and down-to-earth colour, often associated with nature and natural materials like wood. Brands like Costa Coffee leverage these meanings, along with the obvious link to coffee itself, to signal their homely ambience.

Purple is associated with royalty in the West and has associations with quality and luxury. These associations are the reasons for its use by Cadbury, in dark purple, and by Whiskas, in a lighter shade for the food of the Empress or Emperor of the house.

Pink is a sweet and appealing colour, perfect for sugar confectionery. It is also associated with sexiness and femininity in many cultures, which is why it is the perfect colour for the Breast Awareness campaign's iconic ribbon logo.

Grey is associated with business suits as well as age, although it can be considered a gloomy and unattractive colour. In many Asian countries grey is perceived as 'cheap'. It is often associated with and used by technology companies, and can also be used to signal the wisdom of experience.

Integrating the senses

Flavour is just one example of the integration of the senses. It has been shown that 'flavour neurons' in the brain learn to pair (associate) tastes and smell. For example, the sweet taste and strawberry aroma of a strawberry become strongly associated over time, and eventually the aroma of a strawberry automatically triggers the sweetness of its flavour. Similar associations build with the colour, texture and sound of eating a strawberry, although these associations are likely to be less strong as they are not unique to the strawberry.

The integration of the senses is most obvious when there is conflicting information, as we have seen in the 'McGurk effect', visual illusions and the impact of colour and other visual cues on other senses. The reality is that the brain relies on the most salient information when resolving conflicting information, which is usually either the most localizable or most persuasive cue.

That is why we tend to believe our eyes rather than our ears in identifying the source of voices in the cinema, and why we believe our ears rather than our eyes when temporal judgments are required. Auditory cues are our main source of knowledge about time (Roberts, 2002: 3345–54).

Synaesthesia has resurged as a popular topic for research recently, although it has been known about for more than 100 years and was studied by Gustav Fechner and Francis Galton in the 19th century. Fechner, the founder of modern psychophysics, conducted an early empirical study of links between colours and letters among synaesthetes in 1871 and Francis Galton did further work in the 1880s to understand the genetic basis of synaesthesia. More recent work has demonstrated that synaesthesia is much more common among artists, poets and other creatives than among the general population (Ramachandran, 2011: Chapter 1).

There are a number of different forms of synaesthesia, with the most prevalent known as grapheme-colour synaesthesia where letters or numbers are perceived as coloured. Other forms include blending or cross-activation of words, music, smell, taste, colour and order.

In language, cross-sensory metaphors are common, as we talk of 'loud shirts', 'bitter winds' or 'prickly personalities', but such metaphors are not truly synaesthetic. It has been estimated that around 1 in 23 people may experience true synaesthesia, although it is believed that young babies probably experience this naturally, as their brains have a much greater extent of 'cross wiring' which reduces as they grow and as different areas of the brain begin to specialize. It also commonly reported by those under the influence of psychedelic drugs and also as the result of blindness, deafness and strokes.

The effects of synaesthesia teach us something very important about cross-sensory integration. An example of such integration is the *bouba/kiki* effect, which was first investigated by Wolfgang Köhler (one of the founders of Gestalt psychology). He asked people to choose the correct names for two shapes, one of which is named *bouba* and one of which is named *kiki*. Ninety-five to 98 per cent of people choose *kiki* for the angular shape and *bouba* for the rounded shape, and similar experiments have demonstrated these effects with different versions of the shapes and names across different cultures. In other experiments they have been called *maluma* and *takete* with the same results. You can see the shapes in Figure 3.2.

Even young children of 2 to 3 years old show this effect before they are able to read. Ramachandran argues that this effect has implications for the evolution of language, because the naming of objects is not completely arbitrary. The rounded shape of *bouba* or *maluma* is linked to the more rounded mouth shape required to produce the sound, and similarly the sound of the letters 'k' and 't' is harder, angular and more forceful that than of 'b'. These differences suggest a form of sound symbolism, in which sounds are mapped to objects

FIGURE 3.2 *Bouba* and *kiki*

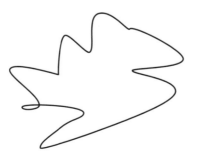
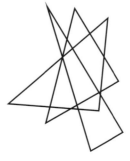

and actions in the world according to the similarity in their 'patterns' (Ramachandran, 2011: Chapter 3).

Arguably, metaphors are a tool for helping us understand abstract ideas in concrete (ie sensory) terms. Are kisses really sweet? The metaphor certainly makes the emotion of love more concrete, relevant and meaningful to all of us, allowing us to understand an abstract idea through very real emotions and perceptions. Put another way, metaphors help us to build imaginary worlds using common 'sense'.

Thus there is a very real connection between the world of ideas, metaphors and stories and our sensory perception. Symbols, including brands, are made real through our senses.

Symbols and signs

04

> *Signs and symbols rule the world, not rules and law.*
>
> **CONFUCIUS**

Symbols of life

I went to the cinema recently to watch the 2013 film *Stoker* by the director Park Chan-wook. Although there are convincing and occasionally disturbing performances from Nicole Kidman and others, the most striking thing about the film is the dense and pervasive use of symbolism and imagery.

Stoker opens and closes with India (played by Mia Wasikowska) stepping across the road and through the fields with hair and skirts moving in the breeze in perfect time to beautiful fields of golden crops wafting in the wind, sometimes in close up and with noticeable distortions of visuals, sound and perception of time. Later in the film there are images of a spider crawling over floors and up legs, a freezer in a dark cellar, paths through dark forests, a key to a treasure, and a wordless piano duet along with more than one murder visualized as sexual acts. Not forgetting a fetish for shoes.

Freud and Jung would have been proud of Park Chan-wook. While his imagery owed much to their ideas, the reality is that our daily lives are full of symbols and signs. Traffic lights are an obvious example. Traffic signals share a universal language that we all understand. Red means 'stop' and green (or green/blue in Japan) means 'go'. Similarly, in other aspects of life, red is often interpreted as a warning sign, standing for danger. If you are a football player it is the signal that you should leave the field, and if you are a student it is a signal that your teacher is unhappy with your work.

Edward Hall considered that his work on perceptions of time and space was about understanding, 'the structure of experience as it is moulded by culture... those deep, common unstated experiences which members of a given culture share, which they communicate without knowing, and which form the backdrop against which all other events are judged' (Hall, 1982: x).

Geert Hofstede said simply that, 'Culture is the collective programming of the mind'. Our mind is always looking for signs in the outside world, from the sound of a car telling us to keep on the pavement, to the sweet sensation telling us that a food or drink contains useful energy, to the face of a friend revealing what they are really thinking, and to the signs on the side of the road which signal the dangers ahead. Signs can be simple, as when gold symbolizes wealth, and also less explicit, as when gold symbolizes the Sun or the masculine life force in the world (in some cultures), or vulgarity and ostentation (the opposite of wealth and power).

Many symbols appear across many world cultures across the world, indicating that they may have common origins, whether that is from a transfusion of ideas, a common ancestor or a natural part of our collective consciousness as Jung claimed. In fact, much more travel happened in the ancient world than we realize, and trade routes often crossed the world sharing art styles, commerce and religious ideas. Islam came to Indonesia, now the biggest Islamic country in the world, in this way as did Buddhism to Japan and why else is Portuguese spoken in the heart of South America? This sharing included the symbols we all use today.

For example, the dragon is a common symbol in China, representing the glory of the Emperor and the Sun, but it has been changed in European Christian art into a more negative symbol of man's baser instincts. Similarly, the image of the bird battling the serpent is found from New Guinea to the Americas, symbolizing the struggle of the sky, waters and Earth, and the *tao t'ieh* (stylized face) of ancient China reappears in the gargoyles of English cathedrals and similar motifs in the Pacific Rim.

Such symbols enrich our lives today, helping us to see objects as representing deeper meanings and more universal and eternal truths about ourselves. A ladder may be a tool for home improvements, but can also remind us of the spiritual climb to greater self-awareness. Similarly, a lamppost may serve as a prop but can also signify the light of truth. It is used for both in market research.

The colour of meaning

While many meanings have changed, much of the symbolism of our ancestors is still relevant, even if in moderated and updated forms. The superheroes of the latest Hollywood and Bollywood blockbusters are strikingly similar to their ancient cultural ancestors. Think of Superman and Harry Potter compared with Theseus and Perseus. All have magic weapons, including magic swords or wands, flying powers, and invisibility cloaks.

At the same time, each country and sometimes city has its own colour and mood, both shaping and reflecting the local culture and behaviours. Colour is packed full of meanings, obvious and hidden, and is arguably the richest of all the sensory signs in terms of cultural as well as personal symbolism.

Take purple for example. Purple appears relatively infrequently in nature (a few fruits and vegetables, flowers, fish and gemstones). Purple can mean sophistication, dignity, elegance, creativity, spirituality, mysticism, magic and imagination. For the Catholic Church, purple is the colour of bishops, rosaries and penitence and until recently it was the colour of mourning in the UK. However, purple is not popular in China, is considered soothing in India, was once prohibited at Japanese weddings, symbolizes homosexuality in Mexico and stands for bravery in the United States.

For me, purple reminds me of the 10 years I spent with Cadbury which was my first employer after finishing my doctorate and has much sensory branding experience to share. Colour and all other sensory experiences are rich in personal and cultural meanings that are primed implicitly through association.

Identity matters

We are all surrounded by symbols and signs every hour of every day. This imagery is rich in deeper truths about our lives and the meanings we extract from even the most ordinary of objects. Our world is full of symbols.

Semiotics is both a science and an art, with basic principles and structured approaches that help brands decode meanings. The word was first used in a very scientific context, by Hippocrates explaining the basis of medical diagnosis in interpreting the signs and symbols of disease symptoms.

Our brains constantly use signs and symbols to access mental shortcuts. These shortcuts allow us to simplify and manage the world in all its complexity. For brands, these shortcuts are important to how customers perceive category and brand identities. Once established, such identities are hard to disrupt.

When we are shopping, we use shelf position and proximity to infer category; size, shape and material of packaging to infer product use ('job to be done'); and colour often to infer brand and other deeper meanings of the category (see Table 4.1). Water brands are typically packaged in clear bottles with wavy lines and designs, blue colours, and images of nature along with names that indicate source. All these symbolize meanings such as clear, pure, fresh, natural and authentic.

The origins of semiotics are in two important late 19th-century and early 20th-century contemporaries, Ferdinand de Saussure, a Swiss linguist, and Charles Sanders Peirce, a US philosopher and polymath. Other philosophers had earlier written about the importance of signs in human life including St Augustine and John Locke, but most of the ideas in currency today are due to de Saussure and Peirce, although their writings are not always easy to understand.

Charles Peirce wrote that, 'The entire universe is perfused with signs, if it is not composed exclusively of signs'. Although buried deep under arcane terminology, academic dryness and general misunderstanding, semiotics is very simply *the study of signs*. That is, semiotic approaches help you understand the meaning of things in the world, including colours, shapes, logos, fonts, materials, graphic devices,

TABLE 4.1 Colour meanings in Asian cultures

Colour	China	India	Japan	Thailand	UK
White	Mourning, coldness, sterility, humility, age	Rebirth, purity, peace, happiness, perfection	Death, coldness, sterility, mourning, sacred	Auspicious, purity	Peace, purity, weddings, angels, hospital
Black	Expensive, trust, honour, water, stability	Dullness, stupidity, death, evil, anger	Fear, expensive, rare, mysterious	Death, mourning, bad luck, unhappy	Sorrow, mourning, formality, power, control
Red	Love, lucky, happy, long life, fertility	Ambition, purity, fertility, beauty, wealth	Love, life, hot, danger, anger	Sunday, extinguishing of desire	Passion, love, danger, energy, power
Yellow	Sacred, royalty, happy, fame, progress	Commerce, sacred, auspicious, spring	Courage, beauty, refined, aristocracy, cheerful	King, Monday, auspicious, Buddhism	Wisdom, warmth, optimism, hope, cowardice
Green	Trust, infidelity, exorcism, youth, jade	Islam, hope, harvest, virtue	Love, happiness, eternal life, youth, fresh	Wednesday	Rebirth, nature, relaxation, lucky, jealousy
Blue	Immortality, feminine, unlucky, high office, heaven	Purity, Krishna, sports	Trust, everyday, ocean, purity, calm	Queen, Friday, compassion, desire	Sadness, soothing, authority, reliability, conservative

TABLE 4.1 *continued*

Colour	China	India	Japan	Thailand	UK
Brown	Earth	Mourning	Natural, *shibui*, earth, home, simplicity	Humility	Wholesome, rural, down to earth, practical, comfort
Orange	Good luck, fate, filial duty, transformation, happiness	Sacred, auspicious, humility, sacrifice, criminals	Love, happiness, energy, balance, warmth	Thursday, Buddhist monks	Sensual, fire, warmth
Purple	Expensive, grief, self pity, nobility, unpopular	Reincarnation, sorrow, comforting	Expensive, fear, sin, privilege, wealth	Saturday, widow mourning	Royalty, spirituality, introversion, wealth
Pink	Sex	Happy, hopeful, Ganesha	Unisex, good health, purity, pornography	Tuesday, enlightenment	Feminine, nurturing, sexy, bankers and barristers
Grey	Cheap	Stone	Masculine, maturity, old age, weapons, hi-tech	Cheap	Anonymous, gloom, meditation

packaging and sounds. Importantly, the words and language we use to share ideas with each other are a system of signs and symbols in themselves (Danesi, 2007, 2008; Chandler, 2002; Oswald, 2012).

What is gold? It is a coloured shiny material with a dictionary definition of yellow, non-rusting, malleable, ductile metal element. However, gold means much more than this. In the modern world, gold can be currency, jewellery, medals, teeth fillings or the 'gold standard'. It can mean wealth, excellence, prestige, prosperity, nobility, divinity, extravagance, pretentiousness, mysticism, Sun or fire. It can have opposing meanings, as in the expressions 'good as gold' and 'solid gold' compared with 'gold digger', 'gold brick' and 'fool's gold'. You see it in China every day (eg on packaging) and in Thailand everywhere (eg covering temples). However, gold is considered garish in Japan.

In semiotics, gold is a *signifier*, attached to many meanings (*signified*), such as wealth, extravagance and divinity. Put together, the *signifier* (gold) and the *signified* (meanings) create a *sign*. A key principle of semiotics is that culture turns all *signs* into coded symbols full of meaning.

For another example, think of the word 'cat'. In English this is a *signifier* for a cat. Together the cat and the word cat (signified and signifier) form a sign. Ferdinand de Saussure was aware that language is a particularly interesting form of sign; as in most cases words (labels) have a completely arbitrary relationship with their meaning. This is slightly different in Asia, where there is often a much more direct link between signifier and signified through the symbolic nature of many languages.

The words 'pusa' and 'chat' can also act as signifiers for a cat in the Philippines and France. So can many symbols such as the sound 'miaow', a picture of a cat or just a pair of pointy ears and whiskers.

Signifying something

All of these signifiers are associated with a cat but in different ways, which is a key part of Peirce's theory of signs. A picture of a cat is *iconic*, looking like the thing it represents (like any portrait, onomatopoeic word or sound effect). The word 'cat' is *symbolic*, in that it has no direct relationship with a cat, and the association is purely arbitrary. This is typical of most languages, as they are based on convention rather than representation. It is also true of numbers, traffic lights and most national flags. Finally, the sound 'miaow' or the graphic of two ears and whiskers is *indexical*, in that there is a direct connection to the *signified* cat (they are iconic of part of the cat or are caused by a cat). Similarly, smoke indicates a fire, a pointing finger indicates where to look and footprints indicate where a cat has been.

The differences between iconic, symbolic and indexical meanings have important implications for marketing, design and research. Imagine you are naming a perfume brand. The name would be *iconic* if it referenced the fragrance itself, for example smelling of roses when the name includes 'rose'. A *symbolic* name would bring associations and connotations, perhaps from memory, childhood or popular culture, which relate to the perfume character. An *indexical* name would point to at least one aspect of the perfume character, so if the name were 'Country Air' it would have an indexical association with a perfume containing notes of cut grass.

1   The first key principle of semiotics is that the world is full of signs that help our minds create mental shortcuts to simplify, manage and predict the world around us. Culture has a key role in turning these signs into coded meanings, rich in associations and hence rich in predictive value for all of us. Signs make life easier.

2   A second principle of semiotics is that any sign needs a context to make its meaning clear. For example, although the word CAT signifies a cat in many contexts, on a building site or in a clothes shop it may signify a construction equipment brand branching into fashion.

The same signifier can have different meanings as context changes. A red dot might just be a red dot. A red dot surrounded by a red doughnut is the logo of the Target retail brand. A lighted red dot surrounded by yellow and green dots on a post at the side of the road signifies 'stop'. A red dot on an Indian lady's forehead is a bindi, protecting the wearer from demons and bad luck and helping her retain energy and concentration. A red dot on a nose might signify a clown or Comic Relief (Red Nose Day) in the UK. A red dot on a white background is the flag of Japan.

Signs come in many forms, called *texts*, which are systems of signs to be read to understand their meaning based on the conventions of the type of text, genre and medium through which the text is communicated. Texts can consist of colour, shape, smell, icon, image, words, language, facial expressions, body language, graphic devices, fonts, materials, formats, size, sounds, weight and substance. Therefore, sensory experiences and sensations are texts, in the same way as words.

Understanding your category

How can semiotics be used to enhance research? One of the easiest and most frequent applications is in the analysis of category codes. Take the energy drink category. Although the number of brands is limited in Singapore, there are many more in Thailand and other Asian markets. The category has consistent themes in the signs used on product packaging and their meanings.

Many brands are in cans, for easy consumption on the go. Many brands use bright colours such as gold, red, yellow and orange to signify the heat of energy. However, there are also brands that use blue and silver colours too, perhaps inspired by the Red Bull international packaging style.

Brand names include Red Bull, Shark, Livita and Naughty G. The use of strong, aggressive animal names is quite common in this category across different markets. What does this signify? The name of Naughty G is perhaps more explicit in pointing to one of the underlying motivations for buying energy drinks.

Many of the drinks mention 'energy' but again some are more explicit in their language. Red Bull (international version) states that it 'Vitalizes body and mind', Shark only states 'Energy drink', Livita states 'Gets you going!' and Naughty G states, 'Work hard, play harder' and also 'Energy, stamina & performance: Supplement drink for him & her'. So while there are differences in the explicitness of the messages, the meanings are consistent and very clear in terms of energy, stamina and their link to sexual performance.

All products explicitly state their formulations and ingredients on the pack, no doubt because of regulatory requirements, and also emphasizing the reason to believe the product claims, based on the active ingredients. There are other medicinal cues in the category too, most explicitly the smell and taste of many of the products which is often closer to medicine than soft drinks, signifying potency and efficacy.

Looking at the alternative versions of the Red Bull packaging the international version is endorsed as 'Made in Europe – Preferred Worldwide' to support its authenticity and quality, while the local version of the packaging claims, 'Singapore's choice' endorsing its local identity.

There is much more that could be said about the packaging in this category, but a very quick analysis reveals many of the key category cues and meanings. This makes a great starting point for developing a brand identity or communication strategy, or simply setting up hypotheses for a research study.

Take any of these signs and put them in a different category or context and they may have different meanings. For example, in the coffee category signs that indicate energy (eg bright colours and wording) are more likely to mean the energy to stay awake than the energy to perform. For the coffee category, red colours are much less common and brown is the dominant colour, but when red is used it indicates the heat of the drink or of the roasting process for beans.

Other signs may have exactly the same meaning across categories. 'Made in Europe' has similar meanings of quality, although the meaning of authenticity may be stronger and more relevant in some categories than others. Names of fierce animals (or sexual predators) are not yet used in the coffee category, as the meaning doesn't match the overall category values. However, that might change as new coffee products explicitly target the energy drink category.

Semiotics is a great way to develop a quick understanding of category values and meanings. Many researchers already use semiotics implicitly, and would benefit from using semiotic approaches more explicitly with structured interpretation.

The structure of signs

Signs and meanings are arbitrary in the sense that there is often no direct connection between the signifier and the signified. However, they are rarely arbitrary in the way that they relate to other signs and meanings as Claude Lévi-Strauss argued. In the energy drink category, there are obvious and important connections between the colours, shapes, materials and words used in the category and the meanings they signify, such as energy, potency, stamina and power. They do not stand on their own, but are intimately linked (Lévi-Strauss, 1974, 1995).

Think of a restaurant menu. In a typical Western restaurant there is always a soup or starter, a main course and a dessert. In Chinese restaurants, the soup may be the last course, and in Italian restaurants, there may be a choice of pasta before the main course and after the starter or soup. However, within each course there are a variety of choices filling the role of starter, main course, pasta, soup and dessert. Some of these choices may be consistent across different menu paradigms (both Western and Chinese menus might include a chicken soup), and some choices may appear across multiple courses, so pasta with arrabiata sauce may appear as a pasta or starter on an Italian menu and as a main course elsewhere. Within all these menu systems, the courses are consistent, although a wide variety of options may be offered within any course. The courses appear in a consistent order within each cuisine paradigm too, but this order is different in other cuisines.

Semiotics talks of paradigmatic and syntagmatic axes of interpretation, referring to the overall structure of courses and the different systems that exist. Luxury brands share many things in common which are the keys to being classified as a luxury brand, and are also differentiated on key dimensions that are important to building brand meaning. All luxury brands have certain social status, personality and relationship with their customers, but these are expressed differently: Dior has a 'celebrity' status, Ralph Lauren a status relating to 'old wealth', Gucci symbolizes nobility and Louis Vuitton is more about the glamour of achievers (Oswald, 2012).

Similarly, product design revolves around the key structures of meaning that a product provides as a customer interacts with the brand through different touch points. Although beauty and functional shampoo are very different, they both have to deliver relevant meanings in terms of the cues they provide at different touch points, called 'moments of truth' in the jargon of some companies. Shampoos deliver relevant meanings when they are first seen and touched, then applied to the hair, lathered into the hair, and then washed and rinsed. Meanings continue to be delivered in the cues they deliver throughout the day.

For functional shampoos, many of these cues are strongly related to the efficacy of the product, reinforcing its effectiveness through smell, texture, colour and skinfeel. By comparison, beauty shampoos reinforce their enhancement of the user's appearance through the same senses but with very different cues relating to the aesthetics of the brand.

TABLE 4.2 Moments of truth for functional and beauty shampoo

Steps	Cues	Sensorials	Functional shampoo	Beauty shampoo
Pour shampoo on hand	Associations with benefits	Feel on hand, fragrance, colour	Light smell, thicker texture, tingling sensation, cooling colour	Strong smell, thinner texture, feminine colour
Apply and massage into hair	Relaxation	Absorption, lightness	Lightness	Fragrance that cues stress relief and perfume
Lather	Perception of product working	Amount of lather, type of lather	Not easy to lather, reaches all corners, coloured	Easy to lather, big bubbles, soft and creamy feel while lathering
After-effects	Long lasting effect	Fragrance	Lingering not cloying smell, shine and no itching	Loud fragrance, silky, no knots

The story of meaning

Myths and stories are highly structured. Western, science fiction, detective and family sitcom are very different genres, but all have a specific time frame, setting, heroic figures (cowboy, astronaut, detective or mother and father), supporting characters, opponents, secondary characters, plots, themes and weaponry (guns, lasers, intelligence or verbal wit (Danesi, 2007: 128). You can compare them in Table 4.3.

I enjoyed *Skyfall*, the latest James Bond film, following many of the conventions of previous films, which in turn follow the plot structure

TABLE 4.3 The structure of stories

Element	Western	Science fiction	Detective	Family sitcom
Time frame	early America	future	present	present
Setting	frontier	space	city	suburbs
Heroic figure	cowboy	astronaut	detective	mother or father
Supporting characters	sidekick, female lover	romantic partner	sidekick	other parent
Opponent	outlaw	aliens, space itself	killer	boss, neighbour
Secondary characters	native Americans, townsfolk	technicians in spacecraft	police, witnesses	children
Plot	restore law and order	conquer or repel aliens	find the killer	solve a problem
Theme	justice and freedom	humanity must triumph	justice must triumph	family values
Weaponry	guns, rifles, fists	space guns, lasers	gun, intellect	insults, verbal wit

of *Overcoming the monster* (read more about this in the next chapter). In most James Bond films there is an initial sequence, which often reviews the action since the last movie, and in the case of *Skyfall* provides some back story for the movie. In Skyfall this moved directly into the credits and theme song, although more conventionally Bond walks on to shoot through the eye first. This scene occurs at the end of *Skyfall*, again subverting expectations. James Bond movies follow a ritual, just as many brands do, although Skyfall plays with some of these conventions, while leaving enough of them intact for everyone to immediately recognize the style of the film. James Bond films have a predictable structure.

Everything in our lives has meaning, and the way we make sense of the world is to structure those meanings into systems. Signs are not entirely arbitrary, and only make sense in the context of other signs, as part of structures that make the world easier to understand and richer in meaning. If you understand these systems, you can re-interpret, transfer and apply them to create powerful brand stories.

Changing times

If you watch several of the James Bond films, which have now spanned more than 50 years, you will be struck by how the portrayal of the central character and his relationships to women has changed over time, despite the consistency in the plot structures.

A third principle of semiotics is that culture is dynamic, and continuously evolving the meanings that we give to signs. Think of the fast food industry and McDonalds, dominated for decades by the idea that 'bigger is better'. It still is in Singapore, where you are always asked if you want to 'upsize', despite changes in other markets and the continuing legal struggle in New York to ban oversized fizzy drinks. McDonalds communication and positioning has changed to match the changing times, using images of fit and healthy adults lying on sun beds and eating salads in some recent advertising. It's debatable whether the film *Supersize Me* was a symptom or a cause of some of the broader changes in society and its attitudes to fast food franchises.

Meanings change over time. At the funeral of George VI in London in 1952 the colour of mourning was purple, although across the world many countries now use black. They haven't always done this and some Asian countries still prefer white or another colour.

When applying semiotic analysis it is common practice to look at the structure of current meanings, separately from the analysis of how those meanings have changed over time and may change in the future. The terms for these analyses are *synchronic*, referring to the structure of meaning for one specific timeframe, and *diachronic*, referring to the evolution of codes over time. In market research, such analyses are often presented to separate the dominant codes, referring to current meanings, from residual and emergent codes, referring to older and dying meanings and newer and future meanings.

James Bond first appeared in 1962, although the books were a decade older. The first James Bond was Sean Connery, who appears in *Dr No* in immaculate dress and bow tie as a well-groomed and stylish man. He has a cigarette in one hand and a smoking gun in the other in one of the posters for the film, signifying his self-assurance, although his forward leaning stance and relaxed pose also signify his approachability. Four scantily dressed women, who signify the promise of sex and titillation, surround him.

Fast forward 50 years and the posters for the three films in which Daniel Craig has played James Bond show a different man. All three have been bathed in greys and darker colours, with a much more serious tone and down-to-earth character. They suggest far more serious times for the hero, with a much more serious pose. In posters for all three films, James Bond is on the move, rather than being relaxed and approachable, and looks as if he has serious intent toward a target he is chasing. Unlike Sean Connery, Daniel Craig is looking for the villain, and not at the viewer of the poster. Similarly, Daniel Craig doesn't have time for women, and appears on his own, or with the shadow of a lady in *Casino Royale*. Daniel Craig's Bond is far more detached than Sean Connery, and seems self-reliant.

Perhaps these are more serious times than 1962? And, of course, the relationship between men and women has changed significantly in 50 years. James Bond retains some meanings and some structural elements, but other meanings have had to change to match the times. Culture is always dynamic and in continuous movement.

Metaphor and meaning

Shakespeare was a master of metaphor, and 'all the world's a stage' is one of his most famous and widely used quotes, linking back to the Roman persona and forward to the modern 'dramaturgical' age as written about by Erving Goffman and others. It's widely used because it makes so much sense as a description of our lives.

Analogy, including metaphor, is the basis of all human thought. George Lakoff and Mark Johnson wrote a whole book on metaphors, and it is the driving idea of Douglas Hofstadter's thinking on a wide range of subjects from computers to music. As Lakoff and Johnson wrote, '... metaphor is pervasive in everyday life, not just in language but also in thought and action. Our ordinary conceptual system, in terms of which we both think and act, is fundamentally metaphorical in nature' (Lakoff and Johnson, 1980; Hofstadter, 2001, 2007).

They open their book with the example of 'argument is war' to show how a concept can be metaphorical and also how it can influence everyday behaviours. They cite many expressions, including 'your claims are indefensible', 'he attacked every weak point in my argument', 'her criticisms were right on target', 'I demolished the argument', 'okay, shoot!' and 'the argument was shot down'. As they say, we don't just talk about arguments as war, it's something we either win or lose, we argue with an opponent and we defend our ground. The metaphor structures our language and behaviour when we argue with someone, and is deeply embedded in our thinking. Similarly, the concept of 'time is money' is deeply embedded in culture.

Associative structures are the key to how we think and the basis of rhetoric, going back 2,000 years to Aristotle who wrote about metaphor, metonymy and irony in his works on *Poetics* and *Rhetoric*. Metaphor and metonymy are important concepts in semiotics, related to the figurative and literal meanings of signs.

Metaphor uses comparison, association or resemblance to make an analogy between one thing and another, such as war and argument or time and money). Metonymy uses an attribute of something to stand for the thing itself, or point to the thing itself by reference to its effects, such as the relationship between smoke and fire or brass and military officers. Synecdoche is a specific type of metonymy where a word for part of something is used to mean the whole, as when sail stands for boat, wheels for car, or face for person.

Although irony is not so commonly written about in semiotics, it is where words are used to convey a meaning contrary to the literal sense of the words, such as, 'I love being tortured' spoken by someone in pain. One of the reasons computers are very bad at semantic analysis is that they just do not get irony, where meaning completely depends on the context.

Metaphor is based on symbolic meanings and metonymy on indexical meanings to use the language of Charles Peirce. Metaphors are commonly found across different languages and cultures, especially relating to our sensory experience of the world. Warm, cold and heavy are commonly used across a wide range of situations in language, although differences in context lead to differences in use. 'Hot' can mean 'rage' in Hebrew, 'enthusiasm' in Chinese, 'sexual arousal' in Thailand and 'energy' in Hausa.

The essence of metaphor is understanding and experiencing one kind of thing in terms of another. Many brands use metaphor and metonymy.

There are huge differences in the way that Eternity and Paloma Picasso perfumes portray their respective brands. Eternity adverts are often in black and white, use realistic imagery, have a more casual feel, and show a girl next door with a maternal and caring relationship. In contrast, Paloma Picasso adverts are colourful and iconic, have an element of fantasy, are artistic and creative and much more formal with a goddess-like image of women. These two brands are almost binary opposites of each other, with Eternity using metonymy and Paloma Picasso using metaphor.

Brands use metaphor and metonymy all the time, often focusing on one or the other in names as well as communication. Some brand and product names are more literal, such as iPhone and others are more symbolic, such as Apple. Many very successful metaphorical brand names end up being metonyms for their own category: Coke, Hoover, Jell-o, Kleenex, Post-It notes, Scotch Tape, Thermos, Vaseline, Walkman and Xerox all started as brand names.

Opposites matter

The *Star Wars* films are packed full of mythic oppositions and themes. George Lucas was an avid reader of Joseph Campbell and the six part series, with parts 4–6 made first, mirrors the structure of Homer's *Iliad*. In the story there are oppositions between young and old (immaturity and idealism versus maturity and wisdom), Luke and the Emperor (the common man versus authority figure), nature and technology, the Force and evil, Jedi and Sith (democracy versus totalitarianism), rebels and empire, freedom and tyranny, love and hate (constructive versus destructive behaviour) and son and father, representing a rite of passage.

Claude Lévi-Strauss argued that such oppositions are the basis of myth, whose purpose is to dramatize contradictions in a structured story format in order to resolve them. As he put it, 'The purpose of myth is to provide a logical model capable of overcoming a contradiction' (Lévi-Strauss, 1974). If you think of the creation myth, God first separates heaven from earth, and then light from dark, land from water and so on, until eventually he creates man and animals and then splits man and woman.

Many binary oppositions are universal (see Table 4.4). These oppositions appear in the mythic traditions of societies around the world, and in the modern storytelling of Hollywood and Bollywood.

These systems of meaning are highly interwoven. Humans have both left and right hands (as well as eyes and feet). In Western thought right is associated with good and light and left with dark and evil. The English word sinister derives from the Latin word for on the left, considered unlucky by Romans too. Left-handedness has often been associated with evil and misfortune. In Michelangelo's Sistine Chapel fresco of the last judgment, Jesus Christ condemns evil sinners to hell with his left hand, and gives passage to heaven for good people with his right. Right is commonly used to convey ideas of correctness, truth and justice (eg in a 'bill of rights'), and a righteous person is someone who is moral and upstanding. Offering a handshake or saluting or taking an oath with the left hand is considered improper and wrong.

TABLE 4.4 Mythic oppositions

masculine	feminine
light	dark
good	evil
self	other
subject	object
sacred	profane
body	mind
nature	history
positive	negative
heaven	hell
beginning	end
love	hate
pleasure	pain
existence	nothingness
left	right

A fourth key principle of semiotics is that meaning often comes from what things are not rather than what they are. As we grow up, we start to understand the world around us by splitting it into pairs of opposites, just as God does in the creation myth. We learn that 'mummy is not daddy', 'hello is not goodbye', 'noise is not quiet' and most importantly that 'no is not yes' (Oswald, 2012).

Binary oppositions are important to the structure of meaning and thinking. They define categories that are logically opposed and there is no middle ground, so something is either one or the other.

This is very typical of Western thought, although arguably does not make sense in Asia, where relationships are more important than attributes. Asians are more comfortable combining conflicting ideas to create harmony, as in the principle of *yin* and *yang*.

In myth, the relationships between different oppositions often reflect strongly held cultural norms. For example, good versus evil and beautiful versus ugly are two important dimensions of meaning, which are strongly linked in myth. Beautiful characters in fairy tales are almost always good: Snow White, Sleeping Beauty and Cinderella. Ugly characters are almost always bad: giants, ogres and goblins. Good and beautiful is a cultural norm, while good and ugly is a cultural contradiction.

However, the Seven Dwarfs and Shrek are far more interesting than typical fairytale characters because they combine good and ugliness and break cultural norms. Similarly, the Wicked Stepmother is interesting because she combines beauty and evil. Such contradictions are the essence of powerful storytelling and the essence of powerful brands.

One of the best-known examples of using cultural contradictions in branding is Omo, although Omo is known by a different brand name in some markets. Omo's 'dirt is good' campaign is one of the most successful campaigns ever in the laundry category. I remember watching the 'Persil mum' ads on TV when I was growing up, without realizing that the campaign was managing to resolve a cultural contradiction between the efficiency of factory-produced high-tech washing powder and the caring of a nurturing mother, into 'caring efficiency'. More recently, Omo resolves contradictions between science and nature, clean and dirty and good and evil. While 'Cleanliness is next to godliness' is the cultural norm, how can any mother allow her children to get dirty even if it is important for their learning. 'Dirt is good' gives permission for mothers (and fathers) to combine the naturalness of learning through play with the science of cleanliness (Oswald, 2012).

Binary oppositions are a great way to think about meanings, and to find innovative ways to break with conventions. However, Eastern philosophies teach that nature is more circular than linear, so sometimes it pays to look for the middle ground.

Squaring the circle

Western thought has always sought to categorize objects as *either* one thing *or* another. Aristotle built systems based on categories, Descartes' dualism focused on the split between mind and body, and Kierkegaard argued for a leap of faith in *Either/Or*. The concept of binary opposition is central to semiotic theory, although Eastern philosophy has always realized that the world is not as simple as this.

Storytellers and filmmakers have always known that it can be much more interesting to look at the middle ground. Many of the most interesting stories and films revolve around things that are 'undecideable', such as zombies. This is also where many of the best new ideas come from.

The phrase 'undecideable' comes from Jacques Derrida, who famously disagreed with structuralism, which is the theoretical underpinning of many semiotic tools (see the article 'Jacques Derrida' on Wikipedia for more on this topic). He argued, along with Michel Foucault, that sign systems are self-referential and do not encode reality. Thus systems that appear stable and logical are illogical and paradoxical. His arguments bear a striking resemblance to the Incompleteness Theory of Kurt Gödel and similar ideas in Quantum Theory that show limits to human knowledge and logical systems.

A central interest in a zombie film is whether zombies are alive or dead, and how this paradox can be resolved. In my favourite film, *Bladerunner*, the story revolves around the differences between man and machine, and where the humans and replicants fall in the continuum between man and machine, and also between emotional and emotionless. In *Bladerunner*, the replicants often appear more human than human, or at least more human than the 'humans' in the story. 'More human than human' is coincidentally the motto of the Tyrell Corporation who designed the replicants in the story. More recently, *Rise of the Planet of the Apes* from 2011 explores the opposition between man and animal (in this case ape).

AJ Greimas and others developed the 'semiotic square' as one way to explore such undecideable oppositions. If you take the opposition of masculine versus feminine, you can draw a connecting 'line' between

FIGURE 4.1 Semiotic square of sexuality

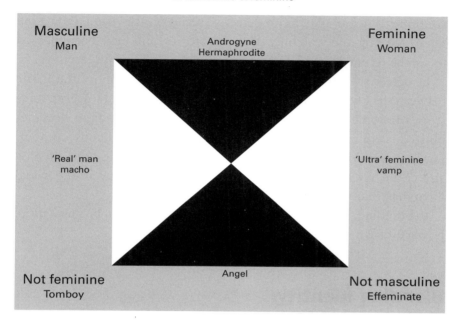

Semiotic Square
of masculine & feminine

Masculine
Man

Androgyne
Hermaphrodite

Feminine
Woman

'Real' man
macho

'Ultra' feminine
vamp

Angel

Not feminine
Tomboy

Not masculine
Effeminate

the two ideas, and then project a square from the line (see Figure 4.1). 'Masculine' implies 'not feminine' and 'feminine' implies 'not masculine' so the other corners of the square can be labelled. The two diagonals of the square are then composed of two contradictions (masculine versus not masculine and feminine versus not feminine) and the bottom of the square has a new opposition or contradiction between 'not masculine' and 'not feminine'. Read Oswald (2012) for more examples of semiotic squares in marketing applications.

The challenge is then to find labels for the different areas of meaning around the square. For example, 'androgynes', 'hermaphrodites' might fall between masculine and feminine poles, or perhaps 'transsexuals', 'metrosexuals' or other labels depending on the frame of reference. Not masculine might be 'effeminate' and not feminine might be 'tomboy'. Masculine and not feminine might be 'macho' while feminine and not masculine might be 'ultra feminine', 'femme fatale' or 'vamp'. The labels depend to a large extent on the objectives and frame of reference, and the process helps to structure thinking around possible blends or combinations of core binary opposition.

Let's go back to story for a final example. Cops and robbers films continue to be popular, as do detective series on television. I am a big fan of reading and watching detective stories, and have been pleased to see the recent success of many Scandinavian authors in recent years.

In detective fiction, the standard paradigm is to show the battle between the good 'law enforcer' and the bad 'criminal'. However, these stories become much more enjoyable when this paradigm becomes blurred, as in many recent examples. Thus, 'corrupted cops' combining law and crime, and 'Robin Hood' figures outside both the law and crime, create paradoxes that can engage audiences in the moral dilemmas that they portray.

In branding, identifying such 'paradoxical' spaces can be much more powerful than focusing on either/or concepts.

Blending identity

Pablo Picasso's *Les Demoiselles d'Avignon* is considered a seminal work of art leading in different ways to modernism and cubism (Picasso always referred to a 'brothel' rather than the more polite 'young ladies' of the usual title). The work borrows ideas from Cézanne, Gauguin, El Greco, Spanish art, Iberian sculpture and African tribal masks and blends them in a unique and provocative way to create a masterpiece, in 1907 and even today. Picasso famously once said that, 'Bad artists copy. Good artists steal'.

Great ideas are always blends of existing ones. As we have seen, the basis of our thinking is in associative memory and metaphor, which is essentially about mixing it up. Steve Jobs once put it this way, 'Creativity is just connecting things'. Cognitive psychologists call this *conceptual blending* and semioticians call it '*intertextuality*', but let me stick to blending.

One of the TV shows that has made me laugh more than most over many years is *South Park*. Each episode takes a theme or idea from elsewhere and plays with it within the context of South Park and the personalities of the four central characters. For example, in the episode *Insheeption* the characters and plot of Inception are blended with those of South Park. Blending of ideas can be through inference, implication, suggestion or more direct association.

Metaphor and metonymy are simple ways of mapping meanings across domains. In metaphor, there are typically two domains, a source and a target. For example, in the metaphor 'people are animals' (ie John is a pig), animals and people constitute two separate domains of ideas, and the metaphor allows us to mentally blend these together. Thus, the form of a metaphor is 'x *is a* y' (eg people are animals). Metonymy is simpler in that it only uses one domain of ideas as in 'x *stands for* y' (eg people are faces).

Conceptual blending often involves more complicated mappings of whole systems of ideas and not just single attributes. When I say, 'his plan backfired on him', I am taking two different sets of ideas and mapping them into a new domain. One set of ideas involves a hunter preparing his equipment, then stalking an animal and finally firing only to experience the bullet coming out of the gun backwards and threatening the hunter. Another set of ideas involves someone who has an intention and carefully plans what to do and then carries out the plan only to find that it fails and there are unintended consequences, even perhaps the reverse of what was expected. The final blended space of 'his plan backfired on him' falls somewhere in between these in a third space of ideas.

Advertising is constantly blending category values with ideas from contemporary culture. The beer category is a great example of this. In one published study, based on work for Diageo, the different themes used in advertising beer around the world were analyzed by Michael Harvey and Malcolm Evans (2001). Although the paper is more than 10 years old, many of the findings remain relevant, certainly in Singapore and other Asian markets. The authors studied markets around the world, and found themes of cosmopolitan lifestyle, alternative humour and tribal totems were common across most of them (see Table 4.5). You only have to look at current advertising of beer to see that many of the same themes are still playing out.

TABLE 4.5   Global themes of beer advertising

Cosmopolitan lifestyle	Alternative humour	Tribal totems
Modern city life	Self-deprecating humour	Bonding focal points
Western clothing and lifestyle	Irony and cynicism	Workplace and after work
Beautiful people	Parody	Nation and icons
New generation (developed markets only)	Surreal inversions of reality	Looking alike
–	Alternative comedians	Regional identity

SOURCE: Harvey and Evans, 2001

Categories and brands regularly blend ideas from each other. Good advertising and creative thinking are all about how we blend ideas. This can be copying, stealing or borrowing. Sometimes it seems obvious and at other times it may be subtle. The results are always a blend of multiple ideas. Creative thinking is all about blending.

Story and archetypes

05

" *Story is about eternal, universal forms.* ROBERT MCKEE

Causality and the mind

David Hume wrote over 300 years ago that, 'Causality is the cement of the universe' (Cron, 2012: 145). Why get up in the morning if you can't assume that the Sun will rise and that everything will be the same as the day before? Our mind makes assumptions about the future based on past experience, or as the neuroscientist Antonio Damasio put it, 'our memories are prejudiced, in the full sense of the term, by our past history and beliefs' (Damasio, 2012: 173).

The patterns that our brain seeks to detect every minute of every day are the patterns of cause and effect. Without cause and effect we would all be lost. Steven Pinker put it this way, 'People assume that the world has a causal texture – that its events can be explained by the world's very nature, rather than just being one damn thing after another' (Cron, 2012: 145).

Importantly, all stories follow a cause-and-effect trajectory from start to finish. Over recent years, storytelling has become a big focus of business communication. From the curated and heavily managed TED talks, with their strong emphasis on narrative structure, to the ever-growing list of business books and services focused on leveraging the power of story (for example Cooke, 2013; Gottschall, 2012; Sachs, 2012; Signorelli, 2012; Smith, 2012; Sykes, Malik and West,

2013). Everybody wants to be a storyteller – something that the most successful brands have always known.

Although the recent avalanche may be a trend to move away from more fact-based approaches to communication, the reality is that stories work. Jerome Bruner famously stated that a fact is 20 times more likely to be remembered if it is part of a story, or as he put it 'anchored in narrative' (Bruner, 1990). Humans have told stories for more than 100,000 years (stories predate language) and written them down for 6,000 or 7,000 years. Every culture in history has created stories. Gerald Zaltman put it this way, 'Storytelling is not something we just happen to do. It is something we virtually have to do if we want to remember anything. The stories we create are the memories we have' (2003: 190).

Jerome Bruner was right about the importance of stories to our memory and behaviour. Research by cognitive scientists has shown that experiences not framed as stories may not be memorized. More recent neuroscience work has shown that stories activate sensory processing areas of the brain (sights, sounds, tastes, movements), unlike facts. In *Story Proof* (2007), Kendall Haven references over 350 research studies across a wide range of scientific disciplines. Every single study showed that stories are an effective medium for motivating, communicating information, and learning.

There is a huge and increasing amount of evidence about the effectiveness of stories for communicating information, memorizing facts and engaging customers. Indeed some argue that stories were crucial to our evolution, and perhaps more important than opposable thumbs, giving us our biggest advantage over other animals. Stories help us to imagine the future and through our imagination prepare for what might happen. It has been shown that our brains are hard-wired for story, and the pleasure stories provide are nature's way of enticing us to listen and learn.

Damasio has written, 'the problem of how to make all this wisdom understandable, transmissible, persuasive, enforceable – in a word, of how to make it stick – was faced and a solution found. Storytelling was the solution – storytelling is something brains do, naturally and implicitly... it should be no surprise that it pervades the entire fabric of human societies and cultures' (Damasio, 2010: 293).

The meaning of stories

Our senses are constantly taking in a vast amount of data, such as the words on this page, the colour of the paper, the weight of the book (or e-reader) in our hands, the smell of coffee from the kitchen, the sounds of conversations downstairs (which we know we shouldn't be listening in on, but which we can't completely ignore). Although all this data is being taken in, it isn't written automatically onto a memory 'hard drive', but gets sorted in different ways, assigned a level of importance, and only gets transferred if we really 'need to know' through a process called consolidation. If we suffer a system crash before consolidation, then we won't remember any of it at all, which is sometimes good and sometimes bad.

The importance of sensory data depends on the meaning that data has for us, and specifically how well it can help us to make specific and accurate predictions about future outcomes. Put another way, prediction is all about understanding cause and effect, which is also the subject of stories.

Thus, meaning is critically linked to emotional state, social and environmental context and the brain's reward system that powers our learning. Emotions are the 'markers' of importance, while context makes information specific enough to provide predictive power, helping the brain to learn new and better ways to navigate events (with better emotional outcomes).

Richard Restak writes about context, 'Within the brain, things are always evaluated within a specific context' (2006: 77). Context is the key to meaning and the secret of the power of story. Similarly, Daniel Gilbert writes about emotion, 'Feelings don't just matter, they are what mattering means' (Cron, 2012: 45), while Steven Pinker has written, 'Emotions are mechanisms that set the brain's highest goals' (1997: 373).

Stories are powerful ways to transmit meaning, containing context, action and emotional reward (cause, behaviour and effect). A story contains all the information the brain needs to make that information useful in making predictions. The meaning of a story is not necessarily diminished by the realness of the events. Imaginary stories are still powerful tools for mental simulation of 'scenarios' that help the brain to increase its predictive powers, and many have argued that one of the greatest gifts of humanity is the ability to create such mental simulations in order to imagine situations and events that have never been experienced.

This is how children learn from fairytales and stories. For example, in many fairytales, children are thrown into a world where their parents are no longer there to help them. The simulation of such stories helps us imagine a world where we cannot rely on our parents to help us, and have to learn to look after ourselves. Arguably, the common theme of the majority of fairytales, myths and legends, is the story of grow-ing up. This is what Joseph Campbell (1993) called the 'monomyth', which he elaborated with examples from cultures all around the world.

Story allowed early humans to imagine dangerous experiences without having to live through them. They have become a useful way to explore our own minds and the minds of others. Steven Pinker has written:

> Fictional narratives supply us with a mental catalogue of the fatal conundrums we might face someday and the outcomes of strategies we could deploy in them. What are the options if I were to suspect that my uncle killed my father, took his position, and married my mother? If my hapless older brother got no respect in the family, are there circumstances that might lead him to betray me? What's the worst that could happen if I were to be seduced by a client while my wife and daughter were away for the weekend? What's the worst that could happen if I had an affair to spice up my boring life as the wife of a country doctor? How can I avoid a suicidal confrontation with raiders who want my land today without looking like a coward and thereby ceding it to them tomorrow? The answers are to be found in any bookstore or any video store. The cliché that life imitates art is true because the function of some kinds of art is for life to imitate it. (Pinker, 1997: 543)

Story and myth

 Joseph Campbell and others have argued that the monomyth or 'hero's journey' is a common pattern found in numerous myths across cultures and time (he borrowed the term from James Joyce's _Finnegan's Wake_). The pattern consists of fundamental structures and stages, which he described in _The Hero with a Thousand Faces_ in this way: 'A hero ventures forth from the world of common day into a region of supernatural wonder: fabulous forces are there encountered and a decisive victory is won: the hero comes back from this mysterious adventure with the power to bestow boons on his fellow man' (Campbell, 1993).

The narratives of Buddha, Moses and Jesus Christ have all been described in terms of the monomyth, as well as epic stories such as _Gilgamesh_ and _The Odyssey_. Campbell (1993) argued that classic myths from all cultures followed this basic pattern. You can see a depiction of the hero's journey in Figure 5.1 below.

FIGURE 5.1 The hero's journey from Campbell, 1993

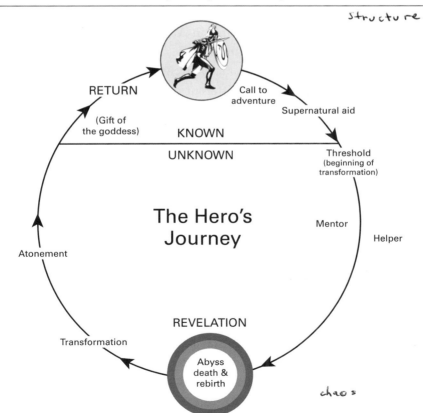

The 'monomyth' is a universal 'archetype'. Campbell's writings have been very influential on Hollywood, most notably with George Lucas and *Star Wars*. For example, the plot of *Star Wars* follows precisely the flow of the monomyth, as you can see in Table 5.1.

Although he has many followers, some believe that the mono-myth is too simplistic in its interpretation of archetypal stories. Most famously, Christopher Booker spent many years writing *The Seven Basic Plots* (2004), which outline seven archetypal story structures, including comedy and tragedy that go back to Aristotle's *Poetics*. The seven are summarized in Table 5.2.

Joseph Campbell was a student of Carl Jung who popularized the idea of archetypes more than anyone else in the last century, although the idea goes back to antiquity. Plato's ideal forms and 'allegory of the cave' have much in common with ideas of archetypes. Campbell (1993) wrote that 'the concept of archetypes was borrowed by Jung from classic sources, including Cicero, Pliny and Augustine. Adolf Bastian called them "Elementary Ideas". In Sanskrit, they were called "subjectively known forms"; and in Australia, they were known as the "Eternal Ones of the Dream".'

Jung wrote extensively about such archetypes as the anima, animus, self, shadow and persona as different aspects of human psychology. He also wrote about the more mythical and cultural aspects of archetypes like the mother, child and trickster (Jung, 1968).

As well as stories and metaphors, the word archetype often refers to characters that have common currency across cultures and time. Jung himself defined archetypes as, 'Forms or images of a collective nature which occur practically all over the earth as constituents of myths and at the same time as individual products of unconscious origin' ('Psychological types' in Jung, 1993: 230–357).

The *Oxford English Dictionary* defines archetype as, 'A symbol, theme, setting or character-type that recurs in different times and places in myth, literature, folklore, dreams and rituals so frequently or prominently as to suggest that it embodies some essential element of "universal" human experience.' My preferred definition of archetype comes from Jon Howard-Spink (2002) who wrote. 'An archetype is a universally familiar character or situation that transcends time, place, culture, gender and age. It represents an eternal truth.'

TABLE 5.1   The hero's journey and *Star Wars*

The hero's journey	Star Wars
The hero exists in an ordinary world	Luke Skywalker is a bored farm boy, dreaming of the space academy
He gets a call to adventure	Luke sees the distress hologram from Princess Leia
He almost refuses	Luke delivers the message and decides to go home
The wise elder (Guru) advises him to heed the call	Obi-Wan advises Luke to come with him
He enters the special world	Luke follows Obi-Wan to the cantina
Where he encounters tests and discovers allies and enemies	Luke meets Han Solo, they escape from imperial stormtroopers, jump into hyperspace and emerge in a meteor storm
He enters the inmost cave	Luke and friends are pulled into the Death Star
Where he encounters the supreme ordeal	Luke and friends are trapped in the 'trash masher' and Obi-Wan is killed by Darth Vader
He seizes the sword	Luke gets the plan to the Death Star
Takes the road back	Luke and friends are pursued by Darth Vader
Almost dies, but is resurrected	Despite being wounded, Luke hits the spot and destroys the Death Star
And returns with the elixir	Luke learns not to rely on machines, but to 'trust the force' and is transformed into a hero

TABLE 5.2   Seven archetypal plots

Archetypal plot	Examples
Killing the monster	*Jack and the Beanstalk, Little Red Riding Hood, James Bond*
Rags to riches	*Aladdin, Cinderella, Shrek*
Quest	*The Odyssey, Indiana Jones, Star Trek*
Voyage and return	*Treasure Island, Peter Rabbit, The Wizard of Oz*
Comedy	*Lysistrata, Pride and Prejudice, Some Like It Hot*
Tragedy	*Hamlet, Madame Bovary, American Beauty*
Rebirth	*The Frog Prince, Beauty and the Beast, The Lion King*

SOURCE: Booker, 2004

I am writing this just after the Chinese New Year celebrations in Singapore, which have brought in the Year of the Snake. The Chinese Zodiac has 12 animals, each of which represents a core idea about human (and animal) behaviour (see Figure 5.2). Snakes are considered charming, even charismatic. You could call them seducers. Although snakes can be very popular, they can also be treacherous, calculating and lazy, and are sometimes considered secretive and somewhat elusive. It is common in many cultures to consider foxes in a similar way (clever, subtle, sly), whereas lions are powerful and fearless and owls are clever and wise.

The characteristics of the snake have much in common with the Western archetype of a 'Shapeshifter' or 'Trickster'. Trickster characters are very common in mythology, across all cultures, from Prometheus and Hermes in ancient Greece, to Leprechauns in Ireland, Robin Hood in England, MacRusgail in Scotland, Gwydion in Wales, Anansi in West Africa and the Caribbean, Saci in Brazil, Hanuman in India and Sun Wu Kong (the Monkey King) in China. Fans of German opera will know the character Loge, who comes from the Loki of Norse mythology. Foxes and related animals are very commonly associated

FIGURE 5.2 Chinese zodiac

SOURCE: Thinkstock reference 88344464

with tricksters, called Reynard the Fox in Europe, Kitsune in Japan, Coyote in North American, and Huli Jing (fox spirit) in China. A quick search would find similar characters in almost every culture.

Such characters remain popular in contemporary culture from Bugs Bunny to Charlie Chaplin's tramp to Jack Sparrow. Tricksters and clowns are often catalysts, creating discomfort and confusion through their antics, remaining untouched themselves. They are usually clever and mischievous, like to have fun, and can be deceitful and tricky, always living on their wits rather than physical strength. They value change and spontaneity, and like to break taboos.

the trickster

- a record of 7 songs based on the plots?
· " " based on prominant archetypal figures

Brand archetypes

Traditionally brands have been developed in a rational and analytical way, using brand attributes, brand pyramids, brand DNA, brand keys and other devices to characterize the brand and what it stands for. However, there are problems with such approaches as they diminish distinctiveness with too many brands trying to portray the same characteristics (eg innovative, exciting, trustworthy), and also because such attributes can get lost in translation meaning different things to different people. They also miss the point that the brain thinks holistically (and mostly non-verbally), and experiences brands in their totality rather than as collections of abstract ideas.

Archetypes have been with us for thousands of years, and are embedded deep in the culture that surrounds us (and therefore embedded deep in our minds too). As we have seen, although each culture has its own stories, fables and legends with their own local characters, they share much in common. Joseph Campbell wrote, 'Why is mythology everywhere the same, beneath its varieties of costume?' The heroes of Indian and Chinese mythology have the same virtues and vices as the heroes of American and European cultures.

The notion of using archetypes as a branding tool has been most famously expounded by Margaret Mark and Carol Pearson in their book _The Hero and the Outlaw_, which was first published in 2001. The book provides a detailed overview of 12 archetypes, their history and mythology and their application to marketing, with many examples (mostly from the US). They group the archetypes into four themes according to a motivational framework, and they describe the four groups of three with the motivations of stability and control, belonging and enjoyment, risk and mastery and independence and fulfillment (or to give them their longer descriptions, 'providing structure to the world', 'no man (or woman) is an island', 'leaving a thumbprint on the world' and 'the yearning for paradise').

Kent Wertime's _Building Brands and Believers_ also describes 12 archetypes, although his selection is different to that of Mark and Pearson, the archetype framework is less structured and he includes shadow archetypes within the 12. Peter Steidl presents 28 archetypes in _Creating Brand Meaning_, including those that are used in the above two books, and adding additional archetypes from a system developed by Young & Rubicam. This creates duplication, and many of his 28 are variations on core archetypes. For example, Wizard, Healer and Enchantress are all expressions of the Catalyst archetype in male and female versions (see Chapter 6), while his Utopian,

Innocent and Enthusiast are different expressions of the Idealist archetype (Wertime, 2002; Steidl, 2012).

Other writers who have referenced archetypes include Mark Batey (2008), Patrick Hanlon (2006), Jonah Sachs (2012) and Jim Signorelli (2012). Mark Batey provides much shorter descriptions of the core archetypes, placing them in a broader context of motivational and emotional theories. Patrick Hanlon places archetypes within a framework of successful brands as 'religions' with mythology and ritual at their core. Jonah Sachs provides brief descriptions of several archetypes as tools for building engaging stories for business. Finally, Jim Signorelli explains the use of archetypal analysis in developing brand stories.

Perhaps the most comprehensive of all of the books on archetypes is *Archetypes in Branding* (2012) by Margaret Pott Hartwell and Joshua C Chen. The book provides a comprehensive overview of 60 archetypes, with five variants of each of 12 fundamental archetypes (which they call Caregiver, Citizen, Creator, Explorer, Hero, Innocent, Jester, Lover, Magician, Rebel, Sage and Sovereign). The book is a great resource for creative development, containing rich descriptions of each archetype.

I will describe the 12 core archetypes fully in the next chapter, but first we should understand why they are so powerful. What is it about these archetypes making them such a useful tool for brand development? And why is it that these archetypes appear so consistently and frequently across different cultures, places and times?

Archetypal frameworks

Carl Jung was not only influential in the development of the idea of archetypes, but also in the development of psychological ideas of motivation and personality. Although the Myers-Briggs Type Indicator (MBTI) has limited scientific evidence, it is the most popular psychometric (personality) test in existence, with reportedly more than 2 million assessments every year based on it. MBTI was developed out of Jung's typologies proposed in 'Psychological Types'. He theorized that we experience the world through four principal psychological functions: sensation, intuition, feeling and thinking. He also claimed that one of the four functions is dominant most of the time (Jung, 1993: 230–357).

The Myers-Briggs typology has lent itself to archetypes. For example, I am an INFP (Introversion, Intuition, Feeling, Perception) type according to the online test I took earlier today, which is called 'The Healer' in the Keirsey Temperament Sorter developed by David Keirsey. I'll leave those who know me to judge the accuracy of this description.

Although MBTI has questionable scientific backing, studies have shown a high degree of correlation between its scales, and other personality measures. In particular, four of the Big Five personality constructs are strongly correlated. The 'Big Five' are often known by the acronym OCEAN and are a conglomeration of characteristics found in nearly all personality and psychological tests. O stands for Openness and is correlated with Sensing/Intuition; C stands for Conscientiousness and is correlated with Judgment/Perception; E stands for Extraversion and is unsurprisingly correlated with Extraversion/Introversion; and A stands for Agreeableness and is correlated with Thinking/Feeling. Only Neuroticism (the N of OCEAN which measures emotional stability) does not have a counterpart in MBTI (McCrae and Costa, 1989).

A brief look at the 12 common archetypes reveals examples that display all of the characteristics of both personality systems. The Guru is strong on Thinking, The Seducer is strong on Sensing, The Caregiver is strong on Feeling, The Artist is strong on Intuition, The Explorer is strong on Openness, The Ruler is strong on Conscientiousness, The Warrior is strong on Extraversion, The Everyman is strong on Agreeableness, and the Rebel is strong on Neuroticism.

The dimensions of stability, change, belonging and individuation are common to many standard psychological models used in market research (eg Censydiam from Ipsos and Needscope from TNS) all of which are based on the work of Jung, Freud and Adler. Whatever the advantages and disadvantages of different models, these dimensions come from the strategies that developed as humans evolved over history. Evolutionary psychologists argue that there are four core strategies that helped humans to be successful: the drive to *acquire* requiring individuation; the drive to *bond* transcending the individual; the drive to *learn* requiring openness to change; and the drive to defend leading to safety and stability (Lawrence and Nohria, 2002; Pinker, 2002).

Thus, evolution is at the heart of understanding human behaviour. Expanding on evolutionary psychology, Jaak Panksepp's work with humans and animals has revealed seven emotions with specific brain circuits, neuronal activity and behavioural outcomes. The most important of these is what Panksepp calls *seeking* (the drive to acquire). The other six are *rage*, *fear*, *lust*, *care*, *panic* (grief) and *play* (Panksepp and Biven, 2012).

These behaviours are consistent with the human values that have been researched by Milton Rokeach (1973) and Shalom Schwartz (1993). The former's work led to the development of the *Rokeach Value Survey*, which measures the importance of 18 'terminal values' and 18 'instrumental values' that drive the beliefs and attitudes of all humans. Rokeach defined terminal values as desirable end states of existence, reflecting the goals that a person would like to achieve during their lifetime. These values vary among different people in different cultures. Instrumental values are preferred modes of behaviour that help people achieve the terminal values. The Terminal Values and Instrumental Values are summarized in Table 5.3.

In the 1990s, Shalom Schwartz summarized the main features of values as beliefs (cognitive structures) closely linked to emotional states and to desirable goals (for example, social equality or fairness) and transcending specific situations or actions. His model of motivation defines 10 different goals and specific values that define them, capturing and simplifying Rokeach's values in a smaller set of values:

1 **Power** is social status and prestige, control or dominance over people or resources (social power, authority, wealth, preserving one's image).

2 **Achievement** is personal success through demonstrating competence according to social standards (successful, capable, ambitious, influential).

3 **Hedonism** is pleasure and sensuous gratification for oneself (pleasure, enjoyment, self-indulgence).

4 **Stimulation** is excitement, novelty and challenge in life (daring, varied life, excitement).

TABLE 5.3 Rokeach's terminal and instrumental values

Terminal values	Instrumental values
True friendship	Cheerfulness
Mature love	Ambition
Self-respect	Love
Happiness	Cleanliness
Inner harmony	Self-control
Equality	Capability
Freedom	Courage
Pleasure	Politeness
Social recognition	Honesty
Wisdom	Imagination
Salvation	Independence
Family security	Intellect
National security	Broad-mindedness
A sense of accomplishment	Logic
A world of beauty	Obedience
A world at peace	Helpfulness
A comfortable life	Responsibility
An exciting life	Forgiveness

SOURCE: Rokeach, 1973

5 **Self-direction** is independent thought and action, creating and exploring (creativity, freedom, curiosity).

6 **Universalism** is understanding, appreciation, tolerance and protection for all (wisdom, social justice, equality, unity with nature).

7 **Benevolence** is preservation and enhancement of the welfare of others in your circle (helpful, honest, forgiving, loyal, responsible).

8 **Tradition** is respect, commitment and acceptance of the customs and ideas of culture and religion (humble, devout, moderate).

9 **Conformity** is restraint of actions, inclinations and impulses likely to upset or harm others or violate social norms (politeness, obedience, self-discipline, honouring parents and elders).

10 **Security** is safety, harmony and stability of society and relationships (family security, national security, social order, cleanliness).

Schwartz also mapped these goals onto a circumplex (see Figure 5.3), closely linked to psycho-evolutionary models of emotion. This two-dimensional model shows the tensions between goals related to self-enhancement and those related to self-transcendence and similarly those related to conservation and those related to openness to change. Schwartz's values have been verified in over 200 samples of respondents from over 60 countries, with over 100,000 respondents in total.

These values are at the top of our personal 'ladders' of meaning, according to means–end chain models. Such models show the path from concrete attributes through to functional and then psychosocial consequences of the attributes that ultimately link to values (long-term goals). For example, in a salty snack, flavour may be linked to perceptions of strength, leading to eating less of the snack which leads to ideas that you will not get fat, meaning that you will have a better figure and higher self-esteem.

FIGURE 5.3   Ten human values from Schwartz, 1993

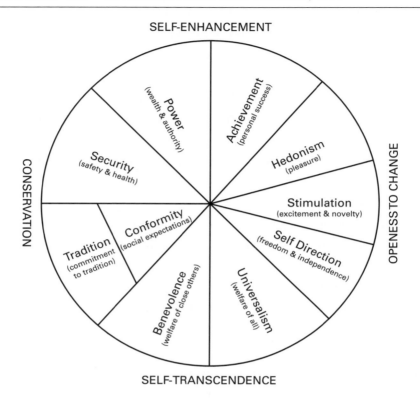

The two dimensions of Schwartz's model are similar to those found in many motivational research models. They encompass a personal dimension between the need for self-expression and the desire for stability and control, and a social dimension between the need for individuation and independence and the need for interdependence and connection with others.

Laddering is a common tool in research, and will be discussed in Chapter 8. In all the research I have conducted using laddering, I have almost always come to values that reflect similar aspirations to those in the models of Rokeach and Schwartz. It is no surprise that all humans crave for the same long-term goals, and a more recent book by Hugh Mackay highlights similar ideas. Mackay uses *What Makes Us Tick* (2010) to reflect on a lifetime in social research to identify the 10 goals that he has found to drive humans across all the different work on which he has been involved. His 10 goals are listed below:

1 The desire to be taken seriously.
2 The desire for 'my place'.
3 The desire for something to believe in.
4 The desire to connect.
5 The desire to be useful.
6 The desire to belong.
7 The desire for more.
8 The desire for control.
9 The desire for something to happen.
10 The desire for love.

In all of the models outlined, the role of brands is to work as symbolic signifiers of identity, lifestyle and taste, depending on the specific identity or role that we wish to play in the consumption context (for example, mother, friend, wife, businesswoman, sports player, gourmand, lover, etc). These roles are exemplified in the archetypes that will be outlined in the next chapter. More importantly, these 12 archetypes relate back to the goals, evolutionary strategies and emotional rewards that consistently appear across all models of behaviour and personality.

In Chapter 6 I will describe 12 archetypes that can be used to create brand stories. The archetypes relate back to all the work discussed in this chapter. They fall into four groups: archetypes of belonging, freedom, ego and order (see Figure 5.4).

Archetypes are not random products of culture and storytelling, but reflect more fundamental human aspirations for finding meaning in the world. This is what makes archetypes such powerful tools for creating brand identity.

FIGURE 5.4 Twelve archetypes

Using archetypes in branding

06

Although not perfect, emotions are better than doing nothing, or than acting randomly, or than becoming lost in thought. Emotions are heuristics.

OATLEY, KELTNER & JENKINS, 2006

Archetypes of belonging

Three archetypes reflect aspirations to connect with others and give and receive love. The Caregiver belongs by supporting, protecting and nurturing those around them, valuing compassion and the stability and security that comes with protecting those who you most love. The Everyman belongs by fitting in with others, being unpretentious and striving for equality. The Seducer belongs by establishing intimacy, with passion, commitment and an enjoyment of sensual pleasure. All three need to belong.

The Caregiver

'The very first requirement in a hospital is that it should do the sick no harm.' – Florence Nightingale

'To us, family means putting your arms around each other and being there.' – Barbara Bush

Florence Nightingale was the founder of modern nursing, but more importantly she was a successful social reformer and a talented statistician (one of the first people to realize the power of data visual-ization). Her earliest public prominence came in the Crimean War where she was a nurse tending to wounded soldiers. She was given the name 'The lady with the lamp' because of her nightly rounds of the wards.

Florence Nightingale established a nursing school at St Thomas Hospital (now part of King's College) in 1860, and laid the founda-tions of the nursing profession, as we know it today. She was respon-sible for reforms that improved healthcare across all sectors of society, advocated better healthcare and hunger relief in India, fought for improvements to the laws governing the lives of prostitutes and also for the expansion of female participation in the workforce. Much of this she did by prodigious campaigning and writing.

Florence Nightingale has been described as 'a true pioneer in the graphical representation of statistics', and is credited with developing a form of the pie chart now known as the polar area diagram (or Nightingale rose diagram), equivalent to a circular histogram, which she developed to show the seasonal sources of patient mortality in a military field hospital she managed. She made frequent use of such approaches to present information to members of parliament and civil servants who did not understand and would not read standard statistical reports.

William and Catherine Booth founded The Salvation Army in 1865, five years after Florence Nightingale established her nursing school. The Salvation Army is a Christian international movement (operating in 126 countries today) known for its charity work and charity shops, as well as its quasi-military structure. Its stated objec-tives are 'the advancement of the Christian religion... of education, the relief of poverty, and other charitable objects beneficial to society or the community of mankind as a whole'. The 'whole' is important here, as although the Salvation Army has a Christian mission, it does work with many of the most disadvantaged and neglected people in the countries where it works.

For example, one Salvation Army campaign was titled 'We see what most don't', with images of desperate people almost hidden against different backgrounds. The copy of several of these posters ran, 'we see the heartbreaking effects of poverty, homelessness, abuse and addiction every day. And most importantly, we see the people who desperately need support and compassion. For us, it's impossible to turn a blind eye to suffering.' The final line is 'Giving hope today'. Other recent campaigns have used the phrases, 'Do good', 'Doing the most good' and 'No dream is too small when you are in need.' These are truly words that Florence Nightingale could have spoken.

The Caregiver archetype appears in many guises and names including Saint, Altruist, Parent, Helper, Supporter, Mother, Sidekick, Caretaker, Protector, Helper, Philanthropist and Good Samaritan. In mythology, Mother Earth is a Caregiver as are many goddesses of fertility, harvest and nature. In Asia, the goddess of rice is also associated with compassion and families, appearing as GuanYin in China and Dewi Sri in Indonesia among other names.

In *The Lord of the Rings*, and more recently *The Hobbit*, Galadriel is the Caregiver, providing protection and shelter for the travellers. In the Harry Potter films, Hermione is often protective and nurturing of the other characters, and Professor Minerva McGonagall is protective of Harry in particular (as is Dumbledore of course). One quote from the first Harry Potter novel (*Harry Potter and the Sorcerer's Stone* by JK Rowling), sums up the highest aspirations and behaviours of The Caregiver archetype:

> Your mother died to save you. If there is one thing Voldemort cannot understand, it is love. He didn't realize that love as powerful as your mother's for you leaves its own mark. Not a scar, no visible sign... to have been loved so deeply, even though the person who loved us is gone, will give us some protection forever. It is in your very skin. Quirrell, full of hatred, greed, and ambition, sharing his soul with Voldemort, could not touch you for this reason. It was agony to touch a person marked by something so good.

Caregivers are compassionate, generous, selfless, empathetic, benevolent, supportive and generous. They offer sustenance and protection to the needy and vulnerable, and value generosity and self-sacrifice. Caregivers are dedicated to the safety, comfort and welfare of others, and are fearful of selfishness and ingratitude. They truly live up to the command, 'Love your neighbour as yourself'.

Caregivers achieve their aims by doing things for other people, driven by the desire to protect and care for others. Their weaknesses are becoming a martyr or being exploited by others.

The Caregiver is an archetypal brand that helps you to help others. That is why the Salvation Army, Oxfam, Amnesty International and other charity and support groups have often used the imagery of the Caregiver in their advertising. The Caregiver archetype also serves brands in the public sector, healthcare, education, and those that are non-profit. It can also be a good archetype for brands that give customers a competitive advantage, support families, or are associated with nurturing and help people care about others or themselves.

Andrex has always been associated with this archetype, with slogans including the famous 'Soft, strong and very long' and also 'Caring for the family'. Similarly, Johnson & Johnson and Pampers have always been Caregivers, with their associations with baby and family products. With their association with baby products, Johnson & Johnson often combine caregiving with idealism (innocence), for example in talking about the 'softest, gentlest, purest language in the world – the language of love' or in imagery such as an umbrella drawn with protective cream to keep a baby in the shade.

Volvo and Campbell's Soup are very different brands, which both emphasize their role in supporting, nurturing and protecting people (and particularly families). Volvo has emphasized the safety and security of their cars for many years. Campbell's use the phrase 'Good for the body; good for the soul.'

The spur for all Caregivers is seeing someone in need or distress, which brings out their caring and nurturing behaviour, especially in those dependent on them. These behaviours grow over time into a more balanced care of themselves as well as others and eventually into true altruism and concern and care for the world as a whole.

The Caregiver is an archetype for brands that help users to care for and nurture others (and even themselves).

The Everyman

'No man is an island, entire of itself; every man is a piece of the continent.' – John Donne

'Let every man be respected as an individual and no man idolised.'
– Albert Einstein

The Everyman is a key character in medieval morality plays at the heart of the story's journey and moral of the piece. Similarly, many people talk about the 'common man' in political theory. The spirit of the Everyman appears in the music of Aaron Copland, later adapted by Emerson, Lake and Palmer. If you want to think of Everyman, think of situation comedies with normal everyday families, Country and Western music, blue jeans, the English pub or the Singapore hawker centre, where everyone is equal and nobody wants to stand out from the crowd. This is the fundamental archetype of democracy (one person, one vote). When Woody Guthrie sings, 'This land is your land' he is speaking to Everyman.

Everyman's Library consists of classic literature published in a format that is affordable for and appeals to everyone, from students to the working classes to the cultural elite. The books follow classic design principles, for example those of William Morris (and the Kelmscott Press) who was equally interested in making fine art and quality designs available to everyone. The name of Everyman's Library was inspired by those medieval plays, and every book contains a quote from the play *Everyman*: 'Everyman, I will go with thee and be thy guide, In thy most need to go by thy side'.

Nothing epitomizes the 'Every family' more than *The Simpsons* and no one is more of an Everyman than Homer. Similarly, the TV show *Cheers* epitomized the 'gang mentality' when kept within bounds, with the setting a third place where 'everybody knows your name'.

One brand that epitomizes the Everyman is IKEA, with its core principle of giving everyone, whatever their status, access to affordable, well-designed furniture and home accessories. In their words, 'The dream is to create a better everyday life for the many people.' IKEA advertising often emphasizes the importance of everyone being equal, as in 'Playin' with my friends'.

IKEA's designs are based on simplicity and self-assembly (allowing them to flatpack for transport and keep costs as low as possible), and more generally they are renowned for cost control and continuous improvement (in design as well as in operations). IKEA stores embody the principle of equality, where everyone has to follow the same route around the store passing by displays of 'everyday' home settings. IKEA currently has more than 300 stores in 38 countries, is the third largest user of wood in the world, and is in the process of expanding into economy hotels across Europe. IKEA's advertising speaks clearly to its archetype.

The Everyman is also known as the Regular gal and Regular guy, Good old boy, Person next door, Regular Jane, the Common man, Realist, Working stiff, Solid citizen, Good neighbour and Silent majority. For the Everyman, all women and men are created equal, and this gives them an empathy and lack of pretence coupled with a very realistic view of the world. Think of Bilbo Baggins in *The Hobbit* and Ron Weasley in the Harry Potter films.

The core desire of the Everyman is to connect with others, so that they can fit in and belong as one of the crowd. By contrast, their worst fear is to stand out from the crowd, put on airs or be rejected. They achieve belonging by developing ordinary, solid virtues and by demonstrating the common touch, allowing the Everyman to blend in with everyone else. Everyman has to be careful not to submerge their own character in their desire to blend in, to give it up for superficial and transient connections or become part of a lynch mob against those who are different.

The Everyman's goal is to belong, and their greatest fear is to be left out or stand out from the crowd. Everyman has ordinary, solid virtues and a common touch. They are always down to earth, unpretentious, realistic, empathic, ordinary, connected and democratic in their behaviour.

The Everyman archetype helps customers be OK just as they are. This is a good archetype for brands that give people a sense of belonging, with everyday functionality, low to moderate prices, produced by solid company and differentiation from elitist or high-priced brands. Wendy's have used the Everyman archetype in the past, and Walmart has built itself into one of the biggest businesses in the world on the basis of its everyday pricing. Here in Singapore, the local brand Fairprice emulates Walmart (with a social mission too), stating on its website:

'Today, with its multiple retail formats serving the varied needs and interests of people from all walks of life, the social mission of NTUC Fairprice has evolved to make the dream of living well accessible to everyone by moderating the costs of a good life.'

Another brand that has built itself on its ordinariness and 'average' credentials is Levi's. Recent adverts have stated, 'Everybody's work is equally important', 'We are all workers', 'For those who toil', 'All I need is all I got' and 'Let the average man be divine'.

The call to action for the Everyman is the feeling of loneliness, isolation or alienation, leading them to seek out affiliations with others to move away from feeling abandoned and alone. This develops into the skill for connecting and fitting in, and the openness to help and friendship. The Everyman can ultimately progress into the humanitarian who believes strongly in the dignity and decency of every person they meet regardless of their circumstances (something that they share with the Caregiver). When taken too far, Everyman can become a victim of the abuse of others because of their fear of being alone, or they may go along with the lynch mob in order to be one of the 'gang'.

The Everyman is the archetype for brands that help anyone to fit in and feel part of a group of equals.

The Seducer

'I'm pretty, but I'm not beautiful. I sin, but I'm not the devil. I'm good, but I'm not an angel.' – Marilyn Monroe

'It is not enough to conquer. One must also know how to seduce.'
– Voltaire

'Beauty is the greatest seducer of man.' – Paulo Coelho

One of my favourite films of all time is *Some Like It Hot*, at the centre of which Tony Curtis tries to seduce Marilyn Monroe, while she appears charmingly innocent and everyone else falls in love with her too.

Marilyn Monroe was and continues to be an archetypal seductress and icon for feminine sexuality. She was born Norma Jean Mortenson in 1926, dying as Marilyn Monroe in 1962 after a very successful career in movies. She had spent much of her life in foster homes, started as a model, eventually managing to get a film contract and using her 'dumb blonde' persona and seductiveness to great effect.

Some Like It Hot was made at the height of her powers in 1959, not long after *The Prince and the Showgirl* for which she received more than one film award. The filming of this was the subject of the 2011 film *My Week With Marilyn.*

The end of her life was marked by illness, personal problems and a notoriety that is the subject of *My Week With Marilyn* (she was unreliable, often late and difficult to work with). Her death was classified as a 'probable suicide', although may have been due to an accidental overdose or something more sinister (and is still the subject of conspiracy theories). She has been a cultural icon and sex symbol ever since.

The Seducer is the perfect archetype for many categories and is commonly used in fragrance, cosmetics, fashion, indulgence food and travel. It is no secret (nor a surprise) that Victoria's Secret follows the Seducer archetype, emphasizing femininity, beauty, experience and, above all, sexuality. Recent advertisements state, 'No one's perfect. Until now', 'I love my body' and 'Good angels go to heaven. Victoria's Secret angels go everywhere.'

As with all the archetypes, the Seducer comes in a number of guises, including Lover, Partner, Friend, Intimate, Enthusiast, Sensualist, Spouse, Team builder, Aesthete, Bon vivant, Hedonist, Matchmaker, Connoisseur and Harmonizer. Although primarily focused on building relationships and enjoying romance, the Seducer can also be about aesthetic appreciation (including food and drink). Beauty is very important to The Seducer, whether it be nature, a night out at a restaurant, a pair of shoes or the right man or woman.

There are many famous seducers in mythology. Rati is the Hindu goddess of love, carnal desire, lust, passion and sexual pleasure, and the female counterpart and consort of Kama, the god of love. She is his constant companion, renowned for her beauty and sexuality, with the power to enchant. She is associated with the excitement and delight of sexual activity, and has given her name to many techniques and positions in Indian literature that derive from her Sanskrit names.

Similarly, Aphrodite was the Greek goddess of love, beauty, pleasure and procreation, called Venus in Roman mythology. Aphrodite arose from the sea foam that came up when Cronos cut off Uranus's genitals and threw them into the sea. The other gods feared her great beauty (depicted by Botticelli and Titian among other great artists), concerned that rivalry over her would lead to the breakdown of good relations among them. Zeus married her to one of the ugliest of the gods in order to avoid such conflict.

Seducers can be male too, and Giacomo Casanova is one of the most famous, an Italian adventurer and writer, who lived and played out many of his exploits in Venice.

Seducers are passionate, sensual, seductive, erotic, affectionate, committed, loving, appreciative and always grateful for the love they receive. They spend all their time seeking true love and pleasure, following their emotions and valuing loving and intimate relationships. *Titanic*, *Romeo and Juliet* (the 'star crossed' lovers), *Casablanca* and *Love Story* are just four of the classic Seducer stories, and Leonardo DiCaprio is definitely a seducer for many (appearing in two of these films).

Seducers are driven by the urge to give and receive love, and their motto, 'I only have eyes for you', speaks to their passionate commitment. Cinderella is one of the classic love stories, although the original fairy tale is a little more gruesome than the Disney version. In the original, Cinderella's sisters are willing to cut their toes and feet to fit into the glass slipper, in their desperation to marry the prince. While some find this gruesome, is it really so extreme when you consider the increasing numbers of people across Asia and the world who use plastic surgery to make themselves look more beautiful or handsome (not forgetting Botox and skin-whitening creams)?

The desire for intimacy and experience can lead Seducers into promiscuity and behaviour that is all about pleasing others, losing their own identity in the process. However, this desire can help them build a relationship with people, work and environments, surrounded by all the things they love. Their greatest fear is to be alone, and to be unwanted and unloved, and for this they are always striving to be more and more attractive, especially physically attractive.

The Seducer helps people give and receive love as well as helping them to belong and to find friends and partners and have a good time. This archetype is perfect for organizations that are freewheeling and fun loving, and is a good way to differentiate you from a self-important or over-confident brand. The Seducer is a good way to create a gender specific identity too (beautiful woman or confident man). For example, Revlon has used the tagline 'Feel like a woman' frequently, and more recently have produced adverts with the lines, '154 shades of woman' and 'My, what beautiful eyes you have.'

Häagen-Dazs is a seducer that focuses on sensual indulgence to great effect, using romantic imagery and language, as in 'Dedicated to pleasure', 'Waiting only makes it sweeter' and 'Do not disturb – slow melting in progress.' They also combine this sometimes with more idealistic virtues, such as 'Made like no other' and 'Anticipated like no other' (talking of the purity of the ingredients and manufacturing process).

Godiva use a similar language of love, seduction and sensual pleasure across all their advertising. Example lines are, 'The only thing missing is you', 'School of fine hearts', 'Say it like you mean it' and 'Bittersweet seduction' (tied to an image of melting chocolate running down someone's back). However, The Seducer is not just about food. Fiat uses the Seducer archetype to sell cars too.

Seduction starts with an infatuation, when you fall in love with a person, an idea, a cause, your work or even a product, which then leads you to the enjoyment of romance (or even to great sex if you are lucky). However, this is only the most basic and superficial level of the Seducer, who can go on to build commitment and a longer-lasting relationship with the person (or thing) that they love, ultimately developing a more spiritual form of love combined with greater self-acceptance, and even sometimes the experience of ecstasy. This is as long as difficulties in the relationship don't lead to obsession, jealousy, envy and all the other bad sides of love and commitment.

The Seducer archetype can help a customer feel the power of love, the commitment of relationship or the sheer enjoyment of a complete sensual experience.

Archetypes of freedom

Three archetypes reflect the desire for spontaneity, discovery and lack of restraint. The Joker values the freedom to be spontaneous and live in the moment, enjoying every minute of the day. The Rebel seeks the freedom to be different and unconventional and break the chains of conformity. The Explorer seeks the authenticity of discovery and the enjoyment of curiosity in the world. All three need to feel free.

The Joker

> 'The only difference between me and a madman is that I am not mad.'
> – Salvador Dali

> 'People ask me, "Steve, how do you get so funny?" I say to them,
> "Before I go onstage I put a fish in each shoe. That way I feel funny." '
> – Steve Martin

Salvador Dali epitomizes the idea of disruptive imagination, combining elements of the Joker and Rebel archetypes with that of the Artist. Similarly, Steve Martin is perhaps one of the funniest comedians I know, seemingly spontaneous on stage and in his many films, such as *Roxanne*.

The Marx Brothers films all thrive on the same anarchy of spontaneity and the need for fun and enjoyment in life. In *A Night In Casablanca* from 1946, they play the staff of a hotel. Groucho Marx (the hotel manager) tells his staff, 'I'm going to change round the numbers of all the rooms.' His staff plead, 'But the guests will go into the wrong rooms. Think of the confusion.' Groucho Marx replies, 'Yeah, but think of the fun.'

Virgin Airlines is a brand that combines the fun and enjoyment of the Joker with the rebellious values of its owner Richard Branson and a little bit of seduction too. These values combine in the Trickster, but Virgin Airlines is primarily a Joker brand using the tagline 'Enjoy'. The Joker permeates their advertising, their copy (both in print and in on-board materials), the naming of on-board kit and of course the service provided on their flights. For example, what other brand would run adverts titled 'Nine inches of pleasure' and 'Play with yourself' for in-flight entertainment. Compare and contrast the 'mates on a night out' service on Virgin with the 'school mistress' service on British Airways, and you can see why Richard Branson is constantly making fun of his 'evil' rival. British Airways and American Airlines have identity; Virgin Airlines has personality.

The Joker archetype includes the Jester, Clown, Fool, Entertainer, Comedian and Satirist (and Trickster). This covers a wide range from the playfulness and spontaneity of young children to Shakespeare's fools (especially King Lear's) to the Yankee tinker in US history and the Trickster characters I introduced in the last chapter (including Bugs Bunny). All share the same spirit of spontaneity and fun, frequently combined with cunning and guile (the Joker uses his head more than his hands).

It's always possible to have fun on your own, but the Joker is all about getting everyone outside to play with one another, and the Joker loves interaction and spontaneous meetings. The Joker is always the life of the party and a perfect archetype for modern life where everyone is hungry for fun and new experiences.

Jokers bring out the kid in you, and always help you to see the funny side of even the most serious of situations. Their core desire is to have fun and enjoyment in life (living life in the moment), and they are on a mission to lighten up the world and everyone around them.

Carl Kerenyi describes the archetype as 'the spirit of disorder, the enemy of boundaries', the person within us who says the unsayable, pokes fun at authority and breaks taboos (that's their rebellious streak coming out). This makes the Joker a good archetype for brands in categories with few or no functional differences, where differentiation has to be sought on lines of personality rather than product features.

The Joker is also perfect for helping people to deal with the crazier and more absurd aspects of modern living and with faceless bureaucracy, taking everything with a pinch of salt and with a fairly easygoing attitude to rules and conventions. Jokers are at heart anarchists (which is why they are next to the Rebel in the circle of archetypes), and they would agree with Emma Goldman that, 'If I can't dance, I don't want to be part of your revolution.' This also means that they can be very innovative, able to think differently from others.

The vice of the Joker is that their jokes can turn into cruel tricks, especially when they feel bored with life (their greatest fear). With the motto, 'You only live once', they will never get tied down, committed or stuck in a rut.

Pepsi's position has always been as a challenger brand, and what better positioning than to be the person that pokes fun at the ruler's pomposity and seriousness, making fun of their smugness and complacency? That's why Pepsi's best advertising has always been in the territory of the Joker, with laughter, spontaneity, pranks, playfulness and fun being the perfect antidote to the responsible, mature, serious, boring and uptight brand leader. Miller Lite is another brand that plays this card and the Joker archetype is common in the beer category with fun being a key category driver (see Chapter 4).

Some of the most successful recent Superbowl advertising has played the Joker card too. Volkswagen's 'The Force' and 'The Dog Strikes Back' are playful and fun, and in 2013 their 'Get Happy' advert mixed this fun with idealism. M&M's 'Just my shell' and 'Love ballad' television spots also play on fun (with a little seduction thrown in with the soundtrack of 'I'm sexy and I know it').

Although the most common use of the Joker is to convey the idea of life as a game and fun, there are more complex and sophisticated layers to the Joker's values, which can lead to the idea of intelligence as a tool to trick others and get out of trouble (some elements of transformation) and ultimately to the experience of life in the moment, one day at a time, with complete spontaneity and freedom.

The Joker archetype can help people belong, have a good time and differentiate a brand from self-important and over-confident brand leaders.

The Rebel

'Every act of rebellion expresses a nostalgia for innocence and an appeal to the essence of being.' – Albert Camus

'Why join the navy if you can be a pirate? Stay hungry, stay foolish.'
– Steve Jobs

Richard Branson, the founder of Virgin, combines the spontaneity of the Joker with the disruptive challenge of the Rebel, and the adventurousness of the Explorer. Steve Jobs was another great entrepreneur, and anyone who reads his biography can't fail to be struck by his unconventional and disruptive behaviour, which emerged in his early hippy adventures, his extreme diets and fads, and his rudeness to those who didn't see the world in the same way as he did.

While Richard Branson is on the more gregarious side of rebellious-ness, Steve Jobs was on the more individualistic side, carving a (sometimes) lonely path to his own vision of freedom.

Jobs would have agreed with Oscar Wilde when he said, 'Disobe-dience, in the eyes of anyone who has read history, is man's original virtue. It is through disobedience that progress has been made, through disobedience and through rebellion.'

Apple's original positioning was completely aligned with Jobs' personality, although it has moved in recent times to a more conventional positioning also incorporating aspects of the Artist. Apple's rebelliousness was seen most strikingly in the famous 1984 Superbowl commercial, but was also the thread through their 'Think Different' campaign which had the following original creed:

> Here's to the crazy ones. The misfits. The rebels. The troublemakers. The round pegs in the square holes.
>
> The ones who see things differently. They're not fond of rules. And they have no respect for the status quo. You can quote them, disagree with them, glorify or vilify them.
>
> About the only thing you can't do is ignore them. Because they change things. They invent. They imagine. They heal. They explore. They create. They inspire. They push the human race forward.
>
> Maybe they have to be crazy.
>
> How else can you stare at an empty canvas and see a work of art? Or sit in silence and hear a song that's never been written? Or gaze at a red planet and see a laboratory on wheels?
>
> We make tools for these kinds of people.
>
> While some see them as the crazy ones, we see genius. Because the people who are crazy enough to think they can change the world, are the ones who do.

The follow up to the 'Think different' campaign, showed a conven-tional (business suited) man and a slightly less conventional man introduce themselves, 'I'm a Mac. And I'm a PC.' Apple continued to focus on being different from the rest for a long time, and this attitude came through in an often quoted remark Steve Jobs made to John Sculley when persuading him to join Apple, 'Do you want to spend the rest of your life selling sugared water or do you want a chance to change the world?'

The Rebel archetype is also known as the Outlaw, Revolutionary, Contrarian, Maverick and Gambler. In mythology, outlaws can be positive figures as well as more negative characters. Think of Zorro and Robin Hood, romantic figures who want to disrupt a society that they see as corrupt, cynical, conformist, repressed or tyrannical; like the protesters at Tiananmen Square or the civil rights and anti-war movements in the Seventies. These 'rebels' truly changed the world we live in now.

Rebel stories are increasingly a part of modern society, especially with a greater focus on individual psychology, In *Rebel Without a Cause* and *On the Road*, the central characters become alienated from society, eventually leading them to break taboos and cultural norms. In *Butch Cassidy and the Sundance Kid* and *Bonnie and Clyde*, the rebels are glamorous figures and the breaking of taboos can feel liberating, while *Goodfellas* and *The Godfather* show the attraction of forbidden behaviours. In *1984*, *Brave New World* and *Brazil*, the central characters rebel against political tyranny and often come to bad ends for themselves.

Of course, there are darker rebel figures, living on the edge of moral and legal norms, such as cyber hackers, mobsters, vigilantes and skin-heads. Both Batman and the Joker share some of these characteristics even though they are on opposite sides of their fight.

If the Rebel had a motto it would be, 'Rules are made to be broken.' They are challenging, outrageous, unconventional, disruptive and different, which is why their greatest virtue is to be at the head of any revolution, helping overturn what doesn't work or has to change. If they take their behaviour too far, this can lead to destruction, their greatest vice. But anything is better than feeling trapped, which is what any Rebel most fears.

This is a great archetype for any insurgent brand, which needs to make its mark in a category dominated by traditional, stable and boring brands. It is also perfect for any brand that wants to disrupt a category, break with existing conventions or help the disenfranchised, but it can be a difficult position to sustain when you become bigger. Somehow Richard Branson and Virgin seem to be able to bridge the contradictions between being a successful brand and a champion of downtrodden consumers. Apple has decided to shift towards a positioning focusing on the freedom of exploration and creativity.

The best-known Rebel brand is Harley-Davidson, which has been the subject of many branding case studies. Harley-Davidson has created an iconic Outlaw feel to their brand (the daredevil rather than the US hero). Rather than try to compete with Japanese makers who sold better products at cheaper prices, Harley-Davidson decided to market meaning (making it much easier to develop brand extensions into clothing and accessories).

Harley-Davidson owners are typically professionals who want to express their wild side. The brand is associated with the Hell's Angels and other outlaw groups and with a complicated personality. For example, a study showed that Harley-Davidson owners thought that riding the brand was a stronger statement of patriotism than obeying the law.

Films such as *The Wild Ones* (Marlon Brando) and *Easy Rider* (Jack Nicholson, Dennis Hopper) helped build the macho image of the brand. The most popular tattoo in the US is a Harley-Davidson symbol. Harley-Davidson imagery and communications are not just about freedom, but freedom from conventions and mainstream values, such as the tagline, 'If you didn't have to answer to anyone, what would you do?' Other Harley-Davidson advertising speaks of 'Air is an air freshener', 'Stop dreaming', 'No cages' and 'Make your own noise.' Riders often sport black leather, heavy boots and body piercings, living the Rebel dream.

Although the most common use of the Rebel is to communicate your status as an outsider, there are more complex layers to this archetype, all of which spring from the trigger of feeling powerless, angry, mistreated or under siege. At the most basic level, Rebels dissociate themselves from group values and societal norms breaking out from traditional behaviour and morality. This can eventually lead to more shocking and disruptive acts, and ultimately to being a revolutionary and changing the world. On the flip side, the shadow of the Rebel is criminal or evil behaviour.

The Rebel archetype works for brands that want to help people break away from existing norms, or disrupt the way they lead their lives. It can help change the rules in a category, especially when there are dominant players with very stable and rigid personalities. Although the Rebel is a great attitude for a challenger brand, it is more challenging to sustain when you become mainstream, but not impossible as Harley-Davidson and others have proved.

The Explorer

'I am prepared to go anywhere, provided it be forward.'
– David Livingstone

'It is not the mountain we conquer but ourselves.' – Edmund Hillary

David Livingstone and Edmund Hillary, along with Sherpa Tenzing, are perfect examples of the Explorer archetype, following in the footsteps of those like Christopher Columbus, who are brave enough to 'boldly go where no man has gone before' in the words of a famous TV franchise (*Star Trek* is all about exploration).

The Explorer is an archetype often used by brands associated with outdoor pursuits (no surprise there). North Face says, 'Never stop exploring', 'Designed for professionals' and 'Never stop facing your fears', while Timberland communicate similar values such as, 'Proper footwear required' and 'Escape and explore'. Similarly, many SUV brands emphasize their rugged and strong design, as in Ford's slogan in the category, 'Built tough'.

The Explorer comes under many names including Seeker, Pilgrim, Wanderer, Pioneer, Individualist, Iconoclast and Adventurer. You will recognize them in Indiana Jones, James T Kirk, Peter Pan, Huckleberry Finn, the Great Gatsby and Marco Polo and they figure in the earliest known stories, *The Epic of Gilgamesh* and *The Odyssey*, where Odysseus is the ultimate Wanderer.

Explorers are authentic, fulfilled, curious, individual, unique, ambitious, autonomous and always true to themselves. Their goal is discovery, to experience a more authentic and fulfilling life by using their freedom to explore the world. They can fall into self-indulgence if they are not given this freedom, because their biggest fear is feeling trapped.

The Explorer is a perfect archetype if your brand helps people to be free, is pioneering, is rugged and sturdy, is used on the road and in the wild, helps people express their individuality, can be purchased and consumed on the go or if you want to differentiate yourself from a more conformist brand.

Amazon.com is an explorer brand with its name evoking the Amazon River and their 'a to z' focus on giving all its customers access to the right choices for them (the long tail of Chris Anderson's book). Heineken's current slogan is 'Open your world' and its communication talks frequently about exploration and discovery. Red Bull thrives on exploration, most notably and recently in the Red Bull Stratos mission to the edge of space and a supersonic free-fall, matching its tagline, 'Red Bull gives you wings'.

Finally, Starbucks' name, imagery and retail experience use the Explorer archetype to great effect. The archetype can be seen in the green colour of the logo (not the original colour) and the image of the sea goddess. Starbucks emphasizes choice and the customization of each drink for every customer. The name is taken from Herman Melville's *Moby Dick* – Starbucks is the name of the first mate on the Pequod. More recently, Starbucks (and its leader Howard Schultz) has worked very hard to express authenticity in its opinions, support of environmental causes and referencing of exotic places as well as in its packaging and retail design.

At the most basic level, Explorers like to hit the open road, get into nature and explore exotic places, to stop themselves from becoming restless, alienated and bored. As they progress they seek their own individuality in order to be more fulfilled, and ultimately are able to express their individuality and uniqueness with complete authenticity.

The grass is always greener on the other side! The Explorer is the brand for those with a constant itch to explore and the need to find their true identity.

Archetypes of ego

Three archetypes reflect the need for individuation and self-mastery. The Artist develops their individuality through creativity and expression, using their imagination to create something new. The Warrior uses their individual will to show their independence in courageous acts and competitive spirit. The Catalyst uses their confidence and charisma to be a change agent in the world. All three use their ego to drive individual success.

The Artist

'If you hear a voice inside you say, 'You cannot paint', then by all means paint, and that voice will be silenced.' – Vincent van Gogh

'Every child is an artist, the problem is staying an artist when you grow up.' – Pablo Picasso

Vincent van Gogh and Pablo Picasso follow all the classic traits of the Artist archetype. Creative geniuses on the edge of madness (particularly in the case of Vincent), living itinerant and difficult lives in order to pursue their own vision.

Vincent's unique style developed over the course of his shorter life, and was highly influential on 20th-century art. It is a personal favourite of mine with its bold colours, raw beauty and emotional directness.

Pablo Picasso lived longer, and developed and redeveloped a number of styles, living a longer life and a full one too (with many partners and much wine – he died with a glass in his hand). In his words, 'Art is a lie that makes us realize the truth.'

Moving to another artistic sphere, Bach, Mozart and Beethoven were very different characters, but share much in common. Bach was a rather sober and serious musician, extremely hard working, perhaps reflecting his religious beliefs and the times in which he lived.

Mozart has been portrayed as rather less serious (especially in *Amadeus*) and was certainly precocious, playing to Kings and Queens from a very early age at the behest of his very ambitious father. Although he lived a relatively shorter life, he was very productive, crafting melodies at the drop of a hat and writing many of his most famous pieces in a single first draft.

Ludwig van Beethoven has often been portrayed as a romantic hero, again reflecting the times he lived in, and was certainly one of the first composers who worked without a 'salary' and lived from commissions and donations from patrons. Although he was often a difficult person, he had a close circle of personal friends, attracted by the strength of his personality and convictions as well as his talent. He was probably one of the first composers to dare challenge authority, expecting to be treated as an equal and would stop performing at the piano if there was any 'chatter' in the room.

All of these artists and composers shared the compulsion to be continually working. As Ray Bradbury has said: 'Don't think. Thinking is the enemy of creativity. It's self-conscious and anything self-conscious is lousy. You can't try to do things. You simply must do things.'

The Artist is also known as the Inventor, Innovator, Creator, Musician, Writer, Dreamer, or more negatively as a Mad Scientist. Some of the earliest, and the most common, of human myths tell the stories of the creation of the world, and we are always fascinated by anyone who creates in any field, be it buildings, music, art, writing or technology.

Technology innovators are revered in modern culture, although often see themselves as very different from more artistic heroes. Even the very un-humble Steve Jobs was quoted as saying, 'Creativity is just connecting things. When you ask creative people how they did something, they feel a little guilty because they didn't really do it, they just saw something. It seemed obvious to them after a while.'

All Artists are driven by the urge to craft something new, and many brands epitomize this urge in positioning themselves as a brand to help users be creative or imaginative. LEGO is the best known of these, with a name that comes from the Danish phrase 'leg godt' which means 'play well'. Much of its communication focused on the imaginative use of LEGO bricks, as well as its various tie-ins with film, TV and literary franchises and the re-creation of the worlds they represent. LEGO is all about the creativity of play and imaginative discovery, as in its different taglines such as 'Unleash your LEGO', 'Just imagine', 'Pure brainfood' and 'Creating little geniuses since 1936.'

Brands relating to children's play frequently use the Artist archetype. Crayola is also well known for its emphasis on invention and imagination, with advertising messages such as, 'The gift of invention', 'Inspire everything imaginable', 'Give everything imaginable' and '120 colours and unlimited possibilities'.

Artists use artistic control and skill to create things of enduring value. Their greatest fear is mediocrity, which explains why they can sometimes become perfectionist, never managing to finish anything. At their best they are expressive, imaginative, original, creative and able to out-innovate anyone else.

The Artist archetype is great for brands that encourage self-expression, foster innovation, are artistic, have an element of 'do-it-yourself', are related to learning and development, or are in creative fields like marketing, public relations or the arts. It is also a great archetype if you need to differentiate from a brand which does everything for customers, leaving no room for choice.

However, the Artist archetype can work for other types of brand too. Sony, Swatch and Crown Paints have used The Artist archetype in the past.

The Artist's call is daydreaming, fantasy and the flashes of inspiration which first lead to creative leaps and innovation through imitation, and then progressively into giving form to their own artistic vision until they are able to create structures that influence culture and society and create larger and longer term impacts.

The Artist is an archetype for those who want to help people be creative, express themselves and build their own vision. In the words of Thomas Edison, 'There is a better way to do it – find it.'

The Warrior

'The point is, not how long you live, but how nobly you live.' – Seneca

'The basic difference between an ordinary man and a warrior is that a warrior takes everything as a challenge, while an ordinary man takes everything as a blessing or a curse.' – Carlos Castaneda

'A hero is someone who has given his or her life to something bigger than themselves.' – Joseph Campbell

Until very recently, Lance Armstrong was a hero to many people. This was not just because of the feat of winning the Tour de France seven times between 1999 and 2005, amazing as that was. It also had a lot to do with his 1996 diagnosis of testicular cancer that spread to his brain and lungs. He was successfully treated with operations and chemotherapy, and declared fit in 1997. At that time he set up the Lance Armstrong Foundation for cancer support. In the way that he faced up to his personal challenges and said 'yes' to life, Lance Armstrong epitomized the Warrior spirit, and Friedrich Nietzsche would have approved.

His many titles were taken away from him recently when it was found that he had been using and distributing performance-enhancing drugs. Does that make him any less a Warrior? I'll let you judge for yourself, but in the words of Joseph Campbell, who wrote the ultimate book on mythological heroes, 'The warrior's approach is to say "yes" to life, "yea" to it all.'

Nike's original name was Blue Ribbon Sports, but in 1978 after 14 years in business the company decided that the Greek Goddess of Victory might give it a more appropriate brand meaning. This was linked to its mission to 'understand and inspire the soul of the athlete'. Its motto 'Just do it' sums up the Warrior's attitude to life, and it has communicated this consistently over the years.

Over the years, Nike has launched campaigns around the themes of 'Anticipate greatness', 'Twice the guts, double the glory', 'Play to be remembered', 'Write the future' and 'Run the elite out of town.' Its most recent campaign, running throughout the 2012 London Olympics, has been around the theme of 'Find your greatness' often showing ordinary people with the courage to push themselves to the limit, overcoming their fears and achieving small but significant wins.

There are many well-known heroes in Greek mythology, including Perseus, Jason and Achilles. In many stories, heroes can become arrogant and bullying, as does Achilles in the *Iliad*. As the saying goes, 'Pride comes before a fall', and this is often the vice of the Warrior, and was undoubtedly the downfall of Lance Armstrong. Indeed, it was at one time almost the downfall of the Nike brand, when its inability to deal with political issues relating to child labour seriously tarnished its image. Perhaps its talk of 'crushing competitors' reflected this hubris.

Each ancient mythology has its Warriors. In China, there are the Eight Immortals and many others. In India, Arjuna and Krishna are the heroes of the Mahabharata. Arjuna is an Idealist as well as a Warrior, and very popular in Indonesia as well as India.

More modern examples of Warriors are John Wayne, James Bond and many of the superheroes we see in the cinema today (including Batman). Hero and Warrior are often synonymous terms, although the word hero can be used in a much broader sense than warrior. I think the term Warrior is appropriate for anyone who is a crusader for a cause (Batman is, after all, the Caped Crusader) or a defender of the underdog or rescuer of any victim, including damsels in distress in medieval courtly romances.

Martin Luther King Jr and Nelson Mandela showed incredible courage in the face of great danger, dealing with it in a different way to more typical Warriors. Although Warriors are often combative, they can also fight for a principle, cause, vision or way of life, in which case they are probably demonstrating characteristics of other archetypes too such as the Idealist who keeps faith.

Mark Twain best summed up the meaning of the Warrior (and Hero) when he wrote:

> Unconsciously we all have a standard by which we measure other men, and if we examine closely we find that this standard is a very simple one, and is this: we admire them, we envy them, for great qualities we ourselves lack. Hero worship consists in just that. Our heroes are men who do things which we recognize, with regret, and sometimes with a secret shame, that we cannot do. We find not much in ourselves to admire, we are always privately wanting to be like somebody else.
>
> If everybody was satisfied with himself, there would be no heroes.

Warriors are driven to prove their worth through courage in the face of difficulty, and therefore their greatest fear is weakness and vulnerability. They want to become strong, powerful and competent by using their courage to do things that others cannot do. They are also known as heroes, crusaders, knights, rescuers, superheroes, soldiers, athletes, dragon slayers and competitors. Warriors are focused, competitive, strong and powerful.

Above all, Warrior brands help you to act courageously. The US Marines is another example of a Warrior brand, with their talk of 'Marines moving toward the sounds of tyranny, injustice and despair', 'Nobody likes to fight, but somebody has to know how' and 'The proud, the few, the Marines'.

There was a very recent example of Warrior advertising in Audi's 2013 Superbowl advert 'Prom', which showed a young man driving his father's Audi to the prom, and then having the courage to kiss the girl he would like to have been his date, before driving home with a black eye. The Audi tagline of 'Bravery. It's what defines us' is a Warrior sentiment, although somewhat different in tone from some of their other communications.

The Warrior archetype works well for brands that help people achieve all that they want to achieve or solve a social, environmental or other major problem (or help others solve it). The archetype also works well when there is a clear 'enemy' to beat, so is often used by challenger or underdog brands. It can also work for innovations that will have a big impact on the world or whose users see them as virtuous. However, Warrior brands have to keep their promises and never back down or renege on promises (unlike other brands).

For the Warrior, the challenge of a defenceless person, underdog, bully or physical trial always beckons, at the first level helping them to develop boundaries and skills that they can use to beat the competition. As their skills develop, they will step up to do their duty for country, community or family, and ultimately use courage and determination to make a difference in the world. Does your brand have what it takes?

The Catalyst

'To be a catalyst is the ambition most appropriate for those who see the world as being in constant change, and who, without thinking that they can control it, wish to influence its direction.' – Theodore Zeldin

'Action is eloquence.' – William Shakespeare

Although Martin Luther and Martin Luther King Jr were separated by almost 500 years, they shared more than their names. Both were catalysts in their own ways, making big changes happen. They both transformed society and culture in hugely significant ways, the former inspiring the Reformation and having a huge influence on Protestant and Lutheran teaching, the latter a winner of the Nobel Peace Prize for his work as a civil rights activist which transformed the United States.

As Martin Luther King Jr said, 'The ultimate measure of a man is not where he stands in moments of comfort and convenience, but where he stands at times of challenge and controversy.' Although both men were also Idealists, they made their impact as Catalysts of change, reaching the highest levels of actuation of this archetype.

Several brands have used the Catalyst archetype, with perhaps Mastercard the best known, with its 'Priceless' campaign. Over time, Mastercard has successfully connected many 'priceless' moments to the brand, and also distanced itself from the reality of the product. It communicates the magical quality of using a credit card to obtain instant satisfaction, while forgetting that you will eventually have to pay a bill. The campaign also very cleverly recognizes the ambivalence that many have towards the more materialistic aspects of modern culture, by letting their customers appreciate that there is more to life than money and consumption. The 'priceless' moments are always free.

Catalysts always want to understand the fundamental laws of the universe, and to harness this knowledge to make dreams come true. Their greatest virtue is the ability to transform situations, although when this power is abused, it turns into the vice of manipulation. The archetype also appears as the Sorcerer, Shaman, Healer, Witch/ Wizard, Magician and Visionary.

Harry Potter is an instant hit with kids today in the same way that watching *The Wizard of Oz* or *Mary Poppins* and reading *The Hobbit*, *The Lord of the Rings* and *The Sword in the Stone* (the King Arthur and Merlin story) were when I was growing up. The modern take on *Merlin* from the BBC is great too. Merlin looks into his crystal ball to see the future of Camelot, has a vision of a peaceful and just society, and develops his own talents, using magical objects to help achieve those goals, such as the round table, Excalibur and the Grail.

The Latin American novels of magical realism have developed this tradition too in films such as *Like Water for Chocolate*, as has the modern interest in more metaphysical ideas in science fiction and other genres. The Catalyst is all about transformation, whether the change is physical, mental or spiritual, and achieves this by harnessing their knowledge and energy to bring change to the world.

Catalysts are intuitive, masterful, confident, magical, charismatic and transformative. They turn visions into reality, value metaphysical solutions and expand consciousness. Prospero in *The Tempest* and Gandalf in *The Hobbit* and *The Lord of the Rings* play this role, helping the real hero of the story achieve their goals by changing situations in positive ways. In the same way, Montgomery Scott (better known as 'Scotty'), the engineer in *Star Trek*, could always fix a problem or make the Enterprise fly faster than it should, as did R2D2 in Star Wars, the robot catalyst who would always open the locked door or switch off the tractor beam so Luke could escape the Death Star.

The Catalyst is a great archetype for any brand that is inherently transformative, consciousness expanding, user friendly or has spiritual connotations. It is also appropriate for new-age brands and very new and contemporary products. However, transformation is a big promise, so brands should always be able to deliver on this.

Other brands have used the Catalyst with varying degrees of success, including Smirnoff, Axe and DuPont. Disney combines Catalyst and Idealist, to bring an innocent magic to their theme parks.

DuPont's slogan is 'The miracles of science', focusing on the power of technology to transform lives. This is a very modern reading of the Catalyst, and DuPont has also used the tag line 'Dreams made real'. In mythology, Catalysts often appear as a Healer, Shaman or Medicine Man or woman, and in the 20th century we have miracle drugs.

In a very different way, Smirnoff focuses on the ability of their brand to transform any situation, visualizing this through the prism of the clear bottle of vodka, and also speaking of the purity of the brand in Idealist terms. Finally, Axe (or Lynx in some markets) talks about the brand's ability to transform interactions with the opposite sex.

Catalysts are highly intuitive, relying on instinct and even extra-sensory perception to provide the hunches that trigger actions for change. At the most basic level, Catalysts provide magical moments and experiences, but at more advanced levels they can fulfill the feeling of being in the moment and ultimately help others move from vision to reality (providing miracles).

The Catalyst archetype works for brands that provide magical moments, or even transform lives as long as they can always deliver on their magical promise.

Archetypes of order

Three archetypes reflect the desire for stability, responsibility and certainty. The Guru values understanding, and uses intelligence, analysis and reflection to build their knowledge of the world. The Ruler values safety, and uses control with responsibility to provide a safe and predictable environment. The Idealist seeks faith and innocence, using their optimism and loyalty to keep the faith. All three seek order amidst the chaos of the world.

The Guru

> 'The syllable gu *means shadows, The syllable* ru, *he who disperses them, Because of the power to disperse darkness, the guru is thus named.'*
> – *Advayataraka Upanishad*

> 'The most difficult thing in life is to know yourself.' – *Thales*

Albert Einstein was one of my heroes as I grew up, and he seemed to embody wisdom with charm, a sense of innocence and a childlike wonder in the world. He appeared very much as a child at heart, yet deeply intellectual. Whatever the reality behind this image, he is probably the most universal contemporary symbol for The Guru. One of my favourite films is *Insignificance*, where the interplay between The Professor, The Actress, The Senator and The Ballplayer is a fascinating play on knowledge, sex, power and fame, with the four characters thinly disguised portraits of Einstein, Marilyn Monroe, Joe McCarthy and Joe DiMaggio. Put another way, the play is about the relationships between Guru, Seducer, Ruler and Warrior archetypes.

The Guru's mission is to use intelligence and analysis to understand the world. Gurus fear ignorance and being duped or misled. There have been many in history, including Socrates, who combined this with Idealism and Rebelliousness, and Plato who also had Ruler tendencies.

Guru is a Sanskrit word meaning 'teacher' or 'master' and is commonly used in Indian religions, where knowledge was always passed from teacher to students. There is a long tradition of Gurus in Asia, including Confucius and Buddha. Reading Karl Jaspers' profiles of Socrates, Buddha, Confucius and Jesus draws out some of the fascinating parallels between these figures (Jaspers, 1962).

In modern US culture, Oprah Winfrey is held in similar regard. Oprah has built on her talkshow reputation by branching into magazines and book clubs rather than cosmetics and fashion, building on her image as a source of wisdom. Like many Gurus, she also combines her wisdom with a dose of spirituality and calmness, just as Einstein did.

We all seek wisdom, and self-help books dominate the shelves of bookstores, especially in Singapore. The X-Files ran for seven series with plots that hinged on finding the difference between truth and illusion, even when the answer is difficult to find. Every episode began with the statement, 'The truth is out there.'

The best-known Guru brand is perhaps CNN, whose mottos 'Be the first to know' and 'Consider the source' could be those of a novice Guru. A more enlightened Guru would say, 'The truth will set you free.' CNN is selling information, in the same way as the *New York Times* ('Where the story always comes first'), and the BBC with its mission 'To enrich people's lives with programmes and services that inform, educate and entertain.'

Gurus have many other identities as teachers, mentors, philosophers, sages, academics, oracles, experts, advisers, contemplatives, scholars, thinkers, researchers and detectives. Sherlock Holmes is another childhood hero.

Gurus are the guardians of truth and sources of wisdom. By seeking and gaining a better knowledge of the world around us, the Guru enlightens all of us and helps us to progress and fulfill our full potential. Gurus can be intelligent, thoughtful, analytical, reflective, expert, philosophical and informative. They seek the truth, share knowledge and always value wisdom and objectivity.

Confusion and doubt are the triggers for the Guru's deep desire to find the truth. The initial search for the truth gradually evolves into critical and innovative thinking and the Guru's elevation to an expert, showing wisdom, confidence and mastery of her or his chosen field. However, they should take care not to be over-confident, as The Guru's gifts can easily disconnect them from reality when they become dogmatic. The business guru Peter Drucker once said, 'I have been saying for many years that we have been using the word "guru" only because "charlatan" is too long to fit into a headline.'

The Guru is an appropriate archetype for brands that provide expertise or information to customers, that encourage customers to think, that are based on new scientific discoveries, that are supported by research or facts and that want to differentiate themselves from brands with questionable quality or performance. Example categories are computer hardware and software, education and training and, in these days of data streaming, mobile telecommunications. Not forgetting, market research and business intelligence. Many research companies use Guru terminology, perhaps overusing the word 'insight', and Ipsos uses the tagline 'Nobody's unpredictable'. Interestingly, IBM now competes in this territory, with their positioning of 'Let's build a smarter planet.'

McKinsey embodies the Guru archetype and consistently communicate its knowledge across a wide range of topics. McKinsey job adverts will regularly test applicants' intelligence with a puzzle (as Google do), using the headline, 'Passionate thinkers wanted'. This enables them to charge many times what market research companies can charge for providing insight-based advice. Whether this is perception or reality is not for me to judge. McKinsey can be dogmatic on occasions too, as Gurus are wont to be.

In summary, Gurus help you understand your world. In the words of René Descartes, 'I think, therefore I am.'

The Ruler

'Most powerful is he who has himself in his own power.' – Seneca

'Nearly all men can stand adversity, but if you want to test a man's character, give him power.' – Abraham Lincoln

'Power is the ultimate aphrodisiac.' – Henry Kissinger

Last year saw the release of two films about the life of the 16th president of the United States. I didn't watch the first, which portrayed Abraham Lincoln as a vampire slayer, but enjoyed the second starring Daniel Day-Lewis (winning his third Oscar for the role).

Lincoln had all the hallmarks of a true leader or Ruler. He led the United States through one of the most difficult periods in its history. He oversaw the American Civil War, managed to preserve the Union while ending slavery and modernized the US economy. In times of change and challenge, he was able to provide stability and safety to the people of the country. What else would a true Ruler do?

His Gettysburg Address of 1863 is the most quoted speech in US history, and remains an iconic testament to the values of nationalism, republicanism, equality, liberty and democracy. Unfortunately, he was also the first US president to be assassinated, but is consistently ranked among the three greatest leaders the country has ever had, along with George Washington and Franklin D Roosevelt.

Many brands, especially those that dominate a marketplace, invoke the Ruler archetype in their personality and positioning. For example, American Express is the 22nd most valuable brand in the world according to *Business Week* and Interbrand. For a long time, it used the slogan, 'Don't leave home without one', using celebrities, politicians and TV stars to promote the card. Often the ads showed the personality having to use the American Express card (or traveller's cheque in older days) in order to gain recognition or status when travelling. Most recently, 'Take charge of your entertainment' and 'My life, my card' have continued this tradition. The implication of all these campaigns is that if you want to be treated like royalty, and live a successful life, you should always carry the right card.

The Ruler is also known as the Boss, Aristocrat, Sovereign, Leader, Parent, Politician, Responsible citizen, Role model, Manager, Administrator, King or Queen. Think of Queen Elizabeth I, Margaret Thatcher, Julius Caesar or Winston Churchill and you will have the right idea. Similarly, Moses, Genghis Khan, Alexander the Great and the Russian Czars all share the qualities of power, control, dominance and leadership as well as the stability and responsibility that go hand-in-hand with them.

All want to create a prosperous and successful community according to their own vision of the world, and all are able to exercise power in order to achieve this. On the flipside of these desires, the Ruler fears being overthrown and the chaos and disorder that might come with that. The Ruler's weakness can be the abuse of power, being authoritarian, tyrannical, manipulative and bossy or, more simply, the inability to delegate to others.

The Ruler is always in charge and in control, portrayed as responsible and able to take charge of events. As Mark Twain said, 'Laws control the lesser man... Right conduct controls the greater one.' Good rulers can inspire responsibility in others and are always able to manage their public and private commitments efficiently. They do not seek status for itself, but rather to wield power and exercise control. The picture of Atlas bearing the weight of the world on his shoulders is the image of the Ruler who takes responsibility for those around them.

The Ruler is a good archetype for high-status products and those used by powerful people to maintain or enhance their power, as well as market leaders and brands that offer a sense of security and stability in today's chaotic world. The Ruler can also work for brands that help people to organize themselves or offer a lifetime guarantee, and can be a good way to differentiate a brand in a category where populist brands dominate. Ruler brands always help you keep control of the world around you.

Mercedes-Benz reflects its status in the world of cars through the tagline, 'The best or nothing' matching the imagery and rhetoric of leadership and authority. In a different way, Microsoft has long talked about power and control, using its market dominance as a lever to sell more software.

For a long time, IBM was a ruler too, but its 'Smarter planet' tagline is now taking it very clearly into the adjacent space of the Guru. It was Francis Bacon who said, 'Knowledge is power' and in the 21st century, that is becoming increasingly true.

The Ruler is always called to action when they see a lack of resources, order, harmony or stability, taking responsibility initially for the state of their own life, and progressively exerting leadership among their family, peer groups and workplace, until ultimately they become a leader of a larger community or society itself.

Perhaps there is a greater need for Rulers now than ever. In the words of Tony Blair, 'the world is ever more interdependent. Stock markets and economies rise and fall together. Confidence is the key to prosperity. Insecurity spreads like contagion. So people crave stability and order.'

The Ruler is the right archetype for brands that can help customers to feel more secure, stable and in control.

The Idealist

'Be the change you want to see in the world.' – *Mahatma Gandhi*

'Every act of rebellion expresses a nostalgia for innocence and an appeal to the essence of being.' – *Albert Camus*

'You may say that I'm a dreamer
But I'm not the only one
I hope someday you'll join us
And the world will be as one.' – *John Lennon*

Mohandas Karamchand Gandhi (known as Mahatma Gandhi) was a true idealist who led India to independence through the use of non-violent civil disobedience, inspiring movements for non-violence, civil rights and freedom around the world. Gandhi first became famous fighting for the civil rights of Muslim and Hindu Indians in South Africa, developing his standard tools of non-violence and civil disobedience in the process. On his return to India, he started organizing peasants to protest land taxes and also reaching out to a wide range of religious groups. He assumed leadership of the Indian National Congress in 1921 and led campaigns for easing poverty, building women's rights, forging links across religious groups, ending 'untouchability' and most famously for the independence of India from British colonial rule.

This came to a head with the Dandi Salt March in 1930, in protest at taxes on salt, and he later led organized protests for the British to leave India during the Second World War (for which he was put in prison). He always lived and dressed modestly (leading Winston Churchill to call him, 'a half-naked fakir'), and was a vegetarian and frequent faster, for both personal and political reasons. Just prior to his death he worked to stop the bloody fighting between Muslims, Hindus and Sikhs on the border with Pakistan, and was assassinated on 30 January 1948 by a Hindu nationalist (now commemorated as Martyr's Day in India). His birthday on 2 October is also a national holiday and worldwide is the International Day of Non-Violence.

When asked to give a message to the people of India, he replied, 'My life is my message.'

The Idealist in Gandhi was supported by a good dash of Catalyst, as indicated in 'Be the change you want to see in the world.' This is another example of the Idealist and Catalyst archetypes working together. In Gandhi, the Idealist took the lead, while in Martin Luther and Martin Luther King Jr it was the Catalyst at the forefront.

John Lennon was also an Idealist, with 'Imagine' the song he is most strongly associated with. Although he lived a very full and successful life, with plenty of interesting experiences, he always retained an innocence, sense of purpose and simplicity about his lifestyle.

The best known recent example of an Idealist brand is Innocent, a company that started in the UK making 'healthy' food and drinks, most famously fruit smoothies. The company sells over 2 million smoothies each week in the UK, accounting for 75 per cent of smoothie sales (a market worth the equivalent of $250 million). Innocent Drinks donates 10 per cent of its profits to charity, and is now majority owned by Coca-Cola. Is Coca-Cola as innocent as Innocent?

The Innocent name in itself speaks to the Idealist archetype, as does the simple packaging (in pure white), the iconic 'baby face' and saint's halo, and the simple and clear labelling which reiterates that the products contain no artificial ingredients. Similarly, the Volkswagen Beetle evokes the innocence of Idealism, in the 'baby face' design of the car front as well as the communication of the brand.

Idealists come in many shapes and forms including Pollyanna, Utopian, Traditionalist, Naive, Mystic, Saint, Romantic, Dreamer, Cheerleader and Child. In Indian mythology, the god Arjuna is the only undefeated hero in the *Mahabharata*, and described as clean of all impurities and with a spotless mind. In the *Bhagavad Gita*, Krishna refers to Arjuna as 'Anagha', meaning that he is pure of heart and sinless. Arjuna is always reluctant to use force, and often hesitates to kill, showing restraint and self-control. He is always magnanimous in victory and compassionate towards his enemies. Although a great Warrior, Arjuna is at heart an Idealist.

In Hollywood mythology, the most famous Idealist is perhaps *Forrest Gump*. The film is full of the implicit belief that it is possible to face any challenge if you keep the simple sweetness of a true innocent. Like other Idealists, Forrest Gump has boundless optimism, and great purity and faith in the future. He is unscathed by all the challenges that life throws at him, including Vietnam, meeting the president and a difficult marriage, following his mother's wisdom that, 'Life is like a box of chocolates; you never know what you're gonna get.'

Being There is another film (and book) that expresses this sentiment, as do songs such as 'Someone to watch over me', 'Summertime' and 'Don't worry, be happy.'

Self-help books such as *Chicken Soup for the Soul* remain popular, full of the homespun wisdom of the Idealist. All reflect the core desire of the Idealist to experience paradise by being happy. Their faith and optimism means that they are also loyal, pure and traditional. This is contrasted with their greatest fear which is to do something wrong, especially if that leads to punishment. Idealism is great, but when weakly expressed the Idealist can appear boring for all their naive innocence, and naivety can lead to blind faith and denial.

Marty Rubin said that, 'Maturity is the moment one regains one's innocence', and it is true that the Idealist is often associated with the very young and the very old. At both these ages we desire purity, goodness and simplicity. Initially an Idealist has childlike qualities of naivety and simple dependence, which grow into a more positive renewal of faith, eventually developing into a mystical sense of wholeness where innocence comes from values and integrity. This is the journey from young child to mature adult. As Queen Elizabeth I said, 'A clear and innocent conscience fears nothing.' Elizabeth's own conscience is open to interpretation.

Does anyone remember the Pillsbury Doughboy or the Jolly Green Giant? Both are Idealists as is the (very old) soap brand Ivory. Disney's motto is 'The happiest place on earth' and embodies the Idealist, with a little bit of the magical Catalyst thrown in because Disneyland is 'Where dreams come true.'

The Idealist helps you retain or renew faith, and is a great archetype for brands that provide simple and stripped down solutions to problems, brands that are associated with goodness, morality, simplicity, nostalgia or childhood, and brands that are produced by companies with very clear and honest values. The Idealist is also good for brands associated with health, cleanliness or virtue and is ideal to differentiate from brands with more tarnished images. Could this be the ideal archetype for a new type of bank?

Coca-Cola may have believed Innocent was a good strategic fit for its brand. Coca-Cola has been an Idealist since the 70s when its ads featuring 'I'd like to build the world a home, and furnish it with love, grow apple trees and honey bees and snow white turtle doves' ran for six years. This was followed by 'It's the real thing' and most recently by its current slogan 'Open happiness'. All have been strongly linked to music in the same theme. Its latest advert 'Security camera' tells viewers, 'Let's look at the world a little differently' showing scenes of heroism, kindness and love to the song 'Give a little bit'. Back to the 1970s?

Ben and Jerry's has always emphasized its purity and simplicity and continues to donate profits to charity like Innocent. Its advertising is full of statements such as 'Granny-like generosity is corporate policy', and visually it has a feel of hippy era love and peace. In a different way, McDonald's is designed for children and families, and promises a fun and safe environment. Arguably, going under the golden arches is like entering a promised land. 'I'm lovin' it' captures exactly the same feeling as 'Open happiness', and Ronald McDonald remains an icon of innocence along with the primary colours and play areas in store.

McDonald's advertised National Breakfast Day on the front of Singapore's *Today* newspaper, and gave away 100,000 free Egg McMuffins with the copy:

> Let's get up. Let's go. Let's seize the day. Let's dream big. Let's laugh. Let's live. Let's live large. Let's change the world. Let's do it now. Let's go the extra mile. Let's never give up. Let's take charge. Let's do the impossible. Let's be strong. Let's be unafraid. Let's push the envelope. Let's do all we can and then some. Let's challenge the status quo. Let's make bold plans. Let's say yes to life. Let's stand tall. But first let's eat. Let's drink. Let's start the day right. Let's get up and go Singapore.

The Idealist is the brand archetype for optimists and for those who want to stay blissfully happy.

07 Finding the esSense of your brand

> *Marketers believe that consumers' thoughts occur only as words. Words do play an important role but they don't provide the whole picture.* GERALD ZALTMAN

How do you find the right archetype for your brand? And how do you then translate that across all brand touchpoints? The final chapters of the book will address these questions, firstly in terms of the research and branding process to identify the right archetype, and then to translate this into specific touchpoint engagements with customers through the esSense framework.

The basis of story is the underlying tensions or contradictions that we all face in our lives. The greater the contradiction, the more powerful is the story. These contradictions can be uncovered through the four-stage StoryWorks process, developed by TapestryWorks.

In the first stage, you build a brand back story, by reviewing the brand's history, if there is one, and relevant research which can help guide the later stages of the process. In the second stage, you plot the category by decoding category communications and values to identify key themes and underlying tensions in the jobs that brands perform for customers. In the third stage, in-depth interviews are used to reveal the deep motivations and hidden contradictions that drive customer behaviour. Finally, workshops are used to build brand identity and individual stories, based on the findings of the first three stages and using creative writing approaches to inspire creative thinking. Co-creation approaches are often used to validate and optimize the outputs of the workshops. Let's look at each stage in more detail.

Building a brand back story

Unless you are entirely new to a category, your brand has history. The start to finding the esSense of your brand is much like that of a biographer researching an historical figure. If you want to fully understand your subject, you need to go right back to their childhood to see how their early years inform their later behaviour.

Such enquiry is mostly based on desk research, reviewing past reports to create hypotheses and questions for later stages. It is often also useful to talk to friends of the brand (stakeholders) to get their point of view, which will also identify any immediate contradictions that may surface in the way that different stakeholders interact with the brand.

Like any good biographer, you need to prepare a set of questions. Here are some that I have found useful:

- Who created the brand and why?
- What was happening in the broader culture at the time the brand was first created?
- How was the brand first positioned, and how has it been subsequently positioned?
- What is the history of brand communications?
- What are the best and most memorable communications created by the brand?
- How have customers related to the brand over time?
- How do they relate to the brand now?
- What brand values or attributes make it stand out from the crowd?
- How is the brand performing versus the competition?
- What are the main triggers and barriers for using the brand?
- What is the brand's character?

- What are the brand's strengths and weaknesses?
- Does the brand have a functional or an expressive role?
- Is the brand part of a low-involvement or high-involvement category?
- Is the brand's use episodic or routine?
- Do customers use the brand exclusively or as part of a repertoire?
- Does the brand owner want to attract new users, retain current users, expand the category overall, increase frequency of use, or create surplus value (charge more)?

These questions are a good start to exploring whatever material is available. Building a brand biography should not take long, but is important to framing the context of the other stages of the process.

Brands are anchored in their past in customer minds, and they can never entirely escape that past. Moreover, the past associations of a brand provide the bedrock for changing perceptions, provided that new directions are attached to existing perceptions, allowing customers to identify communications with their existing network of associations for the brand, as well as building new ones.

To try and change brand perceptions more radically, with little or no consistency with previous brand communications, is to waste time and money unless you have a very large amount of both.

In a recent study TapestryWorks conducted for an Asian telecommunications company, the company had invested considerable resource in an advertising campaign that was proving to have little if any impact on consumer awareness (and, by some measures, was having negative impact). A review of category communications, along with an archetypal analysis of their new campaign, showed that the new communication direction was very far removed from customers' existing perceptions of both their brand and of the category itself. The impact of this was that the advertising was completely unmemorable, despite its strong visual impact. Thus, there was no attachment in consumer minds between the advertising and the brand, and no associations were made. The company immediately stopped the campaign and reverted to more typical category communication.

Cracking the category codes

The next step is to analyze category communications to identify the key plot themes in existing communications and underlying tensions in the jobs that brands perform. It is important to look carefully across the key brands in the category and the range of touchpoints, including television and print advertising, online presence, retail spaces and other brand behaviours. It can also pay to look at new and growing brands too, to see what might be future directions for a category. Again, there are some key questions to ask of the category:

- Are any brands in the category already in archetype territory?
- How deeply are these archetypes communicated?
- Do the brands have clear identities?
- Do the brands have similar identities?
- What archetypal stories do the brands communicate?
- Which archetypes appear most suited to the category and the brands in the category?
- Is there an opportunity for a new archetype in the category?
- Which touchpoints most effectively express the archetypes of each brand?
- Are the touchpoints consistent in what they express or are there contradictions?

Analysis is conducted using CodeWorks, TapestryWorks' proprietary tool for decoding category communications. The approach is based on a semiotic analysis framework. The first step is to list all the signs and symbols being used in the category, including colours, shapes, graphic devices, images, names, language, typefaces, packaging and product formats, packaging and product materials, icons, ambience, lighting, use of sound and music and others.

Once all relevant signs are listed, the meanings, both literal and figurative, are decoded taking note of the context in which the signs appear. For example, in telecommunications advertising an image of a safari or zoo might literally reference exotic places and travel, perhaps a prize competition or roaming plan. The same advertising can also express more figurative brand values such as exploration and discovery, implying that the brand helps each customer to be an authentic and unique individual.

The next stage of the process is to consider whether each meaning has an opposite meaning, and what this might be. Signs are grouped into natural themes and ideas, and are then placed in the context of the development of the category over time, including future directions that are developing.

It can be helpful to think in terms of the different binary oppositions that are implied in the category communications (see Chapter 4), as they map on to the archetypes through the StoryWorks model (see Table 7.1).

TABLE 7.1 Key binary oppositions of StoryWorks model

self	other
individual	collective
home	away
inside	outside
freedom	constraint
life	death
pleasure	pain
health	illness
safety	danger
desire	satisfaction
love	hate
serious	playful
happy	sad
male	female

TABLE 7.1 *continued*

young	old
hero	villain
good	bad
concrete	abstract
natural	artificial
present	absent
appearance	reality
permanent	temporary
similar	different
beautiful	ugly
strong	weak
sacred	taboo
new	old
mind	body
rational	emotional
science	art
order	chaos
conformity	transgression
simple	complex
dominant	subordinate
confident	fearful

Once the key binary oppositions are identified, it is possible to map brands against key themes and ideas, and to explore potential contradictions and interesting combinations through quadrant maps and semiotic squares.

Now you understand the category, the next goal is to get deep into the mind of the customer.

Uncovering consumer stories and underlying conflicts

In *How Customers Think* (2003), Gerald Zaltman explores two central themes that are consistent with our story here. Firstly, the majority of the thoughts and feelings that influence our behaviour occur in the unconscious mind (Kahneman's System 1). Secondly, to gain insight into customer behaviour requires an understanding of how the mind works.

Zaltman believes, as do I, that decision-making is driven more by unconscious feelings than by conscious thoughts. Most of these unconscious feelings and thoughts are non-verbal. They occur as sensations, images, metaphors and stories that are constantly flashing across the mind and interacting with our current experience. Direct question-and-answer approaches are unable to understand these underlying behavioural drivers, and can only capture more limited and shallow surface reasoning (Wilson, Kraft and Lisle, 1990; Wilson and Schooler, 1991; Zaltman, 2003).

Stories, along with the metaphors that Zaltman uses in his research, can invoke and express the images and sensations, including all the different aspects of sensory experience, in non-verbal forms. Such non-verbal expressions may not be literal and direct, and customers may not even be aware of their significance.

Given the importance of vision among the senses, and in human thinking, approaches to uncovering unconscious thoughts focus on imagery and storytelling, although they can also invoke the other senses. This is the basis of the Storyworks approach used by Tapestry-Works, focusing on story and imagery, as well as imagination, in order to probe deeper into the mind. The full approach has five steps plus pre-work.

Homework

One week prior to an interview, participants are advised of pre-work. They are asked to bring a number of pictures that represent their own thoughts and feelings about the topic of interest. These pictures should not be directly related to the topic, but selected from imagery outside the topic area. In some instances, participants might also be asked to bring relevant objects to an interview, or even to make their own drawings of a topic.

Step 1 – Storytelling

The participant is asked how each image represents their thoughts and feelings about the topic, first describing the content of the image and later elaborating on its meaning to them and relevance to the topic. Participants are asked to tell stories relating to the imagery and the topic.

Participants are also asked at this stage to share any images that they would like to have brought, but were unable to find. They are asked to describe the potential image in detail, and given the opportunity to find similar or related images from available magazines, or perhaps to draw what it might look like.

Alternatively, stimulus materials can be pre-prepared for the storytelling exercise, based on the outputs from the semiotic analysis in Stage 2. Visual material, ideally from a wide range of genres, styles and themes can be used for participants to find imagery that depicts the topic of interest. Images can be collected and turned into collages, which can be used as stimulus to help find metaphors to express stories, either with customers or in later workshops.

Such collages can be made more interesting if they are linked to the semiotic analysis of the category, incorporating key binary oppositions within a composite image, with one side of the opposition on one the left of the collage and the opposing side on the right hand side. Such stimulus can really help customers to articulate their feelings based on imagery that is known to be linked to the key themes in the category.

Step 2 – Building the stories

Participants are asked to widen the frame of a selected picture and describe what else might enter the picture (to better understand their story). They are specifically asked what else might be visible if the frame were widened. In addition, they might be asked to describe where they would appear in the frame.

Participants are then asked to sort the various images into different sets based on any groupings or similarities that they feel are relevant. They are asked to describe the reasons for the groupings and to explore alternative groups.

In the next step, participants are probed on the most common and most important elements that have come out of the interview so far. Laddering is used to create a hierarchy of values, using probes such as, 'Why is that important to you?' and 'How does that make you feel?'

Laddering is related to means-end theory, which states that a value chain exists between the attributes of a product or service and an individual's life values. This value chain identifies the associations between the different levels of the value chain, moving from attributes as physical features and characteristics, through to functional consequences of the attributes (results or benefits), moving to emotional consequences of the attributes and ultimately to customer values and goals, called terminal values.

For example, a skin cream might contain an anti-ageing ingredient and a customer remarks that this is important to them in choosing this brand. Further investigation reveals that this is important because they believe that the ingredient makes their skin appear more youthful which helps them to feel and behave like a younger person. Their ultimate goal in this is to feel a sense of well-being and healthiness, and the ingredient helps them achieve this, through this chain of values (Reynolds and Olson, 2001).

Many researchers have proposed that these terminal values are limited in number including being well respected, excitement, fun and enjoyment in life, security, self-fulfilment, self-respect, sense of accomplishment, sense of belonging and warm relationship with others. Others claim there are more, including self-esteem, peace of mind, independence, self-reliance, power, freedom and tradition. In my experience of conducting research there are about 10, and arguably a few more, and hopefully you will see the connection between these terminal values and the values discussed in Chapter 5 from the models of Rokeach and Schwartz as well as the stories of the 12 archetypes (Rokeach, 1973; Schieffer, 2005).

In some interviews, these key dimensions may be further validated using construct elicitation, using probes of three images or three objects, to identify the key dimensions of perception in the topic area. Although these constructs are typically more functional, they help to ensure that all key themes are captured, and they can sometimes lead to new terminal values (Gains, 1994).

Step 3 – Representative constructs

Participants are asked to identify the images that are most representative of the topic and the key groupings that they have identified. They are further asked to identify images that could represent the opposite of these images and hence the opposite of their own thoughts and feelings.

Step 4 – Sensory metaphors

Depending on the topic area, the interviewer might then explore the blending of the senses, with a 'synaesthesia' game. In the game, participants are asked to express their ideas using various different sensory modalities such as colour, taste, smell, touch, sound, temperature, orientation, emotion, and others (see the esSense framework in Chapter 8). A typical interviewer probe would be, 'What sound could you hear that would represent your thoughts and feelings about this topic and the role it plays in your life?'

Step 5 – Short story and summary

In extended interviews, participants are asked to create a story about the topic. A typical interviewer would ask, 'I would like you to use your imagination to create a short story. The story should express your thoughts and feelings about the topic and the role it plays in your life. Please include at least three characters: yourself, the topic and something else in your life that does the same for you as the topic.'

Finally, participants are asked to create a summary collage of their images using images that they brought along and any additional ones that may be relevant.

From these outputs the interviewer would create a summary hierarchical value map for each participant, as well as identifying the key goals and values that the map reveals. If required, these individual maps can be summarized into one overall consensus map.

Although the above approach is relatively detailed, interviews need not take much longer than a standard in-depth interview and my experience is that only a limited number of interviews (8 to 10) is required to capture the key themes driving behaviour, although more might be necessary where there are more diverse populations to be researched.

Validating the right story

For simpler studies, where the brand and category are already well understood, and brands have relatively strong identities, a much shorter and simpler approach can be used to validate hypotheses about the key goals and therefore the most relevant archetypes for customers.

This is done through StoryWorks image cards, which allow participants to pick the most relevant archetype pictures from a set of diverse images, and then to tell the story of that image. As with the full process, laddering can be used to develop participant responses to understand the full chain of value that is driving their behaviour.

Responses can be further validated using a Think Card word game, in which participants pick the words most relevant to what they desire (or avoid) from brands in a category. This word game is also the basis of quantitative validation of archetypes and has also been used to segment customers based on their underlying motivations.

Archetype segments can be quantitatively validated by simple select and ranking tasks using key words and phrases. This approach relies on the brain's unconscious recognition of stimuli more than the more conscious recall of typical rating scales. Validation can also be conducted using implicit testing that measures the speed of response to infer the strength of association between each brand and key words and phrases, and this approach is recommended for measuring emotional responses to brands (Dimofte, 2010).

Building transformational stories

The final stage of the process happens through a StoryWorks workshop or sharing session, where the brand backstory, category codes and customer stories and tensions are synthesized and used as inputs to develop a brand identity and communication stores through a creative writing process. Co-creation approaches are often then used to validate and optimize the workshop outputs.

Most successful brands draw on more than one archetype to create their own brand story. For example, although Coca-Cola is primarily an Idealist brand (Joy to the world), it regularly draws on themes and imagery from other archetypes, such as Everyman (All people are equal), Joker (Let's have fun) and Explorer (Let yourself go). Similarly, although Virgin is at heart a Joker, it draws on the adjacent imagery of the Rebel (Let's break the rules) and Seducer (Let's get intimate).

In these cases, brands think in terms of a primary archetype, which is at the core of the brand, and secondary archetypes that can help express the brands' appeal to different types of customers in different places. It is common that the primary archetype will form the basis of above-the-line communications, contributing the main brand messages, while secondary archetypes may inform tactical marketing and product features and execution.

The StoryWorks archetypes and Think Cards are first used to identify the key archetypes, with each archetype having a number of versions and the key characteristics of the archetype that can be built into a brand identity. When this is done, then the STORY framework can be used as a template for constructing brand stories, through a number of different games, activities and exercises to stimulate creative thinking and writing. The 12 core archetypes are summarized in Table 7.2.

TABLE 7.2   Summary of 12 archetypes

Archetype	Goal	Helps you
Caregiver	Security	Care for others
Everyman	Sense of belonging	Be OK just as you are
Seducer	Intimacy	Find and give love
Joker	Fun and enjoyment in life	Have a good time
Rebel	Revolution	Break the rules
Explorer	Freedom to explore	Maintain independence
Artist	Self-fulfilment	Create something new
Warrior	Self-respect	Act courageously
Catalyst	Sense of accomplishment	Affect transformation
Guru	Discovery of truth	Understand their world
Ruler	Power	Exert control
Idealist	Peace of mind	Retain or renew faith

The STORY framework is used to help construct stories around the relevant archetypes:

- S is for the Star of the story (the customer);
- T is for the Treasure that they seek (their goal);
- O is for the Obstacle they face to obtaining their treasure;
- R is the Right lesson to learn from the story (the moral);
- Y is the whY and the call to action.

For example, in a Nike brand story, the Star might be a well-known athlete or an everyday person, the Treasure is always to achieve greatness through showing courage, and the Obstacle is often fear of failing. The Right lesson to learn is that you can achieve greatness, because Nike equipment gives you the courage to overcome your fear.

As with all stories, the more that is at stake, the more compelling the story. Hollywood scriptwriters believe that death is the ultimate stake in any story, but this can mean any kind of death: physical, spiritual, moral, social or other. Therefore, the more tension that can be built in the story, through setting the target for Treasure high, or creating more difficult Obstacles to overcome, the more gripping will be the story.

There are a number of creative writing techniques that can be used to help build more compelling narratives:

Building characterization

The first tool is to build the characterization of the archetype, either focusing on the brand or on the customer. There are seven variables that can help flesh out the character into a much more developed form:

1 Surface behaviour and personality, in terms of the different quirks, ticks, habits, and visual style of the archetype;

2 The backstory reflecting all that has happened in the past to make them who they are;

3 The character arc showing how the character learns and grows over time;

4 Inner demons and conflicts defining their outlook, beliefs, decisions and actions;

5 Their worldview that shows their belief system and moral compass (this is particularly important for helping define brands);

6 Goals and motivations that drive decisions and actions (eg their terminal values);

7 Decisions, actions and behaviours that summarize the above and are the outcomes of the character in their entirety.

Building plot structures

The seven plots of Christopher Booker can help to build very different versions of similar stories. For example, you can ask, 'What would happen if the brand were to help the customer overcome a monster, instead of moving them from rags to riches?' As a reminder, the seven basic plots are; Overcoming the monster, Rags to riches, Quest, Voyage and return, Comedy, Tragedy and Rebirth.

For added variety, you can consider two additional plot structures that are more recent additions to the canon, and discussed by Booker. These are Rebellion, the 1984 story, and Mystery, which is the basis of the detective story (Booker, 2004).

Related to the plots you can think about character arcs that might happen in your story. Is the Star of the story moving from problem to solution, mystery to solution, conflict to peace, danger to safety, confusion to order, dilemma to decision, ignorance to knowledge or question to answer?

Notice that these character arcs are related to specific archetypes and there are other possible arcs. Also think about how the hero can accomplish their goals in the story. Is it through courage, ingenuity, special capacity, special weapon, self-sacrifice or another way? Again, consider how these relate to the archetypes, their goals, their virtues and their vices.

Playing 'What if?'

In any form of story writing, 'What if?' is always a great question to ask. It can help you connect elements together, but is especially useful for finding initial ideas. The start point might be to read or watch something, and then ask, 'What if?' For example, read a newspaper and at the end of each article ask a 'What if?' question. Watch a competitive television commercial and ask, 'What if?' Over time you can develop a master list of different 'What if?' questions that you can use continually whenever you see something any stimulus. Great writers always ask 'What if?'

The 'socko' ending

The idea of this tool is to start with the end in mind. You visualize a climactic scene at the end of your story. Imagine the music that would go with the scene, feel the full range of emotions bursting out.

Think about how you might add characters to heighten the conflict. Imagine how you can play on the themes and ideas until something truly unforgettable happens.

At this stage, take a step back and ask yourself, 'Who are the characters?' Think about the circumstances that have brought them to where they are, and how you might be able to trace the story back to its logical starting point.

Playing the journalist

Journalists are good at asking questions. The key questions you can ask as you investigate your character are in Table 7.3.

TABLE 7.3 Playing the journalist questions

Who?	Who are the protagonist and antagonist (hero and villain)?
Who else?	Who else is important to the story?
What?	What is happening in the story?
When?	When does the story take place?
Where?	Where is the setting for the story?
Why?	Why is this happening?
How?	How did your character get involved?
So what?	Why should an audience care?

You will see that many of the tools start from asking questions of your brand, customers, characters and story.

Moving to the senses

The final step is to take a brand story and translate this into sensory touchpoints, which is the subject of the last chapter. Before we move to this, here are a couple of workshop activities specifically focused on creating sensory touchpoints:

Bringing moments to life

In this extended exercise, you start with one of your brand stories, or even with a short character sketch of a consumer based on your research.

The aim of the exercise is to identify scenarios for occasions in which a product may be used. Starting with the customer, use the context of the story or the detail of the character sketch to identify occasions of use. For each, identify the key needs of the customer. What does the customer want? How does the customer want to feel? The trick is to be as specific as possible with your answers.

Based on the answers, brainstorm which sensory characteristics would be ideal to meet those needs. Again, be as specific as possible. Don't write 'texture', but rather 'texture that explodes in the mouth and then melts immediately' (or whatever is relevant).

You can then review how well the different brands and products in the category meet these needs, reviewing each one against all key sensory characteristics, and giving them a performance rating. From this you should be able to identify where there are specific opportunities for new products or for improvements to existing brands. You can create a chart of your brand and the key competitors, against each customer segment and usage occasion.

Synaesthesia game

This is a much quicker and more spontaneous activity. You first identify a theme, metaphor or archetype and ask everyone in the room to play the role of one or more of the senses. You can include as many as you want for the esSense framework provided in the next chapter. Someone shouts out the theme, and everyone explains what they are sensing or experiencing.

Someone records all the thoughts and ideas, and you can then brainstorm to build a product identity blueprint. Example senses are colour, shape, smell, taste, sound, texture, temperature, position, orientation, movement and feeling, and there are many others you can use from the esSense framework.

This is a quick and easy way to build your blueprint of sense, symbol and story. Before we move to the final chapter, here are two case studies of building brand esSense from research. These examples illustrate the power of understanding sense, symbol and story to create meaningful differentiation for brands.

Building the story of an Asian food brand

In one recent study, TapestryWorks conducted in South East Asia, a food brand wished to renovate their brand positioning. The brand had a very interesting history, which was the key to developing a successful solution. The brand had originated in one niche target group (young children), and over many years had evolved to span several age and lifestyle groups up to young adults.

The portfolio of sub-brands and product lines was very broad and included everything from single-serve small indulgences to be bought on the street to large family packs targeted at special occasions.

Brand sales had been declining across many of these sub-categories, which had developed individual and diverse communication directions, reflecting the differences in target groups, competitive landscapes and internal ownership.

The history of the brand, and its origins as a product for young children, held the solution to a brand archetype that could build on the past to develop a stronger and consistent identity across all relevant target groups and product formats.

The client had already conducted extensive primary research and TapestryWorks reviewed previous reports and identified the key tension underlying consumer motivations in the category between the need for escape and the desire for comfort. Although there was a strong desire to connect in the broader culture, this was not such a strong category motivation although still important to customers.

Existing category communications revealed further tensions in the messages being communicated by different client product lines, with the majority of brands focusing on 'reality' advertising that reflected a need for safety. However, some brands, including some of the client's product lines, played with themes of fantasy and escape.

In line with other findings, the need for connection did not appear in the advertising of most brands, and never in combination with the need for fantasy.

This created an opportunity for a unique positioning across sub-categories, building on the brand's heritage and creating a platform that could be leveraged across all age groups. The brand's heritage fitted closely with the Trickster archetype (a version of the Joker), as a slightly cheeky young boy who enjoyed life and had been portrayed in the past as somewhat mischievous.

The Joker is an archetype associated with fun and spontaneity, and the joy of living in the moment. These are perfect emotions for communicating the fun of fantasy and escape, combined with the need to connect with other people. Using this platform, the client was able to build a consistent and successful brand communication strategy across all product formats.

During a brand-building workshop, 'The fun of escape' was developed as the esSense of the brand identity. Executions of this identity were developed through brand stories across each of four target groups, each with very different situations where the need to escape and have fun became important. The situations were often associated with boredom and, for example, the most common situation for the oldest consumer group to need to escape was the boredom of office life.

In a follow-up project the client used the esSense framework to develop a stronger product identity across different touchpoints, applying the Joker archetype to re-design packaging across the range, providing consistent and brand-relevant visual style and emotional impact.

Making rice 'nice' for a snack brand

A Chinese snack brand engaged TapestryWorks to help them solve a challenging problem of building a successful product platform with rice as a key ingredient. They had been working on the project for a number of years, and previous launches had failed to capture consumer interest.

A review of previous research identified a set of hypotheses about the previous failures, raising a number of questions for investigation. A detailed semiotic analysis of the rice and confectionery categories, revealed key tensions and challenges for the client in combining the two categories.

Unsurprisingly, rice itself is considered good, healthy, substantial, pure, natural, soft and chewy, while snack products are considered bad, unhealthy, insubstantial, contaminated, artificial, hard and breaking up in the mouth, lacking the chewability of rice. Historical attitudes and beliefs about rice reflected its importance in Chinese culture in providing food security and nurture to people across the

TABLE 7.4 Summary of the meanings of rice

Past	Present	Future
Security	Daily necessity	Balanced health
Energy	Harmony	Gentleness
Home	Peaceful	Cleansing
Family	Satisfaction	–
Hard work	Happiness	–
Balance	Simplicity	–
Integrity	Honesty	–
Natural	Variety	–
Healthy	Gentle	–
–	Comfortable	–
–	Freedom	–
–	Worry free	–
–	Home	–

classes, as reflected in its embedding in everyday language of greetings and customs.

Consumer interviews revealed rich and deep associations with rice across all age groups, connecting consumers with values of home, security and comfort. An exploration of key sensory cues was used to build a product identity framework for building rice values into a snack product through external and internal colour cues, providing substance in mouth feel and the right aftertaste to match the key sensory signals of rice.

Semiotic analysis also revealed an emerging association between rice and cleansing properties, which came from non-food categories. Rice has historically been used with water as a cleanser and is considered to soak up impurities on the skin, in the same way as it soaks up the flavour of the food and sauces eaten with it. This was identified as one of many potential platforms to communicate the 'balancing' virtues of rice as an ingredient in snack foods, overcoming the tensions between comfort and security and the need for pleasure and exploration.

Applying the esSense framework

"Unify. Simplify. Amplify. **KEN CARBONE**

The esSense of branding

Strong brand identity comes from creating consistent customer engagement across all relevant touchpoints, with the goal to unify, simplify and amplify. The esSense approach evaluates how the different senses shape perceptions of your brand by scoring them across 30 key touchpoints, integrating sense, symbol and story. The esSense framework (Figure 8.1) then helps you amplify a brand's core values to forge deeper and more enduring bonds with customers.

Across sense, symbol and story, some touchpoints act as mental 'primers', other touchpoints help engage with customers in the brand experience, and additional touchpoints can help you to grow and amplify to maximize the impression that the brand leaves on the consumer's mind. So always prime, engage and grow the brand experience (PEG).

Sense, symbol and story each have 10 touchpoints, building a complete system for brand engagement. Although labelled sense, symbol and story, all touchpoints are communicated through the senses, although some directly engage the senses, some communicate meaning through symbolism, and others help elaborate the emotional connection of the brand through brand story. Let's start with the senses.

FIGURE 8.1   esSense framework

Brand colours

How do you sense a brand? Your prime should always be colour, which defines the key meanings that are associated with the brand. The flavour (smell and taste), touch (skinfeel) and sound of the brand experience engage closely with the customer's senses. Sensory experience is grown through physical texture (mouthfeel), orientation (balance and direction), movement, temperature, light and intensity of the sensory experience (where these are relevant to the product or service).

We have seen the importance of colour to managing expectations of the experience to come. Colours are often the first way for our brain to identify and differentiate objects in the environment, and many brands are associated with specific colours as in the opening example of Cadbury's purple. Not only is the colour distinctive and now trademarked, but purple also has associations that are relevant to the brand. Purple is a colour of quality and distinction, the colour of royalty and aristocracy (in many, but not all cultures), and often linked to silk and soft fabrics.

All of these impressions enter the mind before the chocolate gets near your mouth! Adding to the feelings of quality, under the purple outer skin, there is usually an inner protective layer of silver foil paper too. Cadbury was a pioneer of this style of composite packaging, which was first introduced in 1950 with an outer layer of stain-resistant paper over an inner layer of foil. In the early days of packaging, it was used only for luxuries for gifting or indulgence, so the quality and colour of packaging was used to create additional value. Colour and images were also good ways to circumvent government regulations in those days (Hine, 1995).

Likewise, the colour red has become strongly associated with Coca-Cola, and is often the default colour for other brands entering the Cola category. That's why Pepsi feels the need to be so emphatically blue, to make it clear that it is different. It has also often used humorous and rebellious advertising (Joker and Rebel) to differentiate itself from the category Ruler (who communicates their Idealist credentials).

Innocent also proclaims its Idealist credentials in its white colour and in the symbolism and stories that it tells about its brand. By contrast, Harley-Davidson colours are overwhelming black, signifying its Rebel status. IKEA is often brown and plain, reinforcing its Everyman archetype, and the light blue of denim proclaims the ordinariness of Levi's. Walking past Victoria's Secret retail outlets in Singapore, you can't miss the use of pink. This is a common colour for the Seducer, and used by the Breast Cancer Awareness Campaign too.

Finally, Tiffany Blue, otherwise known as 'robin egg blue colour' or Pantone PMS 1837, has been used since 1845. The number 1837 comes from the year of Tiffany's foundation, but you won't be able to find it in any Pantone Matching System swatch books as it is trademarked just like Cadbury's purple. Tiffany even sells porcelain versions of the turquoise box with white ribbon in its stores, it carries the colour scheme over to its shopping bags, which are well made and reusable, and mail catalogues in turquoise envelopes to reinforce perceptions of elegance and quality. And its advertising is a master-piece in capturing these brand values – think of the man holding a Tiffany box behind his back, with the line, 'Some days matter'.

Colour primes our mind and body with direct physiological effects as well as less direct symbolic meanings. Red environments are known to increase blood flow and stimulate nervous system responses, changing the way we see the world around us. For example, in one experiment it was demonstrated that those waiting for a red or yellow web page to load were more agitated than those waiting for the same page with a blue background. Red has been shown to increase perceptions of attractiveness and sex appeal in men and women when viewing the opposite sex.

Red clothing also increases your chance of winning in sport. One group of experimenters compared results of the Greco-Roman wrestling, freestyle wrestling, tae kwon do and boxing from the 2004 Athens Olympic Games, where competitors were randomly assigned a blue or red uniform in each bout. Red competitors won more bouts than blue competitors in all four sports, and the effects were especially strong when competitors were evenly matched. In another experiment, sports psychologists showed that uniform colour influenced the scores that referees gave to competitors, with the same participants being rated lower with blue uniforms and higher with red. Although the effects are subtle, across bouts they can have a profound influence on outcomes (Alter, 2013).

Why does the colour red have such a powerful effect on the human body? When asked, subjects tend to reference the similarity of the colour to blood and hence illness, injury and death. In the same way, blue reminds us of the sky, yellow of the Sun and green of grass.

Other studies have shown that blue light can reduce crime rates and mediate the effects of Seasonal Affective Disorder (SAD, also known as the winter blues). Blue is known to lower blood pressure, pulse and respiration rates, having the opposite effect of red. The associations that we have with colour also influence our ability to process information. Seeing the words 'virtue' in black and 'sin' in white slows our reaction times, when compared with seeing them in white and black, as they are more commonly associated (Alter, 2013).

For marketers this means that the congruence between colour, words and other information does matter. When information is congruent, it is processed more rapidly and easily, giving brands a greater chance of capturing attention and influencing decision-making.

Colour primes the other senses more than any other factor. It has a powerful influence over human behaviour.

Brand senses

In Chapter 2 we learnt about the emotional power of smell. Smell engages us directly, often taking us back to formative experiences and powerful memories. For many of us, the whiff of Bazooka gum, Play-Doh or Crayola is an instant transport to the past. In the 1990s Rolls Royce started receiving customer complaints indicating that the new car wasn't as good as the old models. The problem was eventually traced to the smell, and Rolls Royce recreated the aroma of a 1965 Rolls to spray inside all new models (Keller, Apéria and Georgson, 2012: 203).

The smell of Dettol is instantly recognizable to anyone who has ever used the brand, as is the 'ouzo effect' of the white coloured milky emulsion produced when it is mixed with water. These aspects of the sensory experience signal the potency and activity of Dettol's disinfectant chemicals, creating a strong link between product use and efficacy.

The smell is a function of the phenolic chemicals, pine oil and other ingredients that make up the brand, and is forever associated with its disinfectant properties. For this reason, the core of the smell has been kept across a wide range of personal and household cleaning products that are now part of the Dettol brand, supporting the brand's 'mission' to build healthy washing habits. The smell is strong and piercing, matching the Warrior archetype that the brand follows across many of its touchpoints.

Singapore Airlines, Ivory Soap and Thomas Pink also have their distinctive smells, as discussed in Chapter 3. Johnson & Johnson has long used the sweet and clean fragrance of vanilla across its range of baby products and beyond. It's difficult to think of anything that could better signal the mildness, safety and nurturance of a Caregiver brand mixed with an innocent Idealist too. The smell is completely consistent with their brand strategy.

Another famous example of a brand with a signature scent is Colgate-Palmolive which has patented its brand's distinctive taste, although Martin Lindstrom points out that it has not extended this to other products in its dental care range (Lindstrom, 2010: 37).

Smell is intimately bound up with taste, and a final example of how flavour can be used to build brand identity is that of Red Bull. It has never been a preferred taste, but its distinct medicinal flavour reinforces its positioning as an efficacious, performance enhancing drink, along with the small serving size, premium pricing and list of active ingredients. All these elements suggest potency, the key selling point of the brand (Hill, 2008: 144; van Praet, 2012: 230).

Touch has been an underused sense in marketing, and Apple arguably leads the field in using the feel of products in contact with the skin as a key tool in its branding strategy. Of course, its success has been strongly linked to its use of touchscreen technology to create friendly and accessible interfaces with its technology, remembering that this has always been important to it as it pioneered the use of screen icons and user experience.

However, there is much more to Apple's use of touch than this. Think about the way that it packages new products, so that opening your new device becomes completely absorbing, with well-designed packaging that truly engages the senses and creates the expectation of how the product inside will perform. Perhaps its masterpiece is the Apple retail experience, with its completely (designed) open feel, and the licence to touch and play with its products and get the 'feel' of what it would be like to own one for yourself. Once you have felt what it would be like to own something, it is so much easier to buy it with concrete knowledge of what the user experience will be.

Great packaging is not just about looks, but should integrate the fingertips as well as eyeballs in delivering a great sensory experience, and remember that vision depends on what we learn through touch. Touch always makes an experience that much more real.

Touch is important in every experience. Another example of using touch is the way that Starbucks leverages the tactile senses in its stores to reinforce its bond with customers. This is especially true of the seating, with a proportion of comfortable, soft and relaxing seats available in all stores (remember the link between negotiation and style of seating?). The feeling of wrapping your fingers around the coffee cup is an intimate part of the total experience, even when the coffee is to take away and your fingers wrap around the ridged contours of a cardboard insulator for a hot drink.

More recently, Wrangler launched moisturizing jeans in January 2013 with three alternative finishes: Aloe Vera, Olive Extract and Smooth Legs, which aim to prevent cellulite. *Vogue Magazine* reported on 16 January 2012 that all of the jeans have hydrating properties coming from diverse ingredients including natural oils and butters from a wide range of sources. One of Wrangler's models said that, 'They definitely feel cooler than regular jeans... after a day wearing them, my legs feel great – they come out feeling more silky than usual.' The effects of the ingredients are claimed to last up to 15 days, with a reload spray available.

The launch of the Volvo C70 focused on the 'feel' of the new car. The promotional videos associated with the launch are full of texture and touch. B&O have always known about the importance of weight in building perceptions of reliability, quality and durability, and deliberately make its remote controls more heavy than necessary to build these perceptions. IKEA has also recently been using experience of touch to build its own brand, with organized sleepovers in its stores, encouraging customers to experience their mattresses, pillows and bed liner for a whole night and feel the difference. If you sleep well for the night, then why would you not invest in its products?

Hopefully, the sound of a good night's sleep would not register, but many brands rely on the sound of its experience to engage customers. Starbucks notably makes sound a key part of the Starbucks experience. Its staff greets customers in a clear, friendly and standard way, and call orders to other staff so that you can hear your order repeated across the outlet. The sound of coffee grinding and milk steaming can be heard as you order your drink and when you sit down to relax and enjoy. And noticeably Starbucks make great play of its background music, even daring to launch its music label *Hear*

Music when the industry was suffering tough times in 2007 (and launching Grammy award-winning CDs in the process). In Singapore, it makes great play of promoting local artists, displaying their latest CDs and organizing small concerts in key stores and now have tie-ups with iTunes.

Snack products rely on their unique textures to create differentiation, and work that I have done in the UK shows that you can create a great deal of interest by designing unique combinations of textures, adding interest to the eating experience. I am sure that the recent craze for macaroons must have something to do with their unique 'melt in the mouth' texture and, similarly, many Asian snacks are quite bland and a large part of the enjoyment of eating is linked to their interesting textures. For example, think of rice cakes in China and other Asian countries.

In Singapore and China, eating crabs, with black pepper or other flavours, is mainly about the experience of breaking the crab apart and finding the meat and flavours amid the texture. Texture is an integral part of the eating experience, as it is with many meats and vegetables (for example, asparagus).

More fundamentally, touch has been shown to have huge importance to the development of babies. Harry Harlow showed that newborn monkeys clung more to soft cloth mothers with no milk than to wire-made mothers with bottled milk attached to their frame. Their sense of touch, and hence physical intimacy, was more important to them than the need for food (a challenge to Maslow's hierarchy?). More recent research has indicated that the need for physical warmth can compensate for the pain of social isolation, and that cold weather increases the need for more romantic movies (Montagu, 1986: 38–44).

Adam Alter writes on the impact of space on behaviour. As Edward Hall understood, humans like to be sure of their personal space, and respond strongly to physical contact outside their immediate group. In one study by Paco Underhill, shoppers were filmed browsing the aisles of a large department store. He noticed that when shoppers were in narrower aisles, and were jostled by other customers struggling to squeeze through, it was likely that they would just leave the store altogether. When Underhill ran another experiment and asked the shoppers why they had left, they were unable to explain the reasons, although the outcomes were clear. The conclusion is that you need to make aisles wide enough to prevent light collisions between customers (Alter, 2013: 184; Underhill, 1999).

Movement and space can also be communicated through sound. Large spaces are linked to deep, low pitches while small and delicate spaces and objects are more often associated with thin, high-pitched sounds. In general, increasing size is linked to increasing loudness and decreasing pitch.

Starbucks is master at using space to create engaging experiences, with its success in creating a third space between work and home where people can relax and meet. It actively encourages hanging around, at least at some times of day, while other businesses have always focused on 'move em in, move em out' models of customer sales. Starbucks makes a conscious effort to 'stop time' with its store design, layout, music and overall ambience.

Other brands make a conscious effort to disrupt our perceptions of location, balance and direction. For example, Abercrombie & Fitch uses darkness and relatively intimate spaces (or spaces that appear more closed) to create a sense of confined space, making customers focus on the items that they choose to 'spotlight'. If you stand outside an Abercrombie & Fitch store you will notice that you cannot see inside, and once inside you have to work your way through the dark interior with a limited sense of direction and balance. The perception of closeness and claustrophobia is heightened by the use of music, which reinforces the feel of club culture with a DJ using music to drive the behaviour of an audience.

Have you ever considered the importance of temperature in the perception of brands? Few brands use temperature in a systematic way, although one such brand is an Asian icon. If you have ever used Tiger Balm, you will know that the over-riding memory of using the brand is the perception of heat on your skin.

Several research studies have shown that ambient temperature has a strong influence on behaviour. Heatwaves lead to bad tempers in sport and road rage in drivers, either through excitement or discomfort (Alter, 2013: 205–11).

Adam Alter quotes research that shows the impact of lighting on behaviour in test situations, which shows that dim lighting leads to more dishonest behaviour (Alter, 2013). Lighting can have a profound effect on mood. Think of the differences between the lighting in an intimate restaurant, a hospital and a training room, where I spend a lot of my time. Dim lighting would be fine in the restaurant, but would feel very strange in a hospital or training room.

More generally, lighting has a profound effect on perceptions of cleanliness and intimacy, and also plays a huge role in mediating the daily rhythms of life. Abercrombie & Fitch uses a lack of lighting to disrupt perceptions and create a nightclub atmosphere in store. Many restaurants, bars and clubs use lighting to manipulate our perceptions of time and space, often leading to a 'suspension' of real time and space. If you want someone to stay, then convincing him or her that time has slowed down is a good strategy.

Intensity is the third dimension of visual perception (after hue and lightness), but is applicable to all the senses. 'Bright' perceptions include intense colours, but might also apply to a high-pitched sound or loud noise. For example, Abercrombie & Fitch's sound and light are intense, as is the aroma in-store. Its signature men's fragrance is aptly named *Fierce*. McDonald's uses strong lighting and bright colours rather than darkness to give an intense luminosity to its stores, increasing the dynamism of customers.

Intense colours, flavours and sounds stimulate and excite. Lowering the intensity of an experience relaxes, soothes and calms. Pastel shades of colour feel calm and peaceful, and are very popular in Japan. Pastel shades are often associated with higher quality (think of Tiffany Blue), while intense colours and flavours feel gaudy and 'in your face' and therefore less classy.

The intensity of the brand experience shapes your physiological response, either exciting your body into higher awareness or relaxing you into a zone of calm. Collectively the senses help make a brand concrete and real.

Symbolic names

How do you symbolize a brand? Always start with the brand name, which defines the consumer job to be done either directly or perhaps by analogy (with metaphor). The shape, graphic devices (including logos) and sonic iconography of the brand all engage customers with the symbolism you want to build, and sonic icons, fonts, size, formats (including materials), visual icons, pictures and language all nourish and develop the brand's symbolic value.

During his lifetime in the theatre, William Shakespeare coined more than 1,500 new words and modern spoken English is still packed with words, expressions, sayings and clichés that come from his work, including the words lacklustre, bandit and watchdog. He also famously wrote in *Romeo and Juliet*, 'What's in a name? That which we call a rose by any other name would smell as sweet.'

James Bitetto writes, 'Just by naming a process, a level of service, or a new service feature, you are creating a valuable asset that can add to the worth of your business' (Wheeler and Katz, 2011: 84). Names identify by giving meaning (denoting) and suggesting and implying qualities that are beyond the literal meaning (connoting). For example, Cracker Jack is a US brand of popcorn candy. The brand name has the same spelling as crackerjack which is a common term for something that is excellent or first rate. The sound of Cracker Jack is fast and crunchy, suggesting biting into something firm and crispy, and alluding to the sound of popping corn (Rivkin and Sutherland, 2004: 2–3).

McDonald's uses McNames deliberately to strengthen its brand identity. It has Big Macs, McNuggets, McMuffins and McSundaes, and has also launched its own chain of cafes, inevitably called McCafe. The sound of 'Mc' is so strongly ingrained that it immediately triggers thoughts of eating at McDonalds.

Names are powerful, and once they enter the language can become common currency. In fact, many category names were originally brand names that became generic for the product and what it stood for. Cellophane, thermos, celluloid, cornflakes, gramophone, granola, heroin, launderette, milk of magnesia, shredded wheat and yo-yos all started as brands (with a capitalized first letter) but are now just generic names. László Biró's Hungarian name is now used to describe ballpoint pens, velcro and jello are commonly used words, and in the second decade of the 21st century, we don't just search for something on the internet, we 'google' it, even if we are using another search engine.

Names can also evoke the stories and archetypes that are the core of a category. SUVs show this clearly with different brands using names such as Escape, Explorer, Expedition, Everest, Highlander, Liberty, Mountaineer, Navigator, Outlander, Pathfinder, Range Rover, Rendezvous and TrailBlazer. You can guess which archetype they are referring to!

If you wanted to evoke the Catalyst, you could try Magician, Wizard, Wiz or Spell; for Joker you could be Fun, Club, Fiesta, Circus or Party; for Caregiver, Comfort, Home, Hearth, Domestic, Window and Warm would work; for Warrior you can always use Shield, Weapon, Sword, Arrow, Axe, Anvil and Hammer among others; and Rulers are often Count or Countess, Crown, Duke or Duchess, Imperial, Knight, Monarch, Palace, Prince or Princess, Royal, Sceptre, Sovereign, Throne, Tiara or Viscount. All of these work in combination with other words to create the feeling of the archetype and the story behind the brand and its use.

Care should be taken when translating names across different markets. When Coca-Cola first entered China, the original translation of its name meant something like 'bite the wax tadpole', but after searching more than 40,000 characters they found a close phonetic equivalent (ko-kou-ko-le) that means a much more appropriate 'happiness in the mouth' (or literally 'make man mouth happy'). Pepsi managed to get this right first time with a translation that means 'a hundred happy things' (Rivkin and Sutherland, 2004: 158).

Another cultural consideration is that Chinese, and many other Asian languages, are more visual, and therefore typeface and logo can be very important to establishing identity, whereas Western languages and cultures are often more attuned to the sound of the name as the written language is much less symbolic.

When Colgate-Palmolive bought Hawley & Hazel in Hong Kong in 1985, it took over some of the best-selling toothpastes in several Asian countries. Colgate also inherited the brand name Darkie, with a grinning black-faced minstrel as the brand icon dating back to the 1920s when the big toothy smile was considered a positive image. After being besieged with complaints the name was changed to Darlie in 1989, updating the logo to a portrait of a man with an ambiguous race, wearing a top hat, tuxedo & bow tie. It continues to be successful across many Asian countries.

Absolut's name is distinctive as are all its line extension names, using 'misspelling' to create an original and distinctive feel. PayPal is well named as it mimics the effect of the brand on the user. Prozac starts with Pro sounding positive and forceful. Viagra sounds like Niagara, implying the vigour of nature, begins with a V sound which suggests speed and power, and then follows with a very mellifluous rounded r sound, rhythmic, suggesting preparation, action, release and finally rest. The overall sound of the name seems familiar, and you could easily associate the name with a car or running shoes if they had got there first.

Federal Express started its business with a name that was a real asset, bringing credibility to the business. However, over time the name became associated with being slow and bureaucratic and was also rather long with five syllables. The company found that customers were already using a shortened version of the name, so they changed it to FedEx, at the same time updating the typeface and famously inserting the arrow between the E and the x, symbolizing speed of delivery. The name FedEx also sounds fast with the short 'Ex' syllable at the end, reinforcing the positive message of speed and changing perceptions of the brand.

BlackBerry was famously named after a small fruit, alluding to the fact that you can hold it in your hands. The name is symmetrical with two groups of five letters, ends with a 'y' and sounds playful while matching the products' colour scheme. Legend has it that the company had originally considered the name 'Strawberry' as the design of the keyboard was reminiscent of the texture of the seeds on a strawberry's surface. However, blackberry is a faster word than strawberry, signifying the speed of the device. Whether they were inspired by Apple or not, the name is a metaphor for a small, delicious fruit, feeling friendly, ordinary and everyday (Frankel, 2004: 68–70).

Apple itself acknowledges that it came across its logo by accident. It was originally inspired by the story of Isaac Newton, sitting under an apple tree, and this was depicted in the first version of the logo. However, other associations came to the fore later. Jean-Louise

Gassée, the ex-chairman of Apple, was once quoted as saying, 'our logo is a great mystery: it is a symbol of pleasure and knowledge, partly eaten away and displaying the colours of the rainbow, but not in the proper order. We couldn't wish for a more fitting logo: pleasure, knowledge, hope and anarchy.'

Names come from very different sources. Some brands are named after their founders, and this is common for luxury and fashion brands. Such names are easy to trademark and satisfy the ego of the business owner although may be difficult to sustain after they retire. Other names are simply fabricated, such as Tivo, making them easier to trademark, although investment is usually required to educate customers on the meaning. Many names are descriptive, such as YouTube, and directly convey the nature of the business, but are more difficult to use when businesses diversify. Apple has a name that acts as a metaphor, making it a great name for storytelling about the brand and with built in flexibility to diversify the business. Businesses such as IBM have a name based on an acronym. Acronyms are often difficult to remember and trademark and need investment in the same way as fabricated names. There is one other class of name, exemplified by Flickr and Absolut, based on the magic of spelling to create a name that links to a meaning but with a distinctive spelling.

The most effective names combine many characteristics. They are first of all meaningful, conveying a message about the esSense of the brand. They are distinctive: unique, easy to remember and easy to spell and share on social networks. Ideally they should also be future-oriented, and able to sustain their meaning as a company grows. Remember that Apple had to change its name from Apple Computers in 2007 to reflect its development. Good names are also modular, with the potential to name brand extensions, and easy to protect through trademarks. Additionally, good names should have positive connotations across all the cultures in which they are used, and should enable easy visualization of the name (Wheeler, 2013: 23).

What is the origin of Häagen-Dazs? The brand was created by Reuben and Rose Mattus who were Polish immigrants living in New York. They thought the name Häagen-Dazs sounded Danish, although it is completely fabricated. The Danish reference was a tribute to Denmark's treatment of Jews during the Second World War, and a map of Denmark appeared on early labels. The name Häagen-Dazs brings a feel of authenticity to the brand, but has nothing to do with Denmark. For example, there are no umlauts in Danish. The name is unique and original, just as the brand owners intended when they spent hours at their kitchen table making up nonsense words.

Betty Crocker is also a fabricated name, which manages to sound wholesome and folksy, matching the positioning of the brand. Similarly, Godiva trades on a European aspirational and elitist image, despite being owned by Campbell's Soup that has a very different positioning.

Making your brand name distinctive is the most important, and most difficult challenge. But it is definitely worth it. As Danny Altman says, 'Don't pick a name that makes you one of the trees in the forest and then spend the rest of your marketing budget trying to stand out' (Wheeler and Katz, 2011: 84).

Brand symbols

Shapes are important symbols of the meaning of objects and also act as metaphors for other aspects of experience as in the example of *bouba* and *kiki*. Toblerone is distinctive and iconic because of its shape, which was originally inspired by the terrain of Switzerland. Kit Kat has four rectangular bars. We all recognize the three circles that signify Mickey Mouse and his ears without any other information, and the yellow arches of McDonald's are equally familiar.

Coca-Cola's iconic bottle, much discussed by Martin Lindstrom in *Brand Sense*, remains a classic example of packaging design. In 1915, Alexander Samuelson, a Swedish glassblower working for the Root Glass Company of Terre Haute, designed the bottle. He designed the six-and-a-half-ounce bottle so that it could be found in a dark cupboard or icebox by feel alone. The design was heavy and expensive to handle, and eventually was taken over by the can, although the contour bottle outline was eventually brought back to appear as part of the can design.

Absolut vodka pioneered transparent bottles, so you can see what's inside, giving the brand a distinctive profile and silhouette used in advertising. The profile is so distinctive that you can see the profile even when the bottle is not present, and some of Absolut's advertising plays with this by showing the outline from the space that is left by other objects. In many of Absolut's promotions the bottle is the main attraction, so that consumers buy the bottle and not what is inside, making the brand choice a glass beauty contest.

Similarly, Evian's introduction of a premium package shaped like a drop of water is a classic use of shape to build the values of the brand. Previously, I noted that Red Bull's packaging size contributes to the perception of the brand as medicinal and potent, and the brand proposition of Pringles is based on the shape and format of the product, which was unique at the time of launch. Snapple is another example of brands using unique packaging formats and shapes, along with imaginative designs and names, which manage to integrate emotional lifestyle elements into the packaging of the product.

Many brands use graphic devices to build brand identity. Most of us would recognize the characteristic logo of Victorinix, even if we not aware of the brand name. Victorinix is the maker of the Swiss Army knife, which has always had much greater recognition of its logo than name. The white cross on a red background is associated with the Swiss flag, the Christian cross and the shield along with their implied associations with spirit, craftsmanship and protection.

In the words of the company leader, 'Victorinix was not so much "about the marketing" and "all about the product", manufacturing and providing the best knives possible' (van Praet, 2012: 160–61). Although its business was impacted by the events of September 11, 2001, after which its products were banned from flights, it has managed to extend the brand into other businesses, using the logo to leverage the brand's heritage, and still produces 34,000 pocket-knives every day.

IBM launched its 'Smarter planet' platform in 2008. The overall symbol of the planet with five 'rays of light' emerging from its top half has been adapted in a variety of colourful and relevant ways across a wide range of different sectors in which IBM works. Susan Westre of Ogilvy & Mather Worldwide says, 'the icons help communicate complex stories in a simple way that everyone can understand.

Every time there was a new story to tell whether it was smarter transportation systems or a smarter power grid, an icon was developed' (Wheeler, 2013: 17).

The microprocessor market has always been highly competitive and very commoditized, with many brands unknown to mainstream consumers and buyers who focus on the manufacturer of the device to make purchase decisions. Intel changed all this, even though it had become one of the engines powering the industry, through its 'Intel Inside' campaign. The campaign was launched in 1991 as a cooperative marketing programme aiming to stamp the brand name into the minds of end customers through association with device manufacturers. Advertising costs were shared with the manufacturers who had to be convinced to place the Intel trademark and logo in their own materials and on their products.

The campaign produced huge returns in Intel's advertising exposure with sales increasing 63 per cent after one year of the campaign. Awareness of Intel grew from 24 per cent to 94 per cent in the first four years of the advertising, and by 1998, seven years after the campaign's start, Intel had built a 90 per cent share of the world's PC microprocessor market. The 'Intel Inside' sonic logo was a key part of the campaign with high recall, helping to build the company's ownership of associations with 'quality', 'technology leadership' and 'reliability' in the category (van Praet, 2012: 216–17).

There are many other successful examples of sonic logos. The 'bugle call' of Direct Line insurance in the UK is strongly imprinted on many minds, as was the Nokia ringtone, which at one time was the most played tune in the world (judged to be heard 20,000 times each second in 2007). The ringtone was adapted from Francisco Tárrega's *Gran Vales*. The Harley-Davidson engine 'rumble' is also an unmistakable sign of trouble.

Take a look at the three typefaces in Figure 8.2, and I am very sure that you will recognize at least two of the brands without any more information than seeing the typeface or script.

Coca-Cola has a very particular typographic script (known as 'Spencerian') that is memorable and difficult to confuse with any other brand (along with its red and white livery). Likewise, IBM has a very distinctive livery that has stood the test of time, reflecting a

FIGURE 8.2   Distinctive typefaces

modern, solid and bold style. The company has seen many changes in its business model and communication style, and the consistency of the typography has helped build a feeling of reliability, although its more recent communications have tried to soften the harder edges of its identity.

The third typeface, a version of Futura Extra Black, is used by Absolut vodka. It is more difficult to spot, as you will almost always see it with a distinctive colour, as I did recently in the airport that was selling a flavour specially developed for the Asian market with lemongrass as one of the distinctive notes. I remembered the light green colour and distinctive typeface the following week when I was walking down Orchard Road. A window display was using the same combination of colour and typeface and it took me a long time to work out that the store was selling sports shoes and not alcohol.

One of the ways Virgin distinguishes itself from other airlines is in the style and script of the Virgin name. Most airlines, especially Virgin's main competitor in the UK, have stuffy and boring names and stuffy and boring logos. The name 'Virgin' breaks with this tradition, as does the handwritten signature style of the logo, creating a friendly, personal and very 'unstuffy' connection with its customers.

Adam Alter reports an interesting experiment in fonts, which showed fonts that are more difficult to read raise conscious awareness, putting consumers on their guard by deploying more cognitive resources. By contrast, easy-to-read fonts are processed much more implicitly making consumers less risk-averse. In the experiment, the presentation of difficult-to-read fonts improved accuracy on difficult questions and logical problems, exactly because participants engaged more conscious effort than they did when the problems were presented in a clear font (Alter, 2013: 194–95). Most brands should be striving to make decision-making as simple and automatic as possible, and therefore should stick to easy-to-read communications.

Size matters in branding, as the packaging of Red Bull attests. Size is an important signal of intended use and often of target audience too. Coca-Cola is master at channel marketing, creating the right pack size for the right occasion and retail outlet, and in Asia many companies have learnt the power of making single-serve packages for food and drinks, personal care and home-cleaning products that help consumers buy what they need when they need it.

Similarly, Ferrero Rocher have been very smart in the way they have innovated new formats for new occasions and new channels, making the product available for a wide range of 'special occasions' from a big gathering to the occasions when you want to treat yourself (with a small pack of three at the checkout).

Formats and materials can be important too. One of the differences between the iPhone and its competitors is the materials used to construct them. The iPhone and other Apple products continue to use metal casings as a sign of quality and robustness, whereas many competitors use plastics in their own products, to manage costs and keep weight lower.

Formats and materials tell us a lot about the likely quality of products, from the flat-packed, brown cardboard feel of IKEA to the smooth white exterior of Apple's packaging of a new product, we know what to expect from the exterior. As a simple example, drinks *do* taste different from a glass and plastic bottle, even when the contents are identical.

Who can forget the visual style of the 'Got milk?' campaign with its instantly recognizable 'milk moustache', depicting the experience in a vivid and concrete way, directly linked to the senses. The campaign reversed the trend for milk to be unfashionable, combining the visuals with educational 'nuggets' of information about milk. It successfully drove awareness and consumption of milk by creating a positive association with the product from its first airing in 1993. Benetton was well known for their provocative images that were part of a long and successful campaign. Although the images were diverse, the themes were consistent and instantly recognizable as Benetton, under the campaign banner of 'United colours of Benetton'.

Two very different brands use iconic pictures of milk to emphasize aspects of their brand. Cadbury's Dairy Milk has long used the symbol of milk pouring to reinforce its 'glass and a half of real milk' claim. Dove uses a famous 'drop shot' of milk to signify a quarter moisturizing cream. The equally distinctive green arrow pack of Wrigley's Spearmint Gum was introduced in 1905 and is still going strong. It expresses the direct taste and effect of the product and its ingredients pointing to the emotional reward of consumption. Dettol shows its Warrior credentials in the sword that has always played a distinctive part in its logo.

One of the first products to be packaged and marketed in a modern way was Quaker Oats, and the iconic Quaker man was certainly one of the first brand logos. The packaging dates back to the 1870s, when it was described as 'a delicacy for the epicure, a nutritious dainty for the invalid, a delight to the children'. The icon was used for a wide range of marketing activities from its earliest days (Hine, 1995).

In reality brand logos come in a wide range of styles from wordmarks coming directly from the name or acronym, such as Google and IBM; to pictures which are more literal images although perhaps simplified or stylized, such as Starbucks; to letterforms that take a letter like 'U', usually the first letter of the name, and turn it into a picture, such as the Unilever logo; to more abstract symbols that convey a big idea, such as Nike's 'swoosh'.

Perhaps the most famous visual icon of all time is the Marlboro man, who we will return to at the end of the chapter. Another cigarette brand that is famous for its visual iconography is Silk Cut. Facing legislation that would ban cigarette advertising and force the removal of brand logos and messaging, Silk Cut began to position its logo against a background of purple silk in every advert. Once the ban came into effect, it simply turned to outdoor advertising that featured the silk without any logo or message. The logo was no longer needed as consumers had unconsciously learnt the connection between the image and the brand, which was later confirmed by research showing that most consumers were aware of the brand as a result of seeing the ads, confirming that awareness of the brand name had transferred to awareness of the purple silk (van Praet, 2012: 81).

Phil Barden points out the importance of considering visual perception in designing the visual appearance of packaging. In the retail environment, shoppers are on autopilot, and much of what we see is from peripheral vision, and not from looking directly at objects. In reality, peripheral vision is very blurred and used to spot anything in the environment that we should pay more attention to (Barden, 2013: 73–77). However, if the brain cannot pick something out from peripheral vision as being important to notice, then we will walk on by. Barden provides an example of Dettol and Tesco's own label bacterial wipes, which through the lens of peripheral vision are indistinguishable. He recommends manufacturers look at their advertising, packaging and promotions when they have been blurred to see what is really perceptible through peripheral vision.

When Tropicana changed its packaging design in 2009 it made many mistakes, but a critical one was to ignore the importance of peripheral vision on recognition. The instantly recognizable orange with a straw was changed for a more contemporary design featuring a glass of orange, and at the same time the font type was updated too. Consumers then failed to recognize the brands based on the cues they had learnt over a number of years, despite a huge investment in advertising. The exercise cost PepsiCo more than $30 million in two months before they had to withdraw the packaging from the shelves. Phil Barden notes that the packaging redesign reflected a very different consumer goal and archetype, also a significant problem for recognition (Barden, 2013: 205–07).

Language has important symbolic value, and the style of a brand's language reflects important truths about the brand's identity and values. We have seen how the Mc-language of McDonald's has become a brand 'signature', instantly recognizable and even creeping into the dictionary. Apple has its own language too, focusing on thinking differently and expressing this in a variety of ways, including the deliberate comparison with its main competitors, as in 'I'm a Mac, I'm a PC'. It has been relentless in showing how it is different, and it remains to be seen if it can keep this focus on its rebellious heritage.

Disney also has its own language of 'magic', 'fantasy' and 'dreams' that plays to its archetype of the Catalyst. 'When you wish upon a star' and 'Where your dreams come true' invoke the promise of transformation. Virgin Atlantic uses the language of the Joker across all its communications and copy, including instruction manuals and kit names on board. For example, advertising the on-board entertainment with the headlines '9 inches of pleasure' and 'Play with yourself', both finishing with the tagline 'Enjoy'.

Starbucks created its own language to build the 'third place' lifestyle. Tall, Grande and Venti have never been used in Italian espresso bars as terms to describe size. Likewise 'frapuccino' is an invention of Starbucks, successfully giving the store a distinctive feel compared with that of its competitors.

More mundanely, Tesco has always stuck with its 'every little helps' promise in the UK, making the promise real with constant small improvements to its service such as the one-in-front upgrade, leading recycling initiatives, constantly upgrading the clubcard and keeping communications simple, reinforcing its reliability. It is quoted as saying, 'It's not just a catchphrase or marketing slogan, it represents everything we stand for. For our people and our customers, it's how we run our businesses from China to Chorley' (Taylor and Nichols, 2010: 14).

How archetypes answer why

Language leads us neatly to story and how you tell your brand story. The prime should always be the brand archetype, which defines the motivations and rewards that define the brand's role in someone's life. Emotions (including facial expressions), rituals and songs, jingles and music all engage customers with the story you want to tell. Finally, metaphors, navigation, tradition and myth, service style and behaviours, talent and ambience all help to grow and elaborate the brand story.

The power of archetypes is not only to create vivid identities and personalities for all brands, but also to help realize the answer to 'why?' In his book *Start With Why* (2011), Simon Sinek argues that in business it doesn't matter what you do so much as why you do it. He cites Apple as an example of a company that had a clear idea of why from its start in the 1970s, and this hasn't changed over the years.

Sinek makes an interesting comparison of what Apple might say if it were just another company: 'We make great computers. They're beautifully designed, simple to use and friendly. Wanna buy one?' Compare this statement with a more typical Apple communication:

'Everything we do, we believe in challenging the status quo. We believe in thinking differently. The way we challenge the status quo is by making our products beautifully designed, simple to use, and user-friendly. And we happen to make great computers. Wanna buy one?' (Sinek, 2011: 40–41).

As we have seen in previous chapters, Apple has used the Rebel archetype through its history, making a point of being different from other companies.

Dettol is on a 'mission for health' and chooses to use the Warrior archetype in much of its marketing, mixing this with the Caregiver in proclaiming the importance of protecting the family. Its website states, 'We do more not just because we can, but because we must', continuing,

'We know your family means everything to you. You'll do anything to keep them happy and healthy. We believe that health depends on the choices we make every day at home, in our community and beyond. That's why we have started a Mission for Health. Our mission is fuelled by passion and backed by our expertise in disinfection, hygiene and first aid. From the products we make, to the education we provide, and the causes we champion'.

Its passionate mission comes through in the symbolism of its logo and its sword with a flash of light at the tip, the sensory design of the product with its powerful disinfectant smell and visible efficacy in the white clouds that appear on mixing with water, and finally in language that Dettol uses (for example, 'Kills 99.9 per cent of germs' and 'Complete family protection').

IKEA proclaims the importance of the home, with its website tagline 'affordable solutions for better living'. Its stated vision is 'to create a better everyday life for the many people' and it does this 'by offering a wide range of well-designed, functional home-furnishing products at prices so low that as many people as possible will be able to afford them'. IKEA uses the Everyman archetype in all of its marketing, from the communication of inclusion and equality in campaigns such as 'Playin' with my friends' to the experience of shopping. In IKEA stores everyone follows the same path around the store, which displays items in a range of different home environments to show how it might look for different customers in their real homes. Even the restaurant serves cheap and ordinary food at the end of the journey around the store.

Innocent's quest is to 'make natural, delicious, healthy foods that help people live well and die old'. It is an Idealist, proving its values with the symbolism of the packaging, with its white colours, simple and clear layout and communication, the exclusion of any additives and preservatives in the product ingredients, the iconic 'saint' icon with a baby face and halo and its support of charities with 10 per cent of profits given away. It has expanded from smoothies into juice, kids' smoothies, fruit tubes and veg pots all made with the same principles. Its website is packed full of advice on sustainable nutrition including principles of healthier eating and a healthier planet.

Starbucks has always leveraged the romance, adventure and exclusivity of coffee culture in its stores, realizing that it was selling more than a cup of coffee. This has helped it build an emotional bond with customers, and the ability to charge a premium, originally inspired by Italy's espresso bar culture (after a couple of less successful attempts by Howard Schultz). It reinforces the spirit of adventure (the Explorer) using music to create ambience in its stores, imagery of many exotic coffee-growing locations, and welcoming customers to stay as long as they wanted. Starbucks' stated mission is 'to inspire and nurture the human spirit – one person, one cup and one neighborhood at a time', and much of its communication focuses on its 'passion' for what it does.

A final example of the use of archetype is Dove, combining the Caregiver with the Idealist, which share many similar attributes, in its commitment 'to building positive self-esteem and inspiring all women and girls to reach their full potential'. Elsewhere on its website it makes clear its vision as 'Imagine a world where beauty is a source of confidence, not anxiety.' This is supported by 'Dove is committed to help all women realize their personal beauty potential by creating products that deliver real care.' The Idealist shows in the language and the mission of the brand. The Caregiver supports this, as you can see in the imagery that Dove uses to sell the brand. The iconic milk drop visual strongly supports Dove's moisturizing efficacy ('more moisturizing than milk' in the display I saw recently in a Singapore mall). Together with the product sensorials, Dove communications reinforce the gentle and caring nature of the brand.

These examples along with those in Chapter 7 demonstrate the power of being clear on why you are in business, and using that knowledge to define a personality that can embody your own values and match these to customer goals through archetype.

Telling the brand story

In getting to the why, archetypes also help to define the key emotions associated with a brand, through the goals that each archetype re-flects and the frustrations that their goals enable them to overcome. The Rebel feels powerless and trivial and this frustration leads them to seek to change the status quo in order to feel free. Apple was frustrated by the lack of well-designed computers in the world, lead-ing it to be different and create better designed products that met its own requirements.

IKEA is frustrated that many people feel excluded from the ability to have a beautiful home that they can share with others, so it created a way for Everyman (and woman) to have access to well-designed and affordable furniture. Innocent was unhappy with the adulterated and artificial offerings in the drinks category, leading it to develop more pure, innocent and traditional drink offerings, showing its faith in the good taste of consumers.

Emotions are the drivers of human behaviour, linked to the goals we all seek (the 'whys'). Dan Hill cites a study in the *Journal of*

Advertising Research involving 23,000 US consumers, 13 categories and 240 advertising messages that concludes that 'emotions are twice as important as facts in the process by which people make buying decisions' (Hill, 2008: 4). Similarly, Orlando Woods argues that emotional advertising is more effective than message advertising and that emotional response is more predictive of advertising success than traditional measures such as brand linkage, persuasion and cut through (Woods, 2012).

In the IPA's most recent study, the business effects of 1,000 advertising campaigns were examined to measure their business performance in terms of profit, sales and price sensitivity. All the data came from campaigns entered for the IPA effectiveness awards, and concluded that emotional advertising was twice as efficient and delivered twice the profit than rational advertising (as reported in 'IPA study highlights need for research in ad planning process' from **www.research-live.com** on 5 December 2012). Their findings also supported the importance of targeting mass audiences rather than niche markets. Penetration is more important than loyalty as Byron Sharp has often argued (Sharp, 2010).

A recent example of an advertising campaign highlights both the importance of emotion, and the importance of showing the right emotion. Visiting the cinema over the past six months, I have almost always seen a Visa payWave spot in the pre-film advertising reels. There are two different spots, portraying very different emotional spaces.

In the first, which is shown more frequently, people are shown dining in a café, where the ordering, paying and eating are highly synchronized and ordered (in my view, in a similar manner to the drones shown in Apple's famous *1984* spot). The 'hero' of the piece, who behaves in a nerdy and less organized way, doesn't have a payWave card and has to pay by cash, disrupting everyone else in the café and causing people to bump into each other, drinks to spill, and glances across the room. You can feel his embarrassment as everyone looks down at him.

In the second, a man is shown floating around his local supermarket in a state of bliss, with the freedom to turn in the air, pick up items from the shelves, and move wherever he wants. The Visa payWave card allows him to float past a smiling cashier and out of the store, doing a flip turn as he goes.

These executions could not be more different in the emotions that they portray. The first shows order and conformity (the Ruler archetype) and the second freedom and discovery (the Explorer archetype). I know which I prefer, although I should admit that the first probably evokes a stronger emotional response, even if it is negative. Visa's current communication platform of helping customers to 'go' (which would fit the Explorer archetype) seems more consistent with the latter.

Rituals are also important ways to build engagement with customers. Rituals are everywhere in our lives. Think of the crowd singing at international rugby games, and even more strikingly the signature 'Haka' of the New Zealand All Blacks, literally throwing down the challenge to their opponents in the traditional Maori style. In a very different style, a Singapore Airlines flight would not be the same without the towel ceremony before takeoff. And Starbucks is full of rituals, including writing names on the coffee cups, calling the order from barista to barista, and regularly grinding the beans and steaming the milk to create the sound atmosphere of a coffee bar.

James Bond would not be James Bond without certain elements always there. Although Skyfall played with the iconic shot through the eye (moving it to the end of the film), the opening scene followed by the title song and animation sequence followed the James Bond ritual to the letter.

When I worked as a barman, making money to support my student hobbies, I used to look forward to the visit from the Guinness technician who would painstakingly record the time it took to pour a Guinness. The ideal time is supposed to be 119 seconds, making the drink all the more enjoyable when it finally arrives. This ritual, along with the drawing of a four-leaf clover in the white head of the drink creates a strong sense of ritual for the drink. Guinness is also very particular about the temperature at which the drink is served.

Alcohol brands are very strong on ritual. Another example is Stella Artois, which has created a nine-step pouring ritual that you can see in Table 8.1.

TABLE 8.1   Stella Artois pouring ritual

I	The purification
II	The sacrifice
III	The liquid alchemy
IV	The crown
V	The removal
VI	The beheading
VII	The judgment
VIII	The cleansing
IX	The bestowal

The use of Latin numbers and archaic language add to the feeling of a religious ceremony that sounds more like the Quest for the Holy Grail than a pint at your local bar. The Stella Artois description finishes, 'Perfected in nine steps, served in one chalice, beauty by the drop.' There is even a downloadable application game that drinkers can use to follow the ritual on their mobile phones. All of these elements support Stella Artois's claim to be 'Reassuringly expensive', or in the 2013 incarnation of the tagline, 'Perfection has its price.' After all it has been a 'Belgian tradition since 1366'.

Subway has its own ritual, to help customers navigate their menu. Step 1 is 'Your menu choices', followed by Step 2 'Choose your bread', Step 3 'Choose your cheese', Step 4 'Choose your veggies', Step 5 'Choose your sauce' and finally Step 6 'Make it a Meal'. Other fast food outlets structure their menus in similar ways to make decision-making easy and quick.

In a different vein, IKEA manages the way that customers navigate their store in a very structured way, although there are occasional short cuts if you really want to be rebellious.

Songs, music and jingles can all be used to create emotional engagement with customers, and we have seen that sound can be a powerful sensory tool, with a high conscious bandwidth compared with other sensory modalities. Music is much used by alcohol brands, using music and dance as an integral element of event marketing and tying themselves to music festivals and concerts, such as the Guinness Fleadh St Patrick's Day celebrations and Heineken's support of many music events.

Coca-Cola has used music as an integral part of its marketing, often commissioning its own songs and linking the music intimately to the brand archetype. Most famously, 'I'd like to buy the world a Coke', first used in 1971, was reworded and released as 'I'd like to teach the world to sing (in perfect harmony)' by the New Seekers, and was a worldwide hit forever associated with the Coca-Cola brand (Jackson, 2003: 14). More recently, the 'Always Coca-Cola' melody is still instantly recognizable, even if the visuals that went with it are long forgotten.

In 2009, Coca-Cola collaborated with various recording artists, including Panic at the Disco! and Gnarls Barkley, to record different versions of 'Open Happiness'. Remixes of the songs were release in local markets as free downloads, and many became very popular. Leehom Wang's version was the number one in China. In the past year, Coca-Cola has released a new 'Open Happiness' campaign backed by the song 'Give a Little Bit', reinforcing its Idealist brand status.

Marc Gobé cites studies that show that consumers are more likely to buy products that are accompanied by music they like (Gobé, 2009: 74–75). He also cites research that shows the differences in perception of different music styles. Happiness is more strongly associated with fast tempos and larger amplitude modulation, while sadness is more strongly associated with slower tempos and lower pitch levels. Surprise, which is important in grabbing attention, is associated with faster tempos, higher pitches and larger amplitude modulations (Gobé, 2009: 78). Choosing the right music for the right audience and the right emotion is both an art and a science.

Metaphors are linked to the most fundamental patterns of thought (see Chapter 5). One of the best-known examples of the use of metaphor in advertising is the Michelin tyre baby with the slogan 'Because so much is riding on your tyres.' The campaign has had a huge impact over the years, arguably because it references fundamental truths about our evolution and biology, referencing safety, security, kinship and children (van Praet, 2012: 71). Gerald Zaltman argues that the advertising evokes the deep metaphor of 'container', signifying that the tyre keeps the family safe (Zaltman and Zaltman, 2008).

How long has Santa Claus been red? That tradition is about 80 years old now, thanks to the Coca-Cola Company's introduction of a red-clad Santa in print advertising in the mid-1930s. In less than 40 years, Apple has built a whole mythology around its brand, including the 'garage' origins story. Patrick Hanlon considers mythology and origin an important part of building a belief system around any brand (Hanlon, 2006).

Harley-Davidson is a good example of building a mythology around a brand, and to a large extent the Virgin brand has been built on the story of Richard Branson as a lone swashbuckling hero standing up for the ordinary man against large corporations, as Robin Hood did in mythology.

One of the important things that Richard Branson has instilled is a culture and style of behaviours and service that match the promise of the Virgin brand. Compare the teacher and classroom style of service on certain airlines with the mates down the pub style of Virgin and you cannot fail to see the difference. Importantly, the behaviours of Virgin staff are completely aligned with their core values and archetype.

Zappos has built its brand on a certain style of service, and is now embedding its culture in the Amazon brand, although it was Amazon that bought Zappos. That culture is defined by the behaviours that are instilled in staff during training, giving them the freedom to act in whatever way makes sense in order to keep customers happy. It seems to work, and my recent experiences with Amazon suggest that they have taken the lessons on board.

Similarly, Ritz Carlton, Singapore Airlines, Cathay Pacific, Peninsula Hotels and Harrods are all defined by the behaviour of their staff, defining a high level of service for their customers. In most cases, this means delivering consistently to meet or exceed expectations, although the evidence of behavioural economics is that an occasional (pleasant) surprise beats even consistency in terms of delighting customers (Kahneman, 2012).

Abercrombie & Fitch (A&F) is known for its racy marketing photography, with semi-nude males and females creating a highly sexualized tone. It uses the same style of branding in its stores, with male and female greeters as you enter the store, the man with a naked torso. Both look beautiful, with serious facial expressions, yet greet customers in a friendly manner as they enter and exit. A&F only use store employees in all their marketing, holding casting calls for employees who aspire to be models, although you have to work in the store first.

The greeters show the importance of talent in building brand esSense. Dan Hill argues that talent matters more than having famous personalities in advertising, as long as they convey the right attitude and mood.

A&F continues the feel of the greeters in the ambience of its stores, which are closed to the outside, appearing dark and intimate, with spotlights focused only on the products that the store wishes to highlight. A strong smell hits you even standing outside the store, reflecting one of A&F's signature fragrances. A&F shoppers swear that they can recognize the company's clothes from the signature smell that bathes them in-store. In addition to this, electronic dance music creates an upbeat atmosphere with sound levels of 80 decibels according to its corporate policy, a similar level to heavy construction machinery. The fast and lively sound is consistent with its aggressive and attitude-laden branding (Gobé, 2009: 75), drawing heavily on the Warrior archetype, with a little slice of rebellion thrown in.

Its upscale image has allowed it to open stores in high-end locations, such as the one I visited on Orchard Road in Singapore, and price its merchandise more aggressively, especially outside the US. Its CEO calls the image a 'movie' that plays out in-store (as reported in the Wikipedia article on A&F, March 2013).

By contrast, the ambience of the Victoria's Secret store a short walk from A&F could not be more different. The store feel builds on the emotional connection with its customers and their aspirations, centred on supermodels, an updating of the origins of the brand that originally had a more old-fashioned Victorian image. The brand chose a very bright shade of feminine pink, with stripes and a symbolic heart to emphasize the romance of the brand (Seducer archetype). This colour was carried over into pink shopping bags, helping customers to 'come out of the closet' in their purchase of lingerie brands (Gobé, 2009: 152–53). Victoria's Secret retail stores embody all of these design choices in their ambience, creating the ultimate in Seducer brands.

Finally, consider LEGO's use of amusement parks, featuring a range of attractions and interactive games. The parks have a special Imagination zone, emphasizing creativity and exploration, just as the brand does in its advertising and core credo. This is the perfect test bed for new products, and creates a true customer experience, with a huge LEGO store at the end of the journey around the park. This enables LEGO to charge customers to come to shop, as well as creating exactly the ambience of fun and imagination that it seeks to inspire in its brand.

Ambience is the final element of Story, bringing us back to where we started.

Using sense, symbol and story to build brand esSense

LEGO is an inspiring example of the Artist archetype. Its advertising asks viewers to use their imagination to see what a few bricks could become. Its product is colourful and fun, and designed to encourage children to play, create and learn. Its retail stores are fun and packed full of interesting things to see, many from the latest and most popular TV shows and movies. And its play parks show how retail experiences can be designed to create a total brand experience, building the brand image and selling product too. Across all the different touchpoints, LEGO shows consistency and commitment to its core values.

Harley-Davidson has the same consistency and commitment, although it shows this in a very different way. The image of the Harley-Davidson owner, in black leather, unconcerned with social niceties, is strongly imprinted in many people's minds, even if the reality is of mid-level salarymen using the brand as a weekend escape. Its focus on communicating freedom and rebellion keeps the brand on the same track, as does their use of the engine rumble to signify that Harley-Davidson owners want to 'make a noise'. Harley-Davidson continues to live the Rebel lifestyle.

The most famous brand archetype success of all time is also the most documented. In 1924, Philip Morris introduced Marlboro cigarettes as a brand for women, milder and filtered to contrast with the stronger unfiltered brands smoked by most men. The filter was even printed with a red band to hide lipstick stains. The original tagline for the brand was 'Mild as May'.

By 1954, the world had changed, and smokers reconsidered their love of unfiltered cigarettes. This led Marlboro to consider how to leverage its safer filtered cigarette to a wider audience, leading to the creation of the 'Marlboro man' by Leo Burnett. The iconic image of the Marlboro man led to one of the greatest U-turns in branding history, and was found in response to Leo Burnett's question, 'What's the most masculine symbol that you can think of?' to which one of his writers said 'a cowboy'. The ad campaign was launched in 1955 and within two years had increased US sales from 5 billion to 20 billion. Marlboro was the leading global brand by 1972 and is still the number one cigarette brand.

The new image appealed to both men and women, embodying independence, defiance, adventure and authenticity, a combination of Explorer and Rebel, drawing on the mythology of the US Wild West frontier. The imagery taps into human universal themes, creating connections to strongly embedded associations with the American West and the cowboy films and TV shows were popular as the brand grew.

Jerome Bruner wrote that in classic information theory a message is considered informative 'if it reduces alternative choices' (Bruner, 1990: 5). The power of archetypes is to access elaborate networks of associated memories that come from our cultural as well as personal memories. When these networks are aligned with our individual goals, they help us to close down other choices and focus on the brands that are most mentally available, as long as they are physically available to us at the right time.

The secret to building brand esSense is to understand the impact of sense, symbol and story on each customer, and their connection to the customer's values. Does the sensory experience of the brand provide consistent patterns? Are brand symbols sending the right signals to customers? And does the brand personality tell the right story?

Successful brands build brand experiences, brand symbols and brand stories that consistently reflect their core esSense.

REFERENCES

Ackerman, D (1995) *A Natural History of the Senses*, Vintage Books, New York

Alter, A (2013) *Drunk Tank Pink: And other unexpected forces that shape how we think, feel, and behave*, The Penguin Press, New York

Ariely, D (2008) *Predictably Irrational*, Harper Collins, New York

Arnheim, R (1969) *Visual Thinking*, University of Los Angeles Press, Berkeley

Barden, P (2013) *Decoded: The science behind why we buy*, John Wiley & Sons, Chichester

Batey, M (2008) *Brand Meaning*, Routledge, New York

Berdik, C (2012) *Mind Over Mind: The surprising power of expectations*, Penguin, London

Bergen, B (2012) *Louder Than Words: The new science of how the mind makes meaning*, Basic Books, New York

Berkeley, G (1922) *A New Theory of Vision and Other Writings (Everyman's Library edition)*, EP Dutton, New York

Berlin, B and Kay, P (1999) *Basic Color Terms: Their universality and evolution*, CSLI Publications, Stanford

Booker, C (2004) *The Seven Basic Plots: Why we tell stories*, Continuum, London

Brillat-Savarin, J (2009) *The Physiology of Taste* (tr Fayette Robinson), Merchant Books, Milton Keynes

Bronner, K and Hirt, R (2009) *Audio Branding: Brands, sound and communication*, Nomos, Baden-Baden, Germany

Bruner, J (1990) *Acts of Meaning: Four lectures on mind and culture*, Harvard University Press, Cambridge

Brynie, F (2009) *Brain Sense: The science of the senses and how we process the world around us*, Amacom, New York

Buckminster Fuller, R (1978) Children are born true scientists, *Journal of Ekistics* **272** September/October

Campbell, J (1993) *The Hero With a Thousand Faces*, Fontana Press, London

Chandler, D (2002) *Semiotics: The Basics*, Routledge, London

Changizi, M (2010) *The Vision Revolution*, BenBella Books, Dallas

Cooke, P (2013) *Unique: Telling your story in the age of brands and social media*, Gospel Light, Delight, AR

Cron, L (2012) *Wired for Story: The writer's guide to using brain science to hook readers from the very first sentence*, Ten Speed Press, New York

Cytowic, R and Eagleman, D (2011) *Wednesday is Indigo Blue: Discovering the brain of synesthesia*, MIT Press, Cambridge

Damasio, A (2010) *Self Comes to Mind: Constructing the conscious brain*, Pantheon, New York

Danesi, M (2006) *Brands*, Routledge, Abingdon

Danesi, M (2007) *The Quest for Meaning: A guide to semiotic theory and practice*, University of Toronto Press, Toronto

Danesi, M (2008) *Of Cigarettes, High Heels and Other Interesting Things: An introduction to semiotics*, Palgrave Macmillan, New York

Deutscher, G (2011) *Through The Language Glass: Why the world looks different in other languages*, Arrow Books, London

Dimofte, C (2010) Implicit measures of consumer cognition: A review, *Psychology & Marketing*, **27** (10), pp 921–37

Feynman, Richard (1995) *Six Easy Pieces: The fundamentals of physics explained*, Penguin, London

Frankel, A (2004) *Word Craft: The art of turning little words into big business*, Three Rivers Press, New York

Franzen, G and Bouwman, M (2001) *The Mental World of Brands: Mind, memory and brand success*, World Advertising Research Centre, Henley-on-Thames

Frith, C (2007) *Making Up The Mind: How the brain creates our mental world*, Wiley-Blackwell, Chichester

Gains, N (1994) The Repertory Grid Approach, in *Measurement of Food Preferences*, ed H MacFie and D Thomson, pp 51–76, Blackie Academic and Professional, Glasgow

Gibson, J (1950) *The Perception of the Visual World*, Houghton Mifflin, Boston

Gobé, M (2009) *Emotional Branding: The new paradigm for connecting brands to people*, Allworth Press, New York

Godden, D and Baddeley, A (1975) Context-dependent memory in two natural environments: On land and under water, *British Journal of Psychology*, **66**, pp 325–31

Gottschall, J (2012) *The Storytelling Animal: How stories make us human*, Houghton Mifflin Harcourt, Boston

Gregory, R (1998) Brainy Mind, *British Medical Journal*, **317**, pp 1693–95

Gregory, R (2009) *Seeing Through Illusions*, Oxford University Press, Oxford

Hall, E (1982) *The Hidden Dimension*, Anchor Books, New York

Hanlon, P (2006) *Primal Branding*, Free Press, New York

Hartwell, M and Chen, J (2012) *Archetypes In Branding: A toolkit for creatives and strategists*, How Books, Cincinatti

Harvey, M and Evans, M (2001) Decoding competitive propositions: A semiotic alternative to traditional advertising research, *International Journal of Market Research*, **43** (2), pp 171–87

Haven, K (2007) *Story Proof: The science behind the startling power of story*, Libraries Unlimited, Westport

Hawkins, J and Blakeslee, S (2005) *On Intelligence: How a new understanding of the brain will lead to the creation of truly intelligent machines*, St Martin's Griffin, New York

Herz, R (2007) *The Scent of Desire*, William Morrow, New York

Hill, D (2008) *Emotionomics: Leveraging emotions for business success* (Revised Edition), Kogan Page, London

Hill, D (2010) *About Face: The secrets of emotionally effective advertising*, Kogan Page, London

Hine, T (1995) *The Total Package*, Little, Brown and Company, New York

Hoffman, D (1998) *Visual Intelligence: How we create what we see*, WW Norton & Co, New York

Hofstadter, D (2001) Analogy as the Core of Cognition, in *The Analogical Mind: Perspectives from Cognitive Science*, ed D Gentner, K Holyoak and B Kokinov, The MIT Press, Cambridge, pp 499–538

Hofstadter, D (2007) *I Am A Strange Loop*, New York, Basic Books

Howard-Spink, J (2002) Using archetypes to build stronger brands, *Admap*, October, pp 1–3

Hultén, B, Broweus, N and van Dijk, M (2009) *Sensory Marketing*, Palgrave Macmillan, Basingstoke

Hume, David (1993) *An Enquiry Concerning Human Understanding*, Hackett, Indianapolis

Jackson, D (2003) *Sonic Branding: An introduction*, Palgrave Macmillan, Basingstoke

Jaspers, K (1962) *Socrates, Buddha, Confucius, Jesus: The paradigmatic individuals* (from *The Great Philosophers, Volume I*), Harcourt Brace & Company, Orlando

Jung, C (1968) *The Archetypes and the Collective Unconscious: The collected works of CG Jung*, Volume 9, Part 1, Princeton University Press, Princeton

Jung, C (1993) *The Basic Writings of CG Jung*, The Modern Library, New York

Kahneman, D (2012) *Thinking, Fast and Slow*, Penguin, London

Katz, David (1925) *The World of Touch* (tr Lester E Krueger), Erlbaum, Hillsdale NH

Keller, K L, Apéria, T and Georgson, M (2012) *Strategic Brand Management: A European perspective*, Pearson Education, Harlow

Kelly, G (1955) *The Psychology of Personal Constructs*, WW Norton & Co, New York

Kenealy, P (1997) Mood-state-dependent retrieval: The effects of induced mood on memory reconsidered, *The Quarterly Journal of Experimental Psychology*, **50A** (2), pp 290–317

Krishna, A (2010) *Sensory Marketing: Research on the sensuality of products*, Routledge, New York

Krishna, A (2013) *Consumer Sense: How the 5 senses influence buying behaviour*, Palgrave Macmillan, New York

Lakoff, G and Johnson, M (1980) *Metaphors We Live By*, The University of Chicago Press, Chicago

Lawrence, P and Nohria, N (2002) *Driven: How human nature shapes our choices*, Jossey-Bass, San Francisco

Lee, L, Frederick, S and Dan Ariely, D (2006) Try It, You'll Like It, *Psychological Review*, **17** (12), pp 1054–58

Lévi-Strauss, C (1974) *Structural Anthropology*, Penguin Books, London

Lévi-Strauss, C (1995) *Myth and Meaning: Cracking the Code of Culture*, Penguin Books, London

Levitin, D (2006) *This is Your Brain on Music: The science of a human obsession*, Dutton, New York

Lindstrom, M (2005) Broad Sensory Branding, *Journal of Product & Brand Management*, **14** (2), pp 84–87

Lindstrom, M (2010) *Brand Sense: Sensory secrets behind the stuff we buy*, Kogan Page, London

Locke, J (1979) *An Essay Concerning Human Understanding*, Oxford University Press, Oxford

Lusensky, J (2011) *Sounds Like Branding: Using the power of music to turn customers into fans*, Bloomsbury, London

Mackay, H (2010) *What Makes Us Tick? The ten desires that drive us*, Hachette, Sydney

McCrae, R and Costa, P (1989) Reinterpreting the Myers-Briggs type indicator from the perspective of the five-factor model of personality, *Journal of Personality*, **57** (1), pp 17–40

Mark, M and Pearson, C (2001) *The Hero and The Outlaw: Building extraordinary brands through the power of archetypes*, McGraw-Hill, New York

Mehrabian, A (1972) *Nonverbal Communication*, AldineTransaction, New Brunswick

Metzinger, T (2009) *The Ego Tunnel: The science of the mind and the myth of the self*, Basic Books, New York

Montagu, A (1986) *Touching: The human significance of the skin*, Harper & Row, New York

Nesbo, J (2012) *The Bat*, Harvill Secker, London

Nørretranders, T (1999) *The User Illusion: Cutting consciousness down to size*, Penguin Books, London

North, A and Hargreaves, D (1998) The effect of music on atmosphere and purchase intentions in a cafeteria, *Journal of Applied Psychology*, **28** (4), pp 2254–73

North, A, Hargreaves, D and McKendrick, J (1999) Influence of in-store music on wine selections, *Journal of Applied Psychology*, 84 (2), pp 271–76

North, A, Hargreaves, D and Shilock, A (2003) The effect of musical style on restaurant customers' spending, *Environment and Behaviour*, 35 (5), pp 712–18

Oatley, K, Keltner, D and Jenkins, J (2006) *Understanding Emotions*, Blackwell, Oxford

Oswald, L (2012) *Marketing Semiotics: Signs, strategies, and brand value*, Oxford University Press, Oxford

Pallasmaa, J (2005) *The Eyes of the Skin: Architecture and the senses*, John Wiley & Sons, Chichester

Panksepp, J and Biven, L (2012) *The Archaeology Of Mind: Neuro-evolutionary origins of human emotion*, WW Norton & Company, New York

Peck, J and Shu, S (2009) The effect of mere touch on perceived ownership, *Journal of Consumer Research*, 36 (3), pp 434–47

Pine, J and Gilmore, J (2011) *The Experience Economy*, Updated Edition, Harvard Business School, Boston

Pinker, S (1997) *How The Mind Works*, WW Norton & Company, New York

Pinker, S (2002) *The Blank Slate: The modern denial of human nature*, Penguin Books, New York

Prescott, J (2012) *Taste Matters: Why we like the foods we do*, Reaktion Books, London

Purves, D and Lotto, B (2011) *Why We See What We Do Redux: A wholly empirical theory of vision*, Sinauer Associates, Sunderland, MA

Ramachandran, V (2011) *The Tell-Tale Brain: Unlocking the mystery of human nature*, William Heinemann, London

Rentfrow, P and Gosling, S (2005) Message in a ballad? the role of music preferences in interpersonal perception, *Psychological Science*, 17 (3), pp 236–42

Restak, R (2006) *The Naked Brain: How the emerging neurosociety is changing how we live, work and love*, Three Rivers Press, New York

Reynolds, T and Olson, J (2001) *Understanding Consumer Decision Making: The means-end approach to marketing and advertising strategy*, Lawrence Erlbaum Associates, Mahwah, NJ

Rivkin, S and Sutherland, F (2004) *The Making of a Name: The inside story of the brands we buy*, Oxford University Press, Oxford

Roberts, D (2002) *Signals and Perception: The fundamentals of human sensation*, Palgrave Macmillan, London

Rokeach, M (1973) *The Nature of Human Values*, The Free Press, New York

Rolls, M (2006) *Asian Brand Strategy: How Asia builds strong brands*, Palgrave Macmillan, Basingstoke

Rosenblum, L (2010) *See What I'm Saying: The extraordinary powers of our five senses*, WW Norton & Company, New York

Rozin, P and Vollmecke, T (1986) Food Likes and Dislikes, *Annual Review of Nutrition*, **6**, pp 433–56

Sachs, J (2012) *Winning the Story Wars: Why those who tell – and live – the best stories will rule the future*, Harvard Business Review Press, Boston

Schieffer, R (2005) *Ten Key Customer Insights: Unlocking the mind of the market*, South-Western, Mason

Schmitt, B (1999) *Experiential Marketing*, The Free Press, New York

Schmitt, B and Simonson, A (1997) *Marketing Aesthetics: The strategic management of brands, identity and image*, The Free Press, New York

Schwartz, S (1993) Are there universal aspects in the structure and contents of human values?, *Journal of Social Issues*, **50** (4), pp 19–45

Sharp, B (2010) *How Brands Grow: What marketers don't know*, Oxford University Press, Oxford

Shiv, B, Carmon, Z and Ariely, D (2005) Placebo effects of marketing actions: Consumers may get what they pay for, *Journal of Marketing Research*, **17**, pp 383–93

Signorelli, J (2012) *StoryBranding: Creating standout brands through the power of story*, Greenleaf Book Group Press, Austin

Sinek, S (2011) *Start With Why: How great leaders inspire everyone to take action*, Portfolio Penguin, London

Smith, P (2012) *Lead With A Story: A guide to crafting business narratives that captivate, convince and inspire*, Amacom, New York

Steidl, P (2012) *Creating Brand Meaning: How to use brand vision archetypes*, Amazon, Marston Gate

Stein, B and Meredith, A (1993) *The Merging of the Sense*, The MIT Press, Cambridge

Sykes, M, Malik, N and West, M (2013) *Stories That Move Mountains: Storytelling and visual design for persuasive presentations*, John Wiley & Sons, Chichester

Taylor, D and Nichols, D (2010) *The Brandgym: A practical workout to gain and retain brand leadership*, John Wiley & Sons Ltd, Chichester

Treasure, J (2011) *Sound Business: How to use sound to grow profits and brand value*, Management Books 2000 Ltd, Chichester

Turin, L (2006) *The Secret of Scent: Adventures in perfume and the science of smell*, Faber and Faber Limited, London

Underhill, P (1999) *Why We Buy: The science of shopping*, Simon & Schuster, New York

van Praet, D (2012) *Unconscious Branding: How neuroscience can empower (and inspire) marketing*, Palgrave Macmillan, New York.

Ward, Jamie (2008) *The Frog Who Croaked Blue: Synesthesia and the mixing of the senses*, Routledge, London

Wertime, K (2002) *Building Brands and Believers: How to connect with consumers using archetypes*, John Wiley & Sons (Asia), Singapore

Wheeler, A (2013) *Designing Brand Identity*, John Wiley & Sons, Hoboken, NJ

Wheeler, A and Katz, J (2011) *Brand Atlas: Branding intelligence made visible*, John Wiley & Sons, Hoboken, NJ

Wilson, T, Kraft, D and Lisle, D (1990) The disruptive effects of self-reflection: Implications for survey research, *Advances in Consumer Research*, **17**, pp 212–16

Wilson, T and Schooler, J (1991) Thinking too much: Introspection can reduce the quality of preferences and decisions, *Journal of Personality and Social Psychology*, **60** (2), pp 181–92

Woods, O (2012) How emotional tugs trump rational pushes: The time has come to abandon a 100-year old advertising model, *Journal of Advertising Research*, **52** (1), pp 31–39

Zaltman, G (2003) *How Customers Think: Essential insights into the mind of the market*, Harvard Business School Press, Boston

Zaltman, G and Zaltman, L (2008) *Marketing Metaphoria: What deep metaphors reveal about the minds of consumers*, Harvard Business Press, Boston

Zimmerman, M (1986) Neurophysiology of Sensory Systems, in *Fundamentals of Sensory Physiology*, ed R Schmidt, Springer-Verlag, Berlin

Zimmerman, M (1989) The Nervous System in the Context of Information Theory, in *Human Physiology*, ed R Schmidt and G Thews, Springer-Verlag, Berlin

INDEX

NB: page numbers in *italic* indicate figures or tables

Ackerman, D   28, 31–32
Adler, A   108
alcohol brands and ritual   197–98, *198*
Allegory of the Five Senses   28
Alter, A   174, 178–79, 189
Altman, D   185
Andersen, H C   10
Apéria, T   175
Apple (and)   3, 88, 176, 183–84, 189,
        191–92, 193
    design of space   49
    sharing musical tastes   57–58
    Superbowl commercial (1984)   128
    'Think Different' campaign   128
applying the esSense framework   171–204,
        172 see also archetypes; branding
        and brand(s)
    telling the brand story   195–202, *198*
    and use of metaphor   199–200
    using sense, symbol and story to build
        brand esSense   202–04
archetypes (of)   102, *103, 114*, 159,
        160–63, *162 see also* story and
        archetypes
    and archetypal frameworks   107–09,
        111–13, *110, 112*
    belonging   115–24
        caregiver   115–18, 182, 194–95
        everyman   118–21, 161, 194
        seducer   121–24, 161
    brand   105–07, 118, 192–95
    ego   132–40
        artist   133–35, 202
        catalyst   138–40, 182
        warrior   135–38, 182
    freedom   124–32
        explorer   131–32, 161, 194, 197,
        203
        joker   125–27, 161, 173, 182, 192
        rebel   127–31, 161, 173, 193, 195,
        203
    order   141–49
        guru   141–43
        idealist   146–49, 161, 173,
        194–95
        ruler   143–46, 173, 182, 197

    and realizing the answer to 'why?'
        192–95
    as spirit of disorder   126
    and telling the brand story   195–202,
        198
Archetypes in Branding   107
Ariely, D   11–12
Aristotle   28, 39, 92
    Poetics   87
    Rhetoric   87
Audio Branding   28
'Audio Branding: BMW Uses New Sound
        Signature to Help Redefine the
        Brand' (2013)   58

Bacon, F   145
Barden, P   191
Bastian, A   102
Batey, M   4, 107
Berdik, C   10
Bergen, B   6
Berkeley, G   13, 43
Berlin, B   67
Biró, L   181
Bitetto, J   181
Biven, L   109
Black, J W   51
body language   80
    and presentation skills/communication
        61
Booker, C   163–64
Bouwman, M   2
Brand Meaning   4
Brand Sense   3, 185
brand stories (and)   5–7, 165–67
        see also storytelling
    bringing moments to life   166
    synesthesia game   166–67
branding
    archetypes   118
    core values as esSense   2
    esSense of   171, *172*
    names/Post-it notes   88
    salience   2
    using the Catalyst archetype   140
    using metaphor and metonymy   88

brand(s)
colours   172–75 *see also* colours
senses   175–80 *see also* smell; touch
symbolic names for   180–85
symbols, logos and typefaces   185–92, *188*
'Brands Smell Opportunity in Scent Marketing' (2011)   34
Branson, R   125, 127–28, 130, 200
Brillat-Savarin, J A   41
Bronner, K   56, 60
Broweus, N   4
Bruner, J   98, 203
Brynie   4, 32, 39, 42
building brand esSense   5–6
and the golden circle   5, *5*
Building Brands and Believers   106

Cadbury   1, 68, 74, 172–73, 190
see also colour(s)
Campbell, J   100–101, *101*, 102, 106
Carmon, Z   11
Chandler, D   78
Changizi, M   61
Chen, J C   107
Churchill, W   146
Coca-Cola   2, 3, 59, 147, 149, 161, 173, 182, 185, 189, 199 *see also* music
colour(s)   65–68, 74, 78, 76–77, 172–75
blue   1, 67–68, 75, 80, 173–74, 180
brown   67, 68, 81, 173
of carrots and the House of Orange 65–66
gold/yellow   67–68, 78, 80, 174, 185
green   1, 63, 66–68, 72, 132, 174, 188
and Munsell Colour System/*A Color Notation*   66
purple   1, 65, 67, 68, 74, 86, 172–73, 190–91
red   1, 15, 66–68, 72–73, 79, 81, 173–74, 200
trademarking of   1–2
Cooke, P   4, 97
Costa, P   108
Creating Brand Meaning   106
creative thinking   151, 161
and blending ideas   96
Cron, L   97, 99
Cytowic, R   25

Damasio, A   97, 98
Danesi, M   4, 78, 84
definition(s) of
archetype (Howard-Spink)   102
archetype (OED)   102
mental availability (Sharp)   2
music (National Academy of Sciences) 57
physical availability (Sharp)   2
sense (OED)   27
senses (Wikipedia)   27
sensory marketing (American Marketing Association)   2–3
sensory marketing (Wikipedia 2013)   3
de Lairesse, G   28
Delibes, L   56
'Depth perception' (Gibson, 1950)   14
see also Gibson, J
Derrida, J   92
de Saussure, F   75, 78
Descartes, R   92, 143
'Detroit Auto Show Preview: Nissan to debut Brand Scent' (2013)   34
Deutscher, G   67
Dimofte, C   161

Eagleman, D   25
Edison, T   135
Einstein, A   141
Either/Or   92
Evans, M   95
The Experience Economy   20

Faure-Field, S   33
Fechner, G   69
Feynman, R   25, 31
finding the esSense of your brand (and/by) 150–70 *see also* storytelling
building a brand back story   151–52
building transformational stories 161–65, *162*, *165*
consumer stories and underlying conflicts 156–61 *see also* StoryWorks
cracking the category codes   153–54, 156 *see also* StoryWorks *and* Tapestry Works
the senses   165–67 *see also subject entry*
Finnegan's Wake   101
Foucault, M   92
Franzen, G   2
Frederick, S   11
Freud, S   72, 108
Frith, C   10, 13
Fuller, R B   43

Gains, N   159
Galton, F   69
Georgson, M   175
Gestalt   70

Gestalt psychology   29 *see also* Wikipedia
  and the Law of Prägnanz   11
Gibson, J   14, 16, 47
Gilbert, D   99
Gilmore, J   4, 20–21
Gobé, M   4, 199, 201–02
Gödel, K   92
Goffman, E   87
Goldman, E   126
Gosling, S   57
Gottschall, J   4, 97
Gregory, R   10, 13, 16–18, 26, 43
Greimas, A J   92 *see also* semiotics

Hall, E   47, 48–51, *51*, 63, 73, 178
Hanlon, P   107, 200
Hargreaves, D   53
Harlow, H   178
Hartwell, M P   107
Harvey, M   95
Haven, K   98
Hawkins, J   10
hearing   27, 29, 37, 54–55 *see also* music
Henning, H   34, *35*
The Hero and the Outlaw   106
The Hero with a Thousand Faces   101
Herz, R   32, 35–36
The Hidden Dimension   48
Hill, D   3, 4, 21–22, 62, 176, 195–96, 201
Hine, T   173, 190
Hirt, R   56, 60
Hoffman, D   13, 14
Hofstadter, D   87
Hofstede, G   73
How Customers Think   156
Howard-Spink, J   102
Hultén, B   4
Hume, D   13, 97
Hutchence, M   35–36

IBM   143, 145, 184, 186–87, 190
  'Intel inside'   187
  'Smarter planet' platform   186
IKEA   119–20, 173, 177, 189, 194–95, 198
incompleteness theory (Gödel)   92

Jackson, D   4, 56
James Bond/Bond movies   58–59, 84–86,
      197
Jaspers, K   142
Jobs, S   94, 127–29, 134
Johnson, M   87
Joyce, J   101
Jung, C   10, 72, 107–08
  and 'Psychological types' (1993)   102

Kahneman, D   12, 22–23, 201
  and System 1   63
Kandinsky, W   25
Katha Upanishad (Wikipedia)   28
Katz, D   48
Katz, J   181, 185
Kay, P   67
Keirsey, D   108
  and Temperament Sorter   108
Keller, H   30
Keller, K L   175
Kelly, G   18–20
  coined 'constructs'   19–20
Kenealy, P   21
Kerenhi, C   126
Kilian, K   28
King Jr, M L   137, 138, 147
Köhler, W   70
Kraft, D   156
Krishna, A   4

Lakoff, G   25, 87
language (and)   9–10, 51, 54, 61, 67, 70,
      78–80, 87–88, 181–82, 191–92
  brand perceptions   6
  metaphors   25, 46
Lawrence, P   109
Lee, L   11
Lévi-Strauss, C   82, 89
Levitin, D   52, 55
Lindstrom, M   3–4, 30, 60, 176, 185
Lisle, D   156
Locke, J   13, 75
Lotto, B   10, 130
Lusensky, J   4, 57
Luther, M   138, 147

McCrae, R   108
MacDonald, J   63
McGurk, H/McGurk effect   63, 69
Mackay, H   112–13
  ten goals of   113
McKendrick, J   53
Malik, N   4, 97
Mandela, N   137
Mark, M   106
market research   20, 22, 41, 74, 86, 143
  psychological models used in   108
  semiotic thinking in   4
Maslow, A   178
Mehrabian, A   61
Meredith, A   43
metaphors (and)   25, 40, 46, 69–71, 94–95,
      102, 156–57, 180, 192, 199–200
  in advertising   199–200

meaning   87–88
metonymy   87–88, 95
sensory   159
Metzinger, T   48
Montagu, A   42, 46, 178
Müller-Lyer, F-C   17
    illusion   17–18, 17
Munsell, A   66 see also colour(s)
music (and)   52–60, 177–78 see also
        definition(s) of
    advertising   52, 199
    airlines   56
    as branding tool   55
    computer start-up sounds/ringtones   58
    earworms   55
    influence of rhythm and volume
        52–53
    jingles   55–56
    the Mozart effect   52
    physical nature of hearing   54–55
    as shorthand of emotion   57
    sonic logos   58–59, 60
    sound engineering   60
    taste of food   37
Myers-Briggs Type Indicator (MBTI)
    107–08
myths/mythology   89, 91, 90, 117, 122,
        129, 134, 136, 140, 147, 200
        see also story and archetypes
    and the hero's journey   100–102,
        104–05, 101, 103, 104, 105
    and the monomyth   100–102

Newton, I   13, 183
Nichols, D   192
Nietzsche, F   136
Nike   136, 162–63, 190
Nohria, N   109
Nørretranders, T   8
North, A   53

The Odyssey   101
Olson, J   158
Oswald, O   4, 78, 82, 90, 91, 93

Pallasmaa, J   43, 48
Panksepp, J   109
Parmenides   28
Pearson, C   106
Peck, J   41
Peirce, C S   75, 78, 88
    and the theory of signs   75, 78
Penfield, W   44
    and the Penfield Map   44, 45
Pepsi/PepsiCo   126–27, 173, 182, 191

perception(s) (and/of)   8–29, 37, 63–64,
        111, 174, 194
    as active construction   13–18, 17
    associating with the right memories
        24–26
    brand   152, 171, 177, 179–80, 183,
        186
    experience and memory   22–23
    matching the right patterns   20–22, 21,
        22
    nature and nurture   18–20
    patterns in the world   10–13
    the senses   27–28
    signal and noise   8–10, 9
    smell   32–33, 35
    spatial   49–50
    time   72–73
    touch   44, 48
    visual   43, 61–62, 64, 66, 180, 191
Phaedra   28
The Physiology of Taste   41
Pine, J   4, 20–21
Pinker, S   97, 99, 100, 109
Prescott, J   39, 40
Proust, M   32
Proxemics   48
Purves, D   10, 13

Ramachandran, V   25, 48, 69–71
Ratha Kalpana   28
reality of perception see perception
Rentfrow, P   57
research (on) see also studies (on)
    authenticity of celebrities   62
    impact of mood on smell   35
    memories triggered by smell   32
    the Mozart effect   52
    stories and the brain, memory and
        behaviour   98
    touch   41
    visual appearance vs tactile feel   64
Restak, R   99
Reynolds, T   158
Rivkin, S   181, 182
Roberts, D   28, 37, 44, 64, 66, 69
Rokeach, M   109, 111, 110, 112, 159
Rokeach Value Survey   109
Rolls, M   3
Rosenblum, L   63–64
Rozin, P   31
Rubin, M   148

Sachs, J   4, 97, 107
The Scent of Desire   35
Schieffer, R   159

Schmitt, B 4
Schooler, J 156
Schwartz, S 109, 111–12, *112*, 159
The Secret of Scent 35
semiotics 4, 75–76, 78–81, 85–88, 90,
        92–94, 153, 156–57, 169
    see also symbols and signs
    and the semiotic square 92–93, *93*
        see also Greimas, A J
    theory 19
the senses 27–46, 165–67 *see also* hearing;
        smell; taste; touch *and* vision
    number of 27–29, *29*
sensing from a distance (and) 47–71
        see also colour(s); music; space
        and vision
    the *bouba/kiki* effect 70, *70*
    integrating the senses 69–71
    synaesthesia 69–70, 159
sensory branding and marketing 2–4,
        33–34
'Sensory Branding: Luxury Auto-Makers
        Woo with Smell and Sound'
        (2010) 34
Sharp, B 2, 65, 196
Shilock, A 53
Shiv, B 11
Shu, S 41
Signorelli, J 4, 97, 107
Simonson, A 4
Sinek, S 5, 193
    and TED talk 5
Skinner, B F 19
smell 30–36, *35*, 175–76
    comparison across cultures 31
    memories triggered by 32–33
    and sensory branding 33–34
Smith, P 4, 97
space (and) 47–51 *see also* touch
    animal behaviour and distances 49,
        50
    human inter-personal distances 50–51,
        51
    orientation 47
    perception of 49–50
    rubber hand illusion 48
    sense of touch 47–48
    sensory branding 49
Starbucks (and) 132, 176–79, 190, 192,
        194, 197
    music/sound 59, 177–78
    touch 176–77
Start with Why 5, 193
Steidl, P 106–07
Stein, B 43

story and archetypes (and) 97–113, *114*
        see also archetypes *and*
        storytelling
    archetypal frameworks 107–09,
        111–13, *112*
    brand archetypes 105–07
    causality and the mind 97–98
    human values (Rokeach and Schwartz)
        109, 111, *110*
    long-term goals (Mackay) 112–13
    the meaning of stories 99–100
    myth and the hero's journey 100–102,
        104–05, *101*, *103*, *104*, *105*
Story Proof 98
storytelling (and) 4–7, 157–58
        see also StoryWorks
    brand story 5–7 *see also* brand stories
    explorer stories 131
    fairy tales 91
    myths 84–85, *84*
    rebel stories 129
    transformational stories 161–65, *162*,
        165
StoryWorks (and) 150–51, 156–63
        see also storytelling
    archetypes 161–63, *162*
    building characterization 163
    building plot stories 163–64
    homework 157–60
    model 154, *154–55*
    playing the journalist 165, *165*
    playing 'what if?' 164
    'socko' ending 164–65
    Think Cards 160, 161
    validating the right story 160–61
studies (on/for) *see also* TapestryWorks
    advertising (TapestryWorks) 152
    Asian telecommunications company
        (TapestryWorks) 152
    business effects of advertising campaigns
        (IPA) 196
    emotions and buying decisions (*Journal
        of Advertising Research*)
        195–96
    high volume music and food
        consumption 53
    listening to music (Millward Brown)
        57
    music and personality 57
    renovation of positioning of Asian food
        brand (TapestryWorks) 167–68
    sensory marketing (Millward Brown)
        3
    themes used in advertising beer (Harvey
        and Evans, 2001) 95

surveys (on)
  connection between 'crunch' and
    Kellogg's (Brandsense) 60
Sutherland, F 181, 182
Sutherland, R 23, 52
Sykes, M 4, 97
symbols and signs (and) 72–96
  binary oppositions 89–91, 90
  blending identity 94–96, 96
  category codes 80–81
  change in meanings 85–86
  colour 74, 76–77 see also colour(s)
  of life 72–74
  metaphor and meaning 87–88, 95
  paradox of either/or and the semiotic
    square 92–94, 93
  semiotics and signifiers 75, 78–80, 85
  the story of meaning 84–85, 84
  the structure of signs 82–83, 83

Tapestry Works
  CodeWorks 153–54
  project on rice for Chinese snack brand
    168–70, 169
  StoryWorks 150–51, 154–55
    see also subject entry
taste (and) 36–37, 39–41, 38
  brands: Tabasco and Coke Zero 39
  five varieties of 37, 39
  losing your 36–37
  Ney's flavourgram 37, 38
  other senses 37
  sound and music 37
  supertasters 40
  use in metaphors 40
  wine tasters 40–41
Taylor, D 192
temperature 29, 43, 44, 159, 166, 172
  and behaviour 22–23, 179
Theory of Personal Constructs 18
'This is what sensory branding can do for
  your business' (Singapore Business
  Review 2012) 33
Tolstoy, L 57
touch (and) 41–51, 176–79
  comfort 42
  different senses of 44
  as exploratory 43–44
  inter-personal distances 50–51
  metaphors involving 46
  the Penfield Map 44–45, 45
  proprioception 45
  reliance on 42, 43
  rubber hand illusion 48
  shape and weight 41

Touching: The Human Significance of the
  Skin 42
Treasure, J 4, 56
Turin, L 35
Turner, M 25
Twain, M 137, 145

Underhill, P 178–79
using archetypes in branding 115–49
    see also archetypes

Valentine, V 4
van Dijk, M 4
van Praet, D 176, 186, 187, 191,
    200
Virgin 125, 127, 129–30, 161, 168, 188,
    192, 200
Visual Intelligence 14
vision (and) 29, 42–46, 53, 60–65
  blindness and touch 42–43
  as distance receptor 63
  faces in advertising/branding 62
  facial recognition 61–62
  feelings 62–63
  impact of lighting on behaviour
    179–80
  key principles of visual appearance
    64–65
  regained 43
  speech perception/the McGurk effect
    63–64
The Vision Revolution 61
Vollmecke, T 31

Ward, J 25
Wertime, K 106–07
West, M 4, 97
What Makes Us Tick 112
Wheeler, A 181, 184, 185, 187
Wikipedia articles (on)
  depth perception (Gibson) 14
  Gérard de Lairesse 28
  Gestalt psychology 29
  Jacques Derrida 92
  Müller-Lyer illusion 17
  'Sensory branding' 3
Wilde, O 128
Wilson, T 156
Woodruff, R 2
Woods, O 196

Zajonc, R 65
Zaltman, G 6, 25, 98, 150, 156, 200
Zaltman, L 25, 200
Zimmerman, M 8–9, 28